The Agile Organization

*To my dear husband Barney, my late mother
and father, Elsie and Bill,
Thank you for everything.*

The Agile Organization

How to build an innovative, sustainable and resilient business

Linda Holbeche

LONDON PHILADELPHIA NEW DELHI

First published in Great Britain and the United States in 2015 by Kogan Page Limited

2nd Floor, 45 Gee Street
London EC1V 3RS
United Kingdom

1518 Walnut Street, Suite 1100
Philadelphia PA 19102
USA

4737/23 Ansari Road
Daryaganj
New Delhi 110002
India

www.koganpage.com

ISBN   978 0 7494 7131 6
E-ISBN 978 0 7494 7132 3

British Library Cataloguing-in-Publication Data

A CIP record for this book is available from the British Library.

Library of Congress Cataloging-in-Publication Data

Holbeche, Linda.
  The agile organization : how to build an innovative, sustainable and resilient business / Linda Holbeche.
    pages cm
  ISBN 978-0-7494-7131-6 (paperback) – ISBN 978-0-7494-7132-3 (ebk) 1. Organizational change. 2. Organizational behavior. 3. Corporate culture. 4. Organizational effectiveness. 5. Personnel management. I. Title.
  HD58.8.H647 2015
  658.4′06—dc23

                                                                              2015015999

Typeset by Amnet
Print production managed by Jellyfish
Printed and bound by CPI Group (UK) Ltd, Croydon, CR0 4YY

CONTENTS

ACKNOWLEDGEMENTS

I am extremely grateful to all the people, too numerous to mention, who have contributed to this book. These include sources of inspiration, such as the Center for Effective Organizations at the University of Southern California, the Virginia Mason Institute in Seattle, and Dave Francis and Sandra Meredith whose 2000 model originally stimulated my thinking about the nature of organizational agility. They also include participants in various research programmes and those who have kindly helped me to develop case studies. In particular I should like to thank Sarah-Ellen Stacey of the Nationwide Building Society whose practice has been an inspiration and who has kindly acted as a conduit to the development of case studies at RCT Homes and Nationwide Building Society.

In the book I refer to various research projects carried out during my time as Director of Research and Strategy at my former employer Roffey Park, as well as more recent work, for which I would like to thank CEO Michael Jenkins and his team.

I should also like to thank Katy Hamilton, her predecessor Liz Gooster, Lucy Carter and Philippa Fiszzon of Kogan Page for their patience and encouragement. Finally I should like to thank my husband and family for their ongoing support and understanding.

Whilst every effort has been made to contact copyright holders the author and publisher would like to hear from anyone whose copyright may have been unwittingly infringed.

Introduction

Organizational agility is a hot topic these days – and is it any wonder? In a world undergoing continuous and multifaceted change, so fast-moving is the business landscape that organizations must adapt swiftly simply to survive. Organizational agility, or the ability to continuously adjust and adapt strategic direction in a core business, is increasingly considered *the* vital business success factor.

The term 'VUCA' is often used to describe the volatile, uncertain, complex and ambiguous world we now inhabit, with its turbulent financial and commodity markets and geopolitical instabilities. Financial turbulence has increased in intensity and persists longer than in the past.[1] Business cycles are much shorter. The financial crisis that began in 2008 rendered many business models obsolete as organizations throughout the world were plunged into chaotic environments. In a 2010 study by IBM the overwhelming majority of chief executive officers (CEOs) described their operating environment as unlike anything they had seen before.[2] The days when traditional management models – such as strategic planning based on extrapolations from the past – were enough to keep organizations ahead of the curve seem long gone.

In a VUCA world no company consistently beats the market. Megatrends such as demographics, digitization, connectivity, trade liberalization, global competition and business model innovation are leading to the emergence of new competitors and driving new ways of doing business.[3] Organizations are also experiencing unpredictable consumer sentiment, increasing complexity, rising uncertainty, an overload of information and a lack of resources. The impacts of many of these trends are uncertain – but there are some common themes and multiple interdependences between the drivers, which suggest that their effects will be complex and enduring. This combination of factors is forcing many companies to rethink where future business success will come from since previous success is no guarantee of future prosperity.

The only certainty is that before long every organization will be challenged to change in ways for which it has no precedent and the old ways may no longer be the best ways. The ability to change continuously and effectively will be key to survival and future prosperity. Of course the alternative to business transformation is to stand still, Canute-like, in the face of the incoming tide of change; but that might not prove the wisest course. In other words, these profound changes in the global business environment require new ways of leading and managing organizations and fresh answers to the question: what do organizations have to do to survive and thrive in today's fast-moving, complex times?

That's what this book is about.

Essentially, I shall argue that if business leaders and people who work in organizations are to thrive in today's fluid landscape they must adopt agile practices and the mindsets that underpin them. I also maintain that agility is not a stand-alone capability; it must be complemented by organizational resilience, or the ability to learn and recover from significant setbacks. How organizations pursue agility impacts their resilience and their capacity to act. If agility is pursued purely as a cost-saving exercise, people are likely to feel treated as expendable costs and will be less likely to release their discretionary effort to make things happen for the organization. Thus the organization will be unlikely to achieve the beneficial 'value' outcomes of agility such as adaptability, speed, innovation and sustainability. This book points out what to guard against to avoid agility being achieved at the expense of sustainable value. It proposes ways in which organizations and their stakeholders, especially the people who work for them, can attempt to have the best of all worlds.

Who is the book for?

In writing a book it is usual to address one key audience. In the case of organizational agility, there are several audiences and these are the people I consider to be the key players in agile. These include:

- Executives who act as sponsors of strategic change – they play a key role actually and symbolically in forging the way ahead. They need to develop their agile leadership abilities, which include knowing when to step away and let others get involved in decision making.

- Line managers are central to day-to-day operations and for many employees represent the reality of their relationship with the organization. They too need to play different roles in agile, becoming coach and supporter to self-managed teams.

- Functional specialists in HR, Organization Development, Internal Communications, Marketing, Knowledge Management, Finance and IT all have roles to play in designing policies and strategies to support the development of more agile working practices, and must work together to produce well-integrated outcomes.

- The workforce itself, in all its component parts, including outsourced and contract workers. These are the eyes and ears of the organization, on the front line of discovery through their work with customers. They need to be willing to play a proactive role in agile execution and innovation.

- Finally, external stakeholders – boards, shareholders, communities – can only benefit when these internal stakeholders shift the paradigm and breathe life into the agile organization.

In some cases I have highlighted the specific roles of different key players – for instance through case study examples or whole chapters. I have included checklists at the end of each chapter to help different audiences reflect on where they may need to collaborate on specific issues to improve their organization's agility and resilience.

How is the book organized?

This book sets out to answer a number of questions relating to organizational agility, such as:

- What makes an organization agile? Is agile something you do, or something you are?
- Where is the 'people bit' of agile?
- Is there such a thing as an 'agile culture'?
- How does continuous improvement differ from whole system transformation?
- How can you develop organizational 'change-readiness', or increase 'dynamic capacity'?
- What is the system of change that leads to real transformation and what are the principles upon which this is based?

In framing answers to these questions I work through a model that I introduce in Chapter 3 outlining the 'what', 'why' and 'who' of organizational agility and resilience. In developing the model I have built on the work of various theorists to whom I am indebted. In particular I wish to credit the work of Dave Francis and Sandra Meredith, whose 2000 model originally inspired my thinking.[4] The remaining chapters of the book explore the 'how' of organizational resilience and agility.

Chapter 1: Why go agile?

Here I set the context and outline the business case for organizational agility, working through a number of broad cultural, economic and environmental factors and megatrends such as digitization, which are leading to the development of new markets, businesses, channels and consumer expectations – at speed. While some might argue that the need for agility applies only to specific types of business, such as high-technology, I maintain that organizations of every sector and industry will be under increasing pressure to develop greater agility as these context effects grow more substantial.

I define organizational agility and some of its related elements such as innovation. I explore how many organizations aspiring to become agile are pursuing agility through cost-cutting, downsizing, offshoring or outsourcing non-core activities, working through networks of suppliers and 'partner' organizations. I consider what enables an organization to become more adaptable and resilient so that it can respond to a changing environment more quickly and find ways to thrive in that new and challenging environment. The connection between organizational resilience and the employment relationship between employers and employees is discussed. Implications for the skills and mindsets of people working in resiliently agile organizations are highlighted.

Chapter 2: Why are agility and resilience so elusive?

As the chapter title suggests, examples of truly agile organizations are rare while evidence of lack of agility abounds. Here we consider some of the reasons why that might be the case. We start by setting the search for agility in a historical context, looking at the changing nature of the 'white collar' employment relationship between employers and employees and the changing balance of power in that relationship. We then consider a range of structural and cultural practices that add to complexity and anchor organizations in the past. We also examine the new leadership mindsets and skill sets required for leading in fast-moving, ambiguous business environments. Finally we look at some of the people 'push' factors for change, not least talent shortages and changing workforce demographics, which are driving a new focus on getting right 'the people bit'.

Chapter 3: The resiliently agile organization

This is an overview of the resiliently agile model and related capabilities and routines. The model comprises four quadrants – agile strategizing, implementing, linkages and people practices. Central to the model is agile culture and people. The model's elements are explored in turn in later chapters of the book.

Chapter 4: Agile strategizing

We discuss differences between conventional strategy making and the process of strategizing – in particular the importance of involving the people who will execute strategy in its formulation. We draw lessons from long-lived successful companies about the centrality of shared purpose and how this might be developed. We consider the role of top leadership in strategizing, and the skills involved, especially knowing where to go 'tight' and 'loose' with respect to control and enabling greater autonomy.

Chapter 5: Agile implementation

Closing the conventional gap between strategy formulation and implementation will require new ways of operating, new disciplines and the adoption of new routines and high-performance work practices, such as self-managed teams, so that innovation and speed become embedded capabilities in the new, agile 'business as usual'. We discuss lean methodology, agile project management disciplines and how to create an internal climate conducive to innovation. We consider the implications of these agile practices for the roles of line managers in particular.

Chapter 6: HR's role in building a high-performance work climate

In this chapter we look at some of the many ways in which the Human Resources (HR) function can contribute to building a culture of high performance and innovation. Here we focus in particular on how HR strategies relating to performance management, reward and benefits are changing to reflect context shifts and to support specific organizational strategies such as innovation.

Chapter 7: Agile linkages

Organizations increasingly pursue agility and flexibility by working across and beyond conventional boundaries of time and place. We discuss emergent flexible organization forms and focus on the rise of virtual working, looking in particular at the role of the virtual manager. We examine some of the challenges of working in strategic alliances, including their implications for managers, and consider what can help alliances to work effectively.

Chapter 8: Agile people processes

In this chapter we start to look at the 'people' aspects of agility: in particular some of the challenges of attracting and developing a flexible workforce – specifically those people deemed to be 'talent'. All too often these people challenges are addressed piecemeal, with separate, short-term solutions and the temptation is to rush straight into action to 'fix' the problem. A more strategic approach is needed in order to equip organizations with the people they need now and for the future, so here we consider how approaches to strategic workforce planning, talent management, development approaches, retention strategies and succession planning can become more agile.

Chapter 9: Nurturing employee engagement and resilience

Simply having the 'right people' in the 'right' place at the 'right' time is not enough to ensure agility. People need to be willing to give their best and also willing to adapt to changing requirements. Here we consider the central link between employee engagement and employee performance, commitment and retention. We look at what is involved and consider the roles played by executives, line managers, HR/Organization Development (OD) and employees themselves in creating a work context conducive to employee engagement. We also consider typical human responses to change and how organizations can help to maintain employee engagement and build employee resilience during times of change.

Chapter 10: Change and transformation

Conventional planned change based on the idea that organizations are machines that can be 're-engineered' has a poor track record of success yet it remains a preferred management approach. In this chapter we look at how 'planned' change can be effected in a way that achieves win-win outcomes for organizations and employees. In particular we consider the importance of getting stakeholders on board and involving people in the change process.

Chapter 11: Building a change-able culture

In this chapter we look at stimulating the development of a change-able culture, building a receptive organizational context for innovation, change and high performance. We look at what a 'change-able' context might look like and how to build a social movement for change and improvement within organizations. In particular we explore the role of leaders in culture change.

Chapter 12: Agile leadership

The question we consider in this chapter is how to build leadership across organizations – not only by developing people and teams in 'formal' leadership roles, but also catalysing a culture of shared leadership and accountability at all levels. We look at the shifts taking place in leadership practice, including towards values-based leadership. We consider what these shifts mean for the skills and mindsets required of leaders – and how these can be developed. In particular we look at how leaders can build a culture of shared leadership, the bedrock of sustainable agility and renewal.

My aim is to demystify the theme of organizational agility and resilience and to draw some practical insights. I have therefore included checklists throughout the book and case study examples where possible to illustrate how some of the theory can be put into practice.

Notes

1 Sullivan, J (2012) [accessed 30 August 2014] Talent Strategies for a Turbulent VUCA World – Shifting to an Adaptive Approach, *Ere.net* [Online] http://www.ere.net/2012/10/22/talent-strategies-for-a-turbulent-vuca-world-shifting-to-an-adaptive-approach.

2 IBM (2010) Capitalising on Complexity; Insights from the Global Chief Executive Officer Study, IBM & Reinventing the Rules of Engagement: CEO Insights from the Global C-suite Study, IBM Institute for Business Value.

3 Reeves, M and Love, C (2012) [accessed 30 August 2014] The Most Adaptive Companies 2012, *Bcg.perspectives* [Online] https://www.bcgperspectives.com/content/articles/corporate_strategy_portfolio_management_future_of_strategy_most_adaptive_companies_2012/.

4 Francis, D and Meredith, S (2000) Journey towards agility: the agile wheel explored, *The TQM Magazine*, **12** (2), pp 137–43.

Why go agile?

The list of industries engulfed by complex strategic change grows longer every day. Even before the challenging times faced today in 2015, the average life expectancy of a multinational corporation – Fortune 500 or its equivalent – was thought to be between 40 and 50 years.[1] Over the last couple of decades the entire ecosystems of industries as diverse as health care, aerospace, pharmaceuticals, energy, retailing, defence, advertising, financial services, retail and automotive have been transformed in the face of a variety of factors – political, cultural, economic, technological and demographic – that are forcing the pace of change. These forces are global in their scope and far-reaching in their impact, affecting not only the environment in which organizations operate but also redefining what they need to do in future in order to compete successfully.

Technological advances in particular are pressuring costs and prices much faster than in the past through increasingly connected supply chains, squeezing budgets and margins ever tighter. Public sector institutions too are under ever more intense pressure to produce excellent outcomes with decreased budgets. With tighter regulation, shifting public attitudes and growing demands for transparency in their practices and outcomes, even previously venerable institutions are coming under intense scrutiny.

In the current context new rules of the game are being invented; there will be some winners and many losers. Statistics on organizational decline are startling. Research conducted by the Deloitte Center for the Edge indicates that over the last 55 years the average company tenure on the S&P 500 has declined from 61 years to 18 years. Moreover, the rate at which companies have lost their leadership position in a given industry has risen 39 per cent in the same period. Strategic agility is emerging as the essential capacity that organizations must possess if they are to adapt successfully to change.

In this chapter we consider:

- Why organizational agility is important.
- What organizational agility is about.

- What is driving the need for agility.
- Why resilience is such a crucial counterbalance to agility.

The business case for agility

While the current context presents many challenges, success is nevertheless possible. Research by the Center for Effective Organizations (CEO) has found that a few large companies in every industry consistently outperform their peers over extended periods. These companies have the capability to anticipate and respond to events, solve problems and implement change better than what CEO describes as the 'thrashers'. And they maintain this performance edge despite significant business change in their competitive environments.[2] Compare the fortunes of companies such as Eastman Kodak who appear to have waited too long before responding to marketplace developments, leaving them struggling to survive in a diminished form, while others such as Amazon, buffeted by the same challenging winds, manage to reinvent themselves in time to prevent failure. Amazon recognized the changing market trends and transformed itself from a web-based bookseller to an online retail platform to a digital media powerhouse, then became a leader in cloud computing. And this continual change has taken place without a performance crisis, demonstrating an ability to anticipate changes and adapt – instead of the reverse.

What these survivor organizations have in common is agility. Agile organizations are better able to thrive in complex environments because they have developed the ability to spot business opportunities and threats early and to implement change quickly. Agile organizations create not only new products and services but also new business models and innovative ways to create value for a company.

The returns on agility are significant. Agile companies exhibit superior business value relative to their industry groups.[3] Agile businesses have 29 per cent higher earnings per share, with net margins 20 per cent higher, return on assets 30 per cent higher and revenue growth 8 per cent higher than comparable businesses.[4] Not surprisingly, in a substantial 2009 study by the Economist Intelligence Survey the overwhelming majority of executives (88 per cent) cited agility as key to global success and 50 per cent of executives said that organizational agility is not only important but a key differentiator.[5]

Given the changing context, the CEO argues that when the measure of high performance in business is profitability, as measured by shareholder return, it is impossible to sustain over the long term.[6] They propose that return on assets (ROA) is a more meaningful proxy for profitability than either total shareholder return (TSR) or cumulative shareholder return and a better indicator of management's effectiveness. This measure suggests that the management of agile companies takes a longer-term view and is more concerned about investing in value creation processes than attending solely to generating short-term shareholder value.

What is organizational agility?

Agility is a complex construct that can take multiple forms. It captures an organization's ability to develop and quickly apply flexible, nimble and dynamic capabilities. Originally linked with software development, lean manufacturing, just-in-time supply chains and process improvement methodologies in the 1990s agility theory is now informed by complexity science and encompasses more broadly an organization's capacity to respond, adapt quickly and thrive in the changing environment.

Organizations as complex adaptive human systems

For many years modern organizations have been thought of as 'machines' whose processes and output can be controlled in a predictable way. In contrast some of the ideas that have shaped thinking in the Agile community of software developers come from studies of complex adaptive systems that recognize the inherently unpredictable nature of software development outcomes in a fast-changing competitive environment. From a complexity and human systems perspective, an organization is a complex adaptive system. It is therefore not just what an organization *does* but what it *is* that makes it agile.

As with living organisms, organizations self-regulate and change in response to external and internal triggers but the rules and patterns that underpin these responses are complex. In contrast to a mechanical system, where the links between cause and effect are clear and linear, in a complex adaptive system there are multiple interacting and intertwined parts that are non-linear. Change in any part of an organization will affect other parts of the system.

Each organization is made up of a collection of individual agents who have the freedom to act in ways that are not always totally predictable. Where people – the individual agents – have freedom to act, one agent's actions can change the context for others. Individual agents respond to their environment using internalized simple rule sets and mental models that drive action. Patterns of thinking and behaviour and relations between agents are therefore just as much a part of the system as are structures and processes.

In a human system, alongside the formal structures reflected in organization charts there exists the so-called informal 'shadow side' consisting of relationships, power and political networks, and informal communications or 'gossip'.[7] Since this informal system is usually more powerful than the formal system in influencing people's behaviour, efforts to innovate within the formal system are often limited by what is happening in the shadow system. So key to understanding the system is to understand the relationships among the agents.

Ability to adapt

Since organizations are complex adaptive systems, like living organisms they naturally adapt to their context or they die. Evolution theory teaches us that organisms are naturally changing and adapting to their environments all the time, often in infinitesimal ways. They experiment, learn what works, find sources of nourishment and opportune contexts in which to grow. Those that fail to adapt do not survive. According to the theory of evolution it is reasonable to assume that only the 'fittest' organizations – those that can successfully respond to and learn from external events and adapt rapidly to their changing ecosystems – will survive and thrive into the future. After all, Charles Darwin reportedly said that: 'It is not the strongest or the most intelligent who will survive, but those who can best manage change.'[8]

Ability to manage change

Many organizations struggle to manage change and appear ill-equipped to deal with major transformation, especially the kinds of change linked to what D'Aveni calls 'hyper-organization'.[9] The underlying logic of hyper-organization is to focus on staying slim, reducing costs and externalizing risks, stripping out unnecessary positions, outsourcing processes and people, ruthlessly pursuing greater efficiency while keeping up and improving performance levels.

As chief executives work to short-termist agendas and take drastic measures to minimize cost and maximize economic growth, managers consistently tend to pay more attention to the 'process' and 'technology' aspects of transformation than to the 'people' element, with often seriously limiting consequences for the organization and for people. More often than not, rather than creating the new ways forward needed for the organization, the way that change is managed can be so disruptive that it can tear organizations apart. When change results in organizational chaos, initiative overload and employee resistance, the gap between strategic intent and strategic implementation widens, slowing down progress still further.

The key question then is whether the 'natural' ability of human organizations to change can be deliberately accelerated and optimized to benefit all concerned. Can organizations learn to become 'change-able' and adaptable? To some extent at least, yes. As we discuss in Chapter 3, there are many ways to introduce positive change into the system even though direct benefits cannot be guaranteed. In later chapters we look at how various organizations are attempting to become more change-able.

Speed

Given the rapid pace of technological development and growth of global competition, agility is also the ability to move 'quickly, decisively, and effectively in anticipating, initiating and taking advantage of change'.[10] In today's hyper-competitive phase of globalization, organizations need to move swiftly just to keep pace with developments, take advantage of opportunities or avert disaster. In a world where new ideas, technologies and services are emerging all the time, organizations that cannot move fast enough to meet customer needs, or fail to seize opportunities, innovate, trim costs and avoid major errors, soon go out of business. Just look at the UK retail sector where a combination of tough trading conditions, reduced consumer spending and fierce competition from online retailers has led to the closures of well-known high street firms such as Woolworths, Comet and Focus.

Agile organizations are able to react swiftly and decisively to sudden shifts in overall market conditions, to the emergence of new competitors and the development of new industry-changing technologies by developing a range of products that satisfy a range of customers. It is essential to pick out fast what matters and act accordingly. Rapid decision making and nimble execution are therefore defining attributes of an agile business. As noted by Horney, Pasmore and O'Shea, to succeed, 'leaders must make continuous shifts in people, process, technology, and structure. This requires flexibility and quickness in decision making.'[11]

Yet adopting newer, faster, better ways of doing things does not happen overnight; after all, conventional hierarchical organization and governance structures are designed to stabilize and safeguard processes. And as we return to a period of growth many companies and institutions can expect extreme competitive and operating pressures to continue and accelerate further. According to a Deloitte CFO Survey, 'the top priority for CFOs in 2014 is expansion'.[12] But expansion requires investment – and investing in solid infrastructure has, historically, been known to take time.

Innovation

As well as encapsulating the ability to adapt and thrive in fast-changing environments agility is also defined as the ability to 'produce the right products at the right place at the right time at the right price'.[13] The consumer boom of the early 2000s continues apace and the consumer desire for novelty and stimulation is driving the quest for pace, quality and innovation. Consequently, it is no surprise that accelerated innovation now sits high on executive and board agendas in every sector.

Through technology the possibilities for innovation and new business opportunities seem endless. For instance, in April 2014 Google announced that it had bought a company called Titan Aerospace so that the internet's biggest giants are all now 'in' drones. Facebook previously purchased a UK drone-maker called Ascenta, and Amazon is already working on the eighth generation of its Prime Air drone. Though drones are not yet in commercial operation, 'if you're a major multinational corporation, parcel deliverer, army or key emergency services provider and you haven't either invested in a drone manufacturer or at least trialled the things, you're in danger of looking hopelessly out of step'.[14]

Does every organization need to be 'agile'?

Is agility a prerequisite for survival for every organization? After all, it could be argued that some organizations may endemically lack agility and yet they remain successful. Consider universities, for instance. These long-lived elite institutions have been able to select the 'best' students and secure funding in a variety of ways, not least through endowments.

However, in today's globalized knowledge economy, higher education has become a major industry, rapidly expanding, highly competitive and marketized. For instance, in 2012 the maximum tuition fee level was raised to £9,000 at English universities, more obviously transforming students (and their parents) into consumers, if not customers, of higher education establishments. The challenge for today's institutions is to differentiate themselves in an increasingly crowded marketplace in order to attract the numbers of students and other sources of funding they depend upon. Thus, in a relatively short period of time, the dramatic shifts in the higher education landscape have significantly called into question the purpose and infrastructure of higher education, and have enabled new entrants to compete, seize market share and put all but the most financially secure institutions under pressure to change their ways if they are to survive.

That is why I argue that agility and its various components are essential for all organizations. At the very least, we need to change the way we think about change. I agree with Abrahamson that in a world where ongoing disruption can be envisaged as the norm, and change is therefore now a way of life rather than an exception, a useful way of thinking about today's context is to see it as one of 'dynamic stability'.[15] Such a mindset allows for change to be reframed as part of an evolutionary process, as the norm to be embraced positively, without major trauma, rather than a painful add-on to 'business as usual'. Such a perspective will also affect how we enact change, moving away from the kinds of reactive change management that result in radical disruption towards a cultural shift that readily embraces and stimulates change and innovation.

To achieve this shift, Abrahamson argues that a more modulated approach to change is required, what he calls 'pacing', in which major change initiatives are deliberately interspersed with 'carefully paced periods of smaller, organic change'.[16] After all, he suggests, although some change is management-led and occurs within a strategic framework, most change is really happening locally, almost imperceptibly in automatic, spontaneous and reflexive ways at individual and team levels. In later chapters, we explore how embracing change as dynamic stability may require a conscious mindset shift and active learning for employees and managers at all levels.

Forces driving the need for agility

The forces for discontinuous change are multiple – they include the broader politico-economic system implicit in Anglo-American neo-liberal forms of capitalism, global markets, demographics, technology, connectivity, sustainable developments, changing social attitudes, to name but a few – and their effect on business and organizational survival is intensifying.

A global marketplace

Today's marketplaces are ruthlessly competitive, in part because the powerful economic philosophy underpinning the global economy since the 1980s is neo-liberalism, or free-market thinking and practice. This thinking places profit ahead of people, with shareholder value as the dominant goal of organizations, and encourages short-term thinking from top to bottom of organizations. Neo-liberal theory underpins mainstream management theory and practice widely taught in business schools, has affected organizations of every sector, and also appears to have influenced societal values in the West. In the UK in particular, before the onset of the recession in 2008, consumerism and greed – fuelled by easy access to cheap credit – led to widespread individual and public spending and debt.

Since the 1980s knowledge and service industries have become the mainspring of many Western economies. Industries such as financial services have been progressively deregulated to enable global competition. Deregulation enabled the proliferation of new financial products so complex and ultimately ill-founded that prior to the recession few people understood their nature. Early warning signs of what can happen when the prospect of huge bonuses drives ill-judged behaviour, as in the case of several 'rogue traders' whose reckless gambling brought their own employers' businesses to their knees, were ignored.

As discussed earlier, even traditional institutions such as universities are not immune from neo-liberal free-market practices. Denneen and Dretler argue that over the past two decades the higher education industry has followed not 'Moore's Law' (ie the observation that over the history of computing hardware, the number of transistors on integrated circuits doubles approximately every two years) but what they call the 'Law of More': ie *more* and *bigger* are better.[17] Colleges have continuously built up campus facilities and increased campus spending, the numbers of programmes they offer and the size of the administration, hoping to raise their rankings and reputations. In such a competitive marketplace, the only outcome of this, these authors argue, is an increased debt risk.

Disruptive innovation

Almost every aspect of the business environment and business itself is being transformed by disruptive forces. The days when major corporations could dominate markets and provide standardized products at inflated margins seem to be coming to an end. Retaining competitive edge in the face of what Professor Clayton Christensen termed 'disruptive innovation' can be a real challenge.[18] The term originally described how and why some changes in the technology sector (and now more widely in all business sectors) lead, in a relatively short time, to a radical restructuring of the overall system. Christensen found that disruptive innovations in a given marketplace are often triggered by the arrival of new competitors who punctuate the existing equilibrium having spotted opportunities, usually aided by changes to a wider context. Thanks to globalization and technology, new competitors can emerge from anywhere and completely rewrite the laws of competition through innovation.

In Christensen's 1997 book *The Innovator's Dilemma* he distinguished between 'sustaining innovation' (incremental or step changes in an existing order) and 'disruptive innovation' (major changes that ultimately transform an industry sector). So while existing players in a given market might be better at sustaining innovation, it is usually new entrants who become the real winners at disruptive innovation. Those that cannot adapt swiftly enough will struggle. Compare for instance the fortunes of insurgents such as Apple versus established firms such as Nokia. Nokia witnessed the Apple iPhone crush its global business, particularly at the high end of smartphones, which were by far the most lucrative segment of its business. Indeed, things are so fast-moving that manufacturers of high-end smartphones and tablets now fear that consumer demand for their gadgets may be slowing down due to market saturation.

In retailing consumers are looking for the latest products, choice, personalization, quality and low cost. Innovation applies not only to product design but also to delivery mechanisms. Today commuters in many major cities can 'click and collect' goods, which within hours are ready for collection at convenient points such as their local store. The business model involves cutting out the 'middle man' and shortening the supply chain. Of course, home delivery companies will not go without a fight and, partly in response to the spread of click and collect services, couriers are now doing home deliveries every day of the week, thus pushing up costs to delivery companies. So the ability to keep abreast or ahead of customer demand – or better still, to create it – needs to be married with the ability to innovate technically and organizationally, and to plan and execute new courses of action that are cost-effective and fast.

So agile organizations that are able to 'successfully respond to and learn from external events, to innovate technically and organizationally, and to plan and execute new courses of action',[19] are better able to continually and successfully adapt to changing circumstances.

Technology

Technology is at the centre of many business transformations and the rapid development of new advanced technologies is causing the pace of change to accelerate. The digitization of texts, symbols, instructions, patterns, visual images and music allows huge data sets to be marshalled more efficiently than in the past. Many economic activities that once depended on physical proximity and face-to-face encounters can now be conducted at a distance. For the first time, in a 2012 IBM study CEOs identified technology – rather than market forces – as the biggest driver of change.[20] Again in 2014, CEOs ranked technology first, believing that the impact of emerging technologies on their organizations will be profound. Similarly, in a 2014 study of the UK's IT Industry, 63 per cent of 400 UK companies said they intended to invest in technology over the coming year to help them reduce costs and overhead, improve staff capability and productivity, find more effective ways to reach new customers and address other business priorities.[21]

Technology is also enabling social transformations and has wider implications for the way businesses operate and the way we live and work today. Whole industries, businesses, working practices and even definitions of 'work' and 'leisure' are being transformed by the use and effects of technology. Within organizations, hierarchies and jobs for life are being replaced by a knowledge-based network economy bursting with innovative online communication technologies, including mobile devices and cloud computing. Technology is also enabling greater choice for employees, and working lives are changing accordingly. Aided by improved domestic access to high-speed broadband and widespread availability of global devices, an increasing number of people now work from home at least part of each week, as flexible working options have expanded.

In a world in which relationships, business transactions and even political uprisings are being enabled by social media, connectivity is the name of the game. As with the internet, the use of social media brings benefits and new risks – of brand sabotage and cyberbullying for instance. Social media are increasingly used by organizations for recruitment and vetting purposes. Where previously detailed company information was the privileged domain of the most senior management, today the use of social media for internal and external communication purposes reflects profound changes taking place in the ways in which employees expect to be managed and communicated with. Largely gone are the days when companies banned staff from using Facebook and other social networking sites for fear that staff were wasting company time. Now many firms use social media for all company messaging, and many CEOs now regularly connect directly with their workforce through blogging and other social media activities. In comparison to the speed with which messages are co-created and proliferated through the use of social media, conventional internal communications often seem slow and clunky.

In many organizations employees are encouraged to bring their own devices to work rather than the company providing employees with hardware that will soon be obsolete. While saving company costs, such policies reflect the fact that companies can no longer control access to company data by employees. By implication, organizations must trust that employees will not abuse access to previously privileged company information, but will instead help to promote their company brands through the use of such sites. So this democratization of access to information within organizations represents a potential shift of power bases within organizations, in which 'employees' are being reframed as 'customers' and 'partners'.

In the years ahead, rapid technological development will require organizations to continually review their provision in response to changing social attitudes of customers and staff in relation to the use of technology. To return to the example of the higher education (HE) sector, the development and proliferation via the internet of massive open online courses (MOOCs) allows individuals to download 'content' (ie lectures and whole courses from leading universities) free of charge. The market for such services is increasingly competitive and the 'customers' more demanding.

Of course MOOCs are not going to put universities out of business, but they do challenge a business model that assumes the institution holds a monopoly of high-quality content. Increasingly students (and their families) will choose universities that offer a high-quality university experience, with instant provision tailored to their learning and social needs, and for their success in helping students to achieve the desired outcomes of higher education, including qualifications and access to the first step on a career ladder.

A market society

On a broader front, organizations reflect the societies in which they operate and vice versa. Neo-liberalism has become deeply rooted in the public consciousness. Political philosopher Michael Sandel argues that since the early 1980s we have gone from *having* a market economy to *being* a market society.[22] A market society is a place where almost everything is up for sale, where market values dominate every aspect of life, from the private to the civic, driving up inequality. The values, accountabilities and morality of various politicians, corporate and institutional leaders have been called into question.

Similarly, capitalism itself is under the spotlight in the wake of various infamous corporate and institutional scandals and the huge 'rewards for failure' granted to too many organizational chiefs. Of course it could be argued that, carried to an extreme, the neo-liberal pursuit of individual self-interest and placing shareholder value ahead of notions of community or public value was what gave rise to some of the unethical and reckless business practice that has been subsequently identified as a primary cause of the mainly Western economic crisis from 2008 onwards. There have been calls for stronger regulation and better governance as well as higher standards in public life. Company reputations are increasingly recognized as a firm's greatest asset and are easily destroyed by unethical practice.

Despite this, little appears to be changing in practice. It takes a major scandal to really spur businesses into action. An example of this can be seen in the 2012 garment factory fire in Bangladesh, which killed 112 workers producing goods for a variety of global brands. This raised public anger and put consumer pressure onto corporations to use their buying power to improve practice across their global supply chains.

Given the state of the global economy, with tensions in international relations, the deepening threat of climate change, and after a decade or more of unprecedented global economic and geopolitical uncertainty, the time seems right to question the seemingly inexorable flow of neo-liberalism with its extreme gaps between 'winners' and 'losers'. Sandel calls for more collective reasoning around the value and meaning of our social practices. Even some of the guru architects of neo-liberal management theory, such as Michael Porter,[23] now argue for a shift away from a primary focus on shareholder value towards 'shared value' as the principal aim of business. To some extent this search for more meaningful practice is evident amongst potential recruits, where 78 per cent of generation Y are said to look at ethics and values before deciding which company to work for.[24]

David Marquand sees a wider issue: the fall of the public realm.[25] He argues that we are well advanced towards a state of genteel barbarism where the crisis is one of our moral economy as much as of our political economy. He sets out a framework for a new public philosophy founded on civic conscience and cooperation. In such a context, 'new' must genuinely result in 'different' and 'better'.

Demographics

Changing workforce demographics are having a significant effect on organizations across industries and geographies. In the West the population is ageing, and becoming much more ideologically and ethnically diverse, while in developing economies such as China and India the population is younger, growing rapidly and gaining improved educational opportunities.

In many companies, increasing numbers of employees are retiring, taking with them sizable amounts of knowledge whose loss can place the organization at risk. Companies face the challenge of maintaining a productive workforce in the face of potentially shrinking labour pools and the increased mobility of the younger generation of employees. Industries as diverse as utilities, oil and gas producers, health care and the public sector are clearly experiencing the effects of employee retirements and difficulties in sourcing new talent.[26] The changing composition of the workforce and changing expectations of employees are likely to drive the need for a wide range of new approaches to HR practices designed to define, attract, recruit, motivate and develop 'talent'. The relative power in the employment relationship between employer and employee will determine the nature of what organizations offer their employees – or their 'employee value proposition'. What seems increasingly clear is that, notwithstanding desires for fairness, there is unlikely to be 'one size fits all'.

It remains to be seen which of these (and other) influences will prove to be merely incremental 'sustaining innovations' and which will be 'game-changing' disruptive innovations. The impact of each will become apparent as progressive layers of pressure and innovation interact with each other.

Can competitive advantage be sustained?

In this turbulent context, even the very notion of sustainable competitive advantage becomes questionable – as firms such as Microsoft, Nokia and Blackberry bear witness. More than two in five CEOs in the 2014 IBM study now expect their next competitive threat to come from organizations outside their industries.[27] These new competitors are not just set to steal market share; they are upsetting whole industries, redefining how value is created and what constitutes value.

The challenges posed by the potential disruptors will require many existing players in a given market to respond in new and innovative ways. Traditional businesses in particular often struggle to get to grips with potential trends, opportunities and risks to their current business models, yet those that do are more likely to be in the driving seat of change, allowing for evolution rather than revolution. By way of example, a medium-sized UK distribution company specializing in supplying heating and plumbing products to the trade identified some of the following factors as driving change in their business:

- Government legislation, in particular tougher health and safety and climate change/environmental requirements. Only environmentally friendly boilers will sell in future, which means developing partnerships with new suppliers.

- In an e-commerce world with many customers ordering online, some customers will still prefer face-to-face interaction, so a variety of effective channels will be needed and these will need to be maximized, requiring different skill sets and approaches, shared client knowledge and integrated systems.

- The company is well-known for its good relationships with customers. With an ageing traditional customer base a generational change will be needed among customers and staff to expand beyond this. The brand must be rapidly developed to appeal to newer, younger customers – keeping the best of the old alongside the new.

- Mobile technology, personalization and individual relevance mean that 'one size does *not* fit all' – speed of response and flexibility of offer will be required.

- Increasing demands by customers for transparency of pricing mean that margins are likely to be squeezed.

- With competitor consolidation in this mature business, the challenge is to leverage strengths in other areas and develop other partnerships.

In this case, the firm recognized that it needed to better understand its non-traditional yet growing potential customer bases and decided to invest in further market research. Having understood the needs of relevant customer segments, the firm decided to operate through multichannels to meet the more varied needs of tomorrow's mobile customers, trialling some channels ahead of others in order to test customer response. To supply more environmentally friendly products and services and potentially enhance its brand as prime supplier of such products would mean the firm revising its arrangements with long-standing suppliers, finding new sources who could meet requirements of quality, speed and price. Transparency on pricing would mean developing a variety of customer propositions offering greater choice and value and also a more win-win relationship with customers so that trust could be built and maintained. This in turn would require staff development so that branch employees' customer service skills could be taken to the next level.

Yet insurgents can be just as vulnerable to change as existing players if they fall into the 'first-mover trap' (the belief that being first in the market creates a sustainable competitive advantage), one of seven 'misconceptions' in executive thinking identified by Rita Gunther McGrath.[28] Similarly a 2005 McKinsey study[29] found that the probability of market leaders being 'toppled' within five years stood at 30 per cent chance, over three times what it used to be a few decades before.

Some theorists argue that since the need to adapt is part of the evolutionary process, and if a company's competitive advantage is unlikely to be sustainable over the long term, what matters more is its ability to maintain evolutionary advantage over time. After all, old age, obsolescence or changing environmental conditions can cause previously healthy organisms to perish. But at least with human organizations there is the possibility that becoming aware increases leaders' choice about how to deal with the situation facing the organization. All of this is putting pressure on leaders and boards to find new ways to run business in contexts where there are no easy answers, and where recipes of success from the past may not be helpful. So for any business, a useful starting point is to become aware of the trends that might most affect its current and proposed business and to work out what the specific risks and opportunities of different scenarios might represent for the business. We discuss this further in Chapter 4.

Resilience

As we have discussed, strategic agility is vital to any organization aspiring to thrive in today's business environment; it is needed in order to address change that is continuous and relentless. Yet agility alone will not secure sustainable success.[30] In a future defined by ambiguity, unpredictability, complexity, multiple stakeholders and rapid change, organizations also need resilience in order to respond to change that is severely disruptive and surprising.[31] Variously termed organizational 'resiliency' or 'resilience', this is the capacity to deploy different forms of strategic agility when confronted with the unexpected and to respond effectively to changing conditions.[32] It involves taking prompt, creative, situation-specific, robust and transformative actions to minimize the impact of powerful events that are not avoided or avoidable and that have the potential to jeopardize the organization's long-term survival.[33]

Thus, resilience capacity and strategic agility are complementary capabilities that enable organizations to deal with the turbulent environments in which they operate.[34] Key resilience capabilities are 'anticipation' and the 'ability to bounce back'.

Anticipation

Resilient organizations are able to address pivotal events that affect their business because they are alert to, and anticipate, both internal and environmental changes – opportunities as well as challenges – and effectively respond to those changes using available resources in a timely, flexible, affordable and relevant manner. For a notable retailing success story, the John Lewis Partnership, a company founded in 1864, has remained in touch with its customers and ahead of the competition for over a century. It became the largest multichannel retailer in the UK in 2014 through its shrewd anticipation of changing customer preferences and the timely development of its online business ahead of the competition. At the same time, the brand is trusted because the firm delivers its promise to customers and staff to be 'never knowingly undersold'.

Ability to bounce back

Resilience is not only about being able to respond rapidly to unforeseen and problematic change. It is reasonable to assume that, in turbulent circumstances, organizations will not get things right all the time. There may be mistakes, some of them costly, so resilience is also about bouncing back from setbacks with speed and determination.[35] Thus an organization demonstrates resiliency when it experiences a severe, life-threatening setback but is able to reinvent itself around its core values.[36] At organizational level, this is about the robustness of systems; the capacity for resisting, absorbing and responding, even reinventing if required, in response to fast and/or disruptive change that cannot be avoided.[37]

Different levels of resilience may result in different organizational outcomes. While modest levels should enable a firm to recover from disruptions and resume normal operations, high levels of resilience may place an organization ahead of its competition since it has learned to capitalize on environmental disruptions and is able to create new options and capabilities while undergoing a robust transformation in the face of adverse events.

Both strategic agility and resilience are prerequisites for organizations to thrive in a dynamic environment. These concepts share common roots and are built from complementary resources, skills and competencies. While resilient organizations are nimble, flexible and agile, not all agile organizations are resilient.[38] If agility is pursued from a cost-cutting perspective, involving work intensification or job losses, it is likely that the employment relationship between employers and employees will suffer and trust will evaporate. How likely is it, then, that employees will wish to 'go the extra mile' for organizations that see them as costs to be cut or as commodities to be exploited?

Conclusion

Organizational agility – or the capacity for moving quickly, flexibly and decisively – needs to be complemented by resilience, or the ability to anticipate, initiate and take advantage of opportunities while aiming to avoid any negative consequences of change. Together they enable firms to prepare for changing conditions, restore their vitality after traumatic setbacks, and become even more effective as a result of the experience. Combined they represent an organization's adaptive capacity or its 'change-ability'.

Central to an organization's resilience capacity is its relationship with its workforce, and the ways in which the workforce feels 'engaged' or not with the organization and its fortunes. And while people are often stated as a company's greatest asset, few businesses have a clear model of leadership that improves engagement, removes barriers to innovation and uncovers hidden strengths in people and the organization. So how can leaders make the transition to a new way of thinking and working?

In a context where change is a key aspect of the business environment for the foreseeable future, organizations must become change-able. If change is to happen effectively, people at all levels need to embrace change; have a desire for, a mindset oriented towards and a capability for (a way of acting upon) change. All three aspects can be developed to prepare individuals, groups and organizations for change, to render organizations more agile, more resilient and more responsive to change than they might previously have considered possible.

In practice this means that:

- *Everyone needs to be externally aware and alert*, willing to voice and allowed to act on such knowledge.
- *Products and services need to be innovated continuously* in order to meet the demands of the marketplace and customers.
- *Costs need to be kept low on all fronts*, tapping into the goodwill of local staff to implement cost-cutting initiatives while also innovating.
- *Organizations need to be flexible and adaptable* in roles, responsibilities and structures.
- *Key staff need to be able and willing to continuously develop themselves* – flexible sourcing and multiskilling.
- *Organizations need to aim for high engagement with staff* in order to tap into the discretionary effort of all their knowledge workers.
- *Organizational culture needs to be highly adaptable, agile, organic* – with everyone, regardless of rank, willing and able to commit to the organization and contribute to its success.

Plenty of challenges exist, perhaps the greatest of which is assuming that developing agility and resilience are optional. For organizations and individuals that want to survive and thrive in today's fast-changing environment – it is not.

Of course, this is easier said than done – otherwise why are organizational agility and resilience so elusive? This is the theme we explore in the next chapter, where we will consider some of the main barriers to agility before moving on in later chapters to consider what can be done to enable agility.

Checklist

What's happening in your context?

- What are the key environmental factors that are likely to affect your organization in the medium and long term?
- What are the key opportunities and risks you foresee?

- What mechanisms does your organization have to identify and analyse emerging trends?

- How effectively are these trends acted upon and the necessary changes made?

- To what extent do you look out for emergent relevant changes in the environment, using alliances, partnerships and joint ventures?

- What do you see as the role and purpose of your organization?

- Who are its key stakeholders?

- What is the basis of your company's reputation? Where is this at risk?

Notes

1 De Geus, AP (2002) *The Living Company: Habits for survival in a turbulent business environment*, Harvard Business School Press, Boston.

2 Williams, T, Worley, CM and Lawler, EE (2013) [accessed 30 August 2014] The Agility Factor, Strategy + Business, April 15 [Online] http://www.strategy-business.com/article/00188?pg=all.

3 Weill, P (2007) IT Portfolio Management and IT Savvy – Rethinking IT Investments as a Portfolio, MIT Sloan School of Management, Center for Information Systems Research (CISR), Summer Session, 14 June. Research was conducted by MIT via the SeeIT/CISR survey of 629 firms – 329 of these firms are listed on US stock exchanges.

4 Source: Business Agility Portfolios, MIT Sloan School, 2006.

5 Economist Intelligence Unit (EIU) (2009) [accessed 19 January 2015] Organisational Agility: How Business Can Survive and Thrive in Turbulent Times, *Economist Intelligence Unit* [Online] http://www.emc.com/collateral/leadership/organisational-agility-230309.pdf.

6 Williams, T, Worley, CM and Lawler, EE (2013) [accessed 30 August 2014] The Agility Factor, Strategy + Business, April 15 [Online] http://www.strategy-business.com/article/00188?pg=all.

7 Stacey R (1996) *Strategic Management and Organizational Dynamics*, Pitman Publishing, London.

8 See Megginson, LC (1963) Lessons from Europe for American business, *Southwestern Social Science Quarterly*, **44** (1), pp 3–4.

9 D'Aveni, R (1994) *Hypercompetition: Managing the dynamics of strategic maneuvering*, Free Press, New York.

10 Jamrog J, Vickers, M and Bear, D (2006) Building and sustaining a culture that supports innovation, *Human Resource Planning*, **29** (3), pp 9–19.

11 Horney, N, Pasmore, W and O'Shea, T (2010) Leadership Agility: A business imperative for a VUCA world, *People and Strategy* (HRPS), 33 (4), pp 34–42.

12 Deloitte [accessed 26 January 2015] Q4 2013 Global CFO Signals™; Time to accelerate? [Online] http://www2.deloitte.com/content/dam/Deloitte/global/Documents/Finance-Transformation/gx-ft-Q42013-global-cfosignals-report-021214.pdf.

13 Roth, AV (1996) Achieving strategic agility through economies of knowledge, *Planning Review*, 24 (2), pp 30–36.

14 Herriman, J (2014) Game of Drones, *London Evening Standard*, 28 April 2014.

15 Abrahamson, E (2000) Change without pain, *Harvard Business Review*, July, pp 75–79.

16 Ibid.

17 Denneen, J and Dretler, T (2012) [accessed 19 January 2015] The Financially Stable University, *Bain & Company* [Online] http://www.bain.com/Images/BAIN_BRIEF_The_financially_sustainable_university.pdf.

18 Christensen, CM (1997) *The Innovator's Dilemma: When new technologies cause great firms to fail*, Harvard Business School Press, Boston.

19 Williams, T, Worley, CM and Lawler, EE (2013) [accessed 30 August 2014] The Agility Factor, Strategy + Business, April 15 [Online] http://www.strategy-business.com/article/00188?pg=all

20 IBM Institute for Business Value (2014) [accessed 30 August 2014] Reinventing the Rules of Engagement: CEO insights from the Global C-suite Study [Online] http://public.dhe.ibm.com/common/ssi/ecm/en/gbe03579usen/GBE03579USEN.PDF.

21 Comptia [accessed 26 January 2015] 4th Annual State of the Channel, published Monday, 20 October 2014 [Online] http://www.comptia.org/resources/4th-annual-state-of-the-channel.

22 TED blog [accessed 26 January 2015] The Real Price of Market Values: Why We Shouldn't Trust Markets With Our Civic Life: Michael Sandel at TEDGlobal 2013 [Online] http://blog.ted.com/2013/06/14/the-real-price-of-market-values-michael-sandel-at-tedglobal-2013/.

23 Porter, ME and Kramer, MR (2011) Creating shared value, *Harvard Business Review*, January.

24 Source: Cone Communications Survey.

25 Marquand, D (2014) *Mammon's Kingdom: An essay on Britain, now*, Penguin Books, London.

26 Closing the Generational Divide (2012) [accessed 30 August 2014] IBM Institute for Business Value [Online] http://www-935.ibm.com/services/us/gbs/bus/pdf/g510-6323-00_generational_divide.pdf.

27 Ibid.

28 Gunther McGrath, R (2013) Transient advantage, *Harvard Business Review*, June.

29 Defined as being in the top quintile by revenue in a given industry.

30 Hamel, G and Valikangas, L (2003) [accessed 19 January 2015] The quest for resilience, *Harvard Business Review,* September [Online] hbr.org/2003/09/the-quest-for-resilience/ar/1.

31 McCann, JE (2004) Organizational effectiveness: changing concepts for changing environments, *Human Resource Planning Journal*, March, pp 42–50.

32 Lengnick-Hall, CA and Beck, TE (2009) Resilience capacity and strategic agility: prerequisites for thriving in a dynamic environment, Working Paper series Wp# 0059MGT-199-2009, The University of Texas at San Antonio, College of Business.

33 Heifetz, R, Grashow, A and Linsky, M (2009) *The Practice of Adaptive Leadership*, Harvard Business Press, Boston.

34 Weick, KE and Sutcliffe, KM (2007) *Managing the Unexpected: Resilient performance in an age of uncertainty*, 2nd edn, Jossey-Bass, San Francisco.

35 Marcos, J and Macauley, S (2008) Organisational Resilience: The key to anticipation, adaptation and recovery, Cranfield School of Management paper.

36 Alpaslan, CM and Mitroff, II (2004) Bounded morality: the relationship between ethical orientation and crisis management, before and after 9/11, in *Current Topics in Management*, Vol. 6, ed M. Afzalur Rahim, Kenneth Mackenzie and Robert Golembiewski, pp 13–43, JAI Press, Greenwich.

37 McCann, J, Selsky, J and Lee, J (2009) Building agility, resilience and performance in turbulent environments, *HR People & Strategy*, 32 (3), pp 45–51.

38 Jamrog J, Vickers, M and Bear, D (2006) Building and sustaining a culture that supports innovation, *Human Resource Planning*, 29 (3), pp 9–19.

Why are agility and resilience so elusive?

In Chapter 1 we looked at some of the reasons why agility and resilience are needed if organizations are to survive and thrive. For leaders, there is a growing sense of urgency about finding ways to succeed in today's volatile context and, as the pace of change continues to hot up, leaders will have even less time to make an impact. Disruption is – and will continue to be – a fact of life for all industries, as new technologies and regulations cause major changes to many markets, placing ever greater pressure on organizations to deliver – and fast. And as we move deeper into the 21st century, we can realistically expect that pressures to change the culture, purpose and shape of organizations will intensify as the needs for flexibility, competitiveness, innovation and speed become even greater.

Today, the most important question for any organization is not, 'do we need to change?' but 'are we changing as fast as the world and the competition around us?' For most organizations, the answer would be 'no', as findings from the 2009 EIU study highlight.[1] While most executives in this study recognized organizational agility as a competitive necessity, many admitted that their companies were not sufficiently flexible to compete successfully.

So why are agility and resilience so elusive?

In this chapter we look at some of the reasons why many organizations struggle to become resiliently agile. While some of these can be found in the tangible aspects of organization, such as structures and talent shortages, some of the main endemic barriers to agility and resilience are to be found in the 'intangible' aspects of organization – in people's mindsets and behaviours, in organizational culture and history and also in the nature and health of the employment relationship between employers and workforces. In particular, we explore some of the barriers to agility and resilience in:

- structures and routines;
- the conventional strategy-making process;
- the implementation gap;
- organizational culture;
- neglecting the human aspects of change;
- talent shortages.

These add to complexity and the challenge of responding to external demands in a timely way.

Setting the context: evolution of agility theory

First let's set these barriers in context by considering a brief account of where agility theories come from and what preceded them. These different theories reflect the times in which they emerged, though it could be argued that these intertwined social and business trends continue to influence people's thinking and expectations today.

The 1990s

The global economy was increasingly operating along free-market lines, aided and abetted by the deregulation of industries such as financial services and the opening up of many previously protected markets. In terms of management theory, processes were now recognized as an important element of business success and a raft of approaches from manufacturing, often described as 'Japanese management practices' – such as total quality management, continuous improvement, business process re-engineering and lean methodologies – were increasingly adopted, usually by large organizations. Toyota was a leading exponent of such methods in the West. Putting the customer first became the rationale for 'delayering' organizations – making them flatter and more horizontal in terms of the customer process, removing many hierarchical management jobs that were often described as 'checkers checking checkers'. Limited amounts of outsourcing began in 'non-core' areas, enabled by technology and facilitated by the diminishing power of trade unions and lack of collective protections for employees.

What did this mean for the employment relationship?

These increasingly common organizational downsizings started to undermine the white-collar notion of a 'job for life'. Given the fluidity of organizational environments, the old psychological contract or employment 'deal' of job security and career progression in exchange for hard work and loyalty was becoming an expensive liability for employers who were now looking for more flexibility and cost-effectiveness with regard to the workforce. While people were regularly described as their organizations' 'biggest asset', they were increasingly treated as its greatest cost.

The emergent psychological contract (or 'new deal'[2]) implied that employees should no longer expect job security or career progression within the same company unless they were exceptional. Instead they should continuously upgrade their performance and take responsibility for their own careers by developing themselves to become 'employable' – internally, or elsewhere when no longer needed. Rather than looking for employee loyalty, employers now wanted commitment from their employees. The assumptions behind the new employment relationship were unitarist: that the interests of business and those of employees were aligned: ie that what was good for the business was good for the people.

HR policies embedded these new approaches to the employment relationship. As performance management became more widespread, people's performance ratings became the justification for decisions about their continuing employment or promotion. The link between seniority (time served) and career and pay progression was largely disaggregated and performance-related pay was introduced in many sectors. The UK became the easiest country in Europe in which to hire and fire employees. What was good for the business was perhaps not always good for employees.

Many highly skilled white-collar workers felt disillusioned about the loss of the 'old deal' and, as the jobs market improved, now felt free to shop around, leading to medium labour flexibility. So much so that by the end of the 1990s business growth in some knowledge-based sectors, particularly consultancies, was being constrained by the lack of sufficient skilled people to do the work. Thus began what McKinsey dubbed the 'War for Talent', as employers vied with each other to attract and retain the best available 'talent'.

The rise of agile

The concept of agile arose in response to the needs of modern businesses to operate in predictable ways even in the face of extreme complexity. The arrival of the internet and other advanced technologies led to a huge increase in the scale and types of competition for organizations large and small, enabling even tiny enterprises based in developing countries to compete on a global scale.

An Agile movement came into being that was synonymous with the intensive use of IT and software development. An Agile manifesto was developed by a growing community of specialists in Utah. Agile applies to a specific methodology – iterative project management methods, lean tools and continuous improvement approaches – that is applied to develop many kinds of systems, including web-based applications, mobile applications and business intelligence systems.

By the time discussion of the agile enterprise arose in the early 2000s, it was against a backdrop of widespread lack of trust in employers and, increasingly, institutions and their leaders in the wake of various corporate and other scandals. A profusion of literature has since been generated on the broader concept of agility, much of it generated by consultancies and describing the mindset shifts required to run an agile organization.

The metaphor of organizations as well-oiled machines that can control their destinies remains dominant in management thinking, though it is starting to be questioned as organizations struggle with its limitations and search for new approaches fit for the current context. The wider notion of an agile organization is still being developed.

What increases complexity in organizations?

There is a growing mismatch between the demands of the external environment and the slower pace at which organizations are able to respond. Let's turn our attention now to look at some of the factors that are driving complexity and often represent fundamental barriers to agility.

Structures and routines

By their very nature traditional hierarchical structures are not built to be flexible and adaptable. In true machine-style they are set up to stabilize, minimize disruption,[3] and ensure efficient management control over execution, discipline, coordination and cost-effectiveness. They seek to avoid instability in the system by concentrating control and power at the top. They also find optimal ways to allow some players to exercise a degree of autonomy while blocking power to others. In a knowledge-based hierarchy, specialized knowledge workers get to solve the more difficult or more specialized problems.[4] 'Winners' in conventional hierarchies are usually people who have learned to play the game by the current rules, or who subvert them to their own ends.

In slow-moving conditions, hierarchies can be highly efficient. However, in a dynamic environment, the longer established, larger and more complex the organization, the more likely it is to become too internally focused and fall out of step with the demands of the external context. Symptoms of such disconnections include 'silo' mentality, conflicting departmental priorities and goals, slow response times, processes becoming disconnected from the customer or from each other, duplication of effort, lengthy decision making, political behaviour and lack of accountability. Strong vertical divisions can make it difficult for departments and units to effectively collaborate because they don't understand each others' objectives, priorities and needs.

If outcomes are not measured appropriately, or poor behaviour gets rewarded, teams may come to mistrust their management or lack confidence in other departments. Similarly, cross-border partnerships and working arrangements can easily be undermined by lack of trust, teamwork or collaboration. Hierarchical structures tend to discourage much-needed innovation and initiative from entry-level and mid-level employees who are not 'empowered' to act. Managers too can suffer from perceived powerlessness – when they believe they lack the authority and power to make important decisions.

Hierarchical structures tend to work on the cascade principle of internal communication. In the Information Age the ability to access the right information at the right time is crucial to getting work done. At the very least, clear goals and measures are needed to help guide employee performances. Without this, hierarchies get in the way. For instance, in 2013 a major study into the culture and behaviour in Britain's National Health Service (NHS) found that unclear goals, excessive box-ticking, regulation and poor organizational and information systems left staff wasting valuable time hunting for information, struggling to deliver care effectively and disempowered from initiating improvement since they lacked valid insights into the quality of the care they provide.[5]

Alongside structures, organizational routines either enable or limit the work that companies, organizations and even markets can accomplish.[6] Most theories of routines conceptualize them as stable,[7] since they are based on repetition of behaviour patterns.[8] Routines help organizational participants to understand how the organization operates and then use this insight to guide their performances within the routine. In changing circumstances, if an organization substitutes old unhelpful routines with new routines – of collaboration versus competition; flexibility versus rigidity – it is more likely to be capable of adapting appropriately to the changing context and generating resilient responses.[9]

The conventional strategy-making process

When it comes to direction-setting and strategy-making routines, hierarchical management approaches still prevail despite the volatile context. After all, the conventional strategy-making process is seductively rational; it assumes that a plan to deliver strategic goals (usually set at the top and 'engineered' with the help of expert advisers) can be implemented successfully. In essence, conventional strategy-making involves using data to identify business and organizational challenges and opportunities, deciding on strategic goals then developing plans to achieve them, working towards some idealized future state over the forthcoming time frame (typically 12–18 months for business planning, 3–5 years for corporate strategy).

The process usually relies heavily on analysis: drivers for change in the current and emerging business context are identified, including competitor analysis, then possible strategic options are tested using scenario planning. Problem-solving techniques such as root cause and gap analyses help to identify where action is required, then 'stretch' goals are set, individual business unit plans are submitted and aligned within the overall plan, and resources are allocated. The business strategy is then cascaded to managers and the rest of the organization via various communication channels, so that – in theory at least – the strategic direction is clear to all.

So what is wrong with such a process? After all, there is some comfort in familiar, tried and tested legacy approaches. Let us look at some of the inherent challenges in conventional approaches to making and implementing strategy.

Leadership mindsets

The challenge to industrial-era linear 'engineering' models of planning and implementation is that the pace of change today is so fast that plans are often superseded by events before they can be delivered. The ability to make sense of complexity is often undermined by leadership mindsets that lack strategic sensitivity. In complex environments, previous experience is insufficient to guide us. Sydney Finkelstein ascribes many business failures to the 'flawed executive mindsets that throw out a company's perception of reality [and] delusional attitudes that keep this inaccurate reality in place'.[10] Similarly, the ability of the top team to make bold decisions is often undermined by damaging in-fighting and 'win-lose' politics. Professor Andrew Kakabadse, in his research with chief executives, suggests that 66 per cent of executives find it hard to talk about uncomfortable issues, even those that could seriously impact the business.[11] He has also found that eight out of ten board directors could not agree – or did not even know – the basis of competitive advantage for the firm on whose board they sat.

Other common leadership mindset barriers to agile decision making include short-termism, complacency, risk aversion and analysis paralysis, as set out below.

Short-termism

Tenure is short at the top, with turnover amongst CEOs in the world's top 2,500 companies averaging at about 15 per cent per year – meaning that one in seven is moving on every 12 months, usually because they are deemed not to have delivered shareholder value. Given quarterly reporting ('quarterly capitalism'), demanding shareholders and executive bonus cycles, leaders typically have little time to make an impact and, if they cannot produce quick results, boards replace them rapidly. As a result, the average tenure of a senior leader is just three years. Not surprisingly, executives tend to be very short-term focused.

The limited time horizons of many executives and boards tend to make executives reactive rather than proactive. This is all the more obvious in periods of rapid change, when senior managers tend to focus only on short-term strategy, cost-cutting and transition planning. However, the forces now in play may have long-term consequences, potentially altering the shape and nature of diverse markets. Firms continue to place far more emphasis on defending and extending today's core business at the expense of creating tomorrow's exciting new growth platforms that transform the lives of customers and create new markets. McKinsey research found that directors still spend 70 per cent of their time on quarterly reports, audit reviews, budgets and compliance – instead of on matters crucial to the future prosperity and direction of the business.[12] Thus executives and boards are likely to miss the chance to influence their context and reshape their propositions for success over the longer term. Achieving the right balance of short- and long-term vision is crucial.

This was most evident following the financial crisis that began in 2008. Many formerly market-leading businesses proved to be the least resilient when the deep-ensuing recession hit. This may have been because their boards were negligent, overoptimistic or ill-informed, looking in the rear-view mirror and not scanning the road ahead, making them blind to what lay around the corner. Consequently they failed to take corrective action when it was needed because they did not know that a correction was needed.

Complacency

Another reason why some organizations fail is if they swallow their own success propaganda and ignore changing consumer patterns, which are often subtle but rapid. As a result they may underestimate the strength of new competition or the potential of new technology applications to change consumer tastes. In the UK supermarket sector, for instance, the major supermarket chains, often referred to as the 'Big Five'[13] have mostly pursued a strategy of (physical) expansion for almost three decades. Megastores and out-of-town retail spaces were developed across the country as the big five supermarkets competed to lure customers for their 'big weekly shop'. They transformed the way we shopped, changing supermarkets from being places we went to buy a few groceries to a one-stop destination for everything from a washing machine or a duvet to a barbecue or a computer.

But in recent times it appears that the age of the megastore may soon be over. Shoppers are rejecting the 'big weekly shop' model and choosing to buy less more often, in so-called 'top-up' shops. The transition has led to the rising popularity of smaller, convenience-style stores – and a decline in the popularity of out-of-town stores. Moreover, shoppers are also increasingly turning to budget supermarkets, which plan to double the number of their smaller retail stores in the next decade in order to take advantage of their record sales, forcing the big five to rein in their expansion plans overall, leaving them sitting expensively on nearly 30 million square feet of unused space.

Risk aversion and analysis paralysis

To develop even short-term advantages, what organizations really need to do is innovate. This can, of course, seem inherently risky – are we backing the right horse? Many large organizations are headed by very risk-averse CEOs and boards who made their way to the top in business through wheeling and dealing politically, rather than by being bold and innovative leaders. Thanks to internal complexities and politics many senior teams struggle to make the courageous decisions that will help their organizations get into growth faster. When it comes to grasping the key technologies relevant to their industry, many top teams are rooted in the past. Perceived risks and barriers to the adoption of new technology can slow things down, such as concerns over data security, the cost of deploying new technologies and clumsy implementation of new systems. In particular, with respect to investing in major change programmes many senior management teams have become inherently timid.

Especially during the recession triggered in 2008 it seems that the role of many a CEO, even in entrepreneurial organizations, became more like that of a controlling chief financial officer (CFO) than an innovative and dynamic business leader. Today's business environment is a more heavily regulated environment than in the past so there is a strong governance emphasis on risk management, which often masks intolerance of risk. If people are held too tightly to account they are unlikely to use their initiative, which will stifle innovation and the potential for testing new options in a timely way.

According to the *EMC Leader* report 2020, analysis paralysis is one of the key problems in delivering results.[14] The management preference for analysis is hardly surprising given that the rational, technical approach to leadership and management has been perpetuated to the current day via business school and executive education. However, many of the dilemmas and challenges facing managers in today's complex times are far from simple; reason and logic alone may no longer be the best basis for decision making. In our modern connected world, with its conditions of high uncertainty and complexity, things are too easily disrupted by the unforeseen, and the links between cause and effect are difficult or impossible to detect. When the future is less an extrapolation of the past, the conventional linear models of planning and executing strategy promoted by business schools may actually inhibit organizations from moving towards desired outcomes in fits and starts.

Risk-averse managers usually demand an overwhelming body of evidence before making decisions. In the era of 'big data' there is no shortage of information available – quite the contrary. Knowing what to do with the data and what questions to ask is a different challenge. Often the quality of data is limited by the effectiveness or otherwise of the technical infrastructure of the firm; whether databases are well maintained and legacy systems fit for purpose. Nevertheless, there remain often unrealistic stakeholder expectations that executives will be able to wave their magic wands and provide a clear path forward through a confusing landscape and build their organization's capacity to act. In practice, as Patrick Hoverstadt points out, when it comes to making potentially brave and risky decisions: 'Management, fearing a loss of control of the situation, press the sub-systems for information and reports... [resulting in] operations undermined by micro-management... prompting ever more micro-management.'[15]

So, arguably, we now need a different kind of leader who can actively seek to understand broader trends outside their own organization and industry; who is prepared to take risks and is brave enough to make those decisions that enable change and innovation on a continuous basis. In particular, agile organizations need what Heifetz and Laurie call 'adaptive' leaders who have a 'stomach for failure'.[16] Especially in a fast-moving context, if you wait too long to take corrective action, the longer you fall behind the curve and risk running out of time. Thus strategic error and the inability to recover become intertwined as slow decision making and over-clunky governance structures entrap managers.

Complex times

If decision making is hard even in 'normal' times, how much tougher will it become in today's context where organizational changes tend to be broad-based (ie systematic and requiring broad support), fast-paced (so everything seems urgent) and have unpredictable outcomes? This layer of complexity, together with the absence of past predictors, adds to the difficulty of decision making and strategic execution. As Plsek suggests, 'much of our current frustration around adoption of innovation... is a consequence of our largely unconscious application of machine-metaphor thinking to what is inherently a complex adaptive system'.[17]

As management teams attempt to get to grips with complexity and to steer the 'correct' course, they often struggle to coalesce around a shared agenda. If there is little or no agreement on how to address challenging situations, organizations risk ending up operating in what Ralph Stacey calls the 'zone of complexity', where chaos, anarchy and confusion reign (see Figure 2.1).[18] Conversely, if there is too much order, with too many formal contacts, rules, siloed behaviour and command and control management styles, organizations can stagnate.[19]

Arguably a more propitious place to be is at the 'edge of chaos', walking the tightrope between social and technical complication, avoiding both the extremes of complacency and of panic. This is the zone of dynamic stability where there is just enough order that people know broadly what is happening, but where things are not so stable that people see no reason to change. While being at the edge of chaos is not necessarily a comfortable place to be, it is

FIGURE 2.1   Ralph Stacey: agreement and certainty matrix

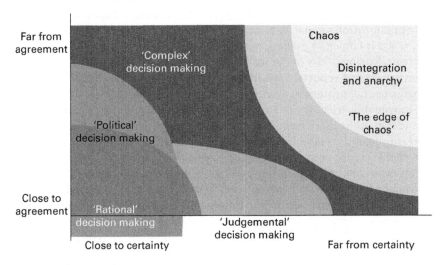

Far from
agreement

'Complex'
decision making

Chaos

Disintegration
and anarchy

'The edge of
chaos'

'Political'
decision making

Close to
agreement

'Rational'
decision making

'Judgemental'
decision making

Close to certainty

Far from certainty

SOURCE RD Stacey (2002) *Strategic Management and Organisational Dynamics: The challenge of complexity*, 3rd edn, Prentice Hall, Harlow

here that people are most open to new knowledge and learning, experimentation and innovation. As Arthur Bartram points out: 'The edge is a risky place to be: but can any organization afford not to spend some time there'?[20]

The implementation gap

Even if a clear strategic plan emerges, a yawning gap usually opens up between strategic intent and strategic execution. For instance, budgets get slashed before implementation is under way, conflicting priorities emerge, people identify potential problems and possible solutions but somehow these don't get acted on so the organization's capacity to act is reduced or brought to a standstill. John Kotter's famous reasons why change efforts fail include not establishing a sense of urgency; not creating a powerful enough sponsorship group; lack of vision; undercommunicating by a factor of 10; not removing obstacles to the vision; not planning systematically for short-term wins; declaring change to be over too soon before anchoring changes in the company's culture.[21]

Other typical causes of the 'implementation gap' include:

- Implementation takes longer than originally allocated.
- Major problems surface during implementation that had not been identified beforehand.
- Coordination of implementation activities is ineffective.

- People fail to recognize good ideas as potential solutions and they therefore do not get the backing needed.
- Organizational politics and vested interests get in the way.
- Initiative overload, with competing activities and crises distracting attention from implementation.
- Capabilities of the employees involved are insufficient.
- Training and instruction given to lower-level employees are inadequate.
- Uncontrollable factors in the external environment have an adverse impact on implementation.
- Key implementation tasks and activities are not defined clearly or in enough detail.
- Information systems used to monitor implementation are inadequate.

In particular, strategic execution is often hampered by lack of consistent management support, leadership and direction by departmental managers. In many cases there is little communication, a lack of clear priorities, poor coordination and untapped capability. Traditional management models typically place multiple and often conflicting responsibilities on managers – to do their technical 'day' jobs as well as manage the productivity and output of their team. Consequently many managers and their teams struggle to juggle priorities and many have a bias towards activity rather than results – so people come to prefer the security that comes with following standard operating procedures over using initiative and achieving meaningful results for customers and the business.

Technology: the 'holy grail'?

The use of advanced technologies opens up the potential for accessing new markets, innovation, improving production and cost-effectiveness. Yet competitive advantage does not materialize simply through acquiring new technology; the people, processes and structure aspects of the operating model are still the key determinants of operational effectiveness. If people's skills have not kept pace, then the potential of technology is unlikely to be realized. For instance, Big Data is a concept that is generating a high profile and information volumes are growing by 60 per cent per year. Two in three employees are reported to lack the analytical skills to apply good judgement,[22] and developing (or acquiring) vital talent takes time.

Moreover, the rapid spread of best practice allows competitors to quickly imitate efficient techniques; competitors soon begin to look identical and a war of attrition can result in a race to the bottom. So innovating and establishing a differentiated offer in the marketplace is the best way to outperform the competition. That is why strengthening the link between strategy and operations, and building a culture conducive to innovation, is a vital component of sustainable competitive advantage.

Organizational culture

Culture, often defined as the assumed beliefs and norms that govern behaviours or 'the way we do things around here', can be a powerful force for stability, since familiar practices are reinforced over time and become habits and routines that maintain the status quo, whether or not these serve the business well. So how meetings are conducted, punctuality, tolerance of underperformance, levels of challenge, how power is really exercised, what gets rewarded and who gets promoted are all aspects of culture that new recruits learn to navigate in order to be accepted and succeed within the dominant culture.

Some leading companies are proud of their strong cultures and believe that these set them apart from their competition. However, the shadow side of strong organizational cultures is that they can also stifle dissent if people come to identify so closely with the company culture that they don't 'rock the boat'. Journalist Madeleine Bunting described the cultural practices at telecoms company Orange – such as staff being encouraged to show their loyalty by wearing orange T-shirts at work – as 'cultish'.[23]

Strong cultures tend to focus people's minds internally, which means that weak external signals about when it is time to change strategy and approach can easily be missed. If a company's strategy and culture are not aligned, then, as per the well-known phrase attributed to Peter Drucker: 'culture eats strategy for breakfast'. So if a company in a highly competitive market attempts to differentiate itself on the quality of its customer service, but its cultural practices suggest that customers are way down the pecking order, it will struggle to succeed. Similarly, strategic innovation is unlikely in organizations with highly risk-averse, low-trust cultures.

Culture change?

Even though many organizations acknowledge the importance of culture, few explicitly use it as a way to drive business performance and achieve breakthrough results, or even believe it could make sense to do so. After all, conventional wisdom suggests that culture change is complex and can take years, since there are usually many interests vested in maintaining the status quo. In a 2014 Roffey Park survey three-quarters of HR managers (77 per cent) indicated that their organizations had attempted to change their culture in the previous five years, principally to improve efficiency and respond to financial challenges.[24] Respondents talked about the need to do things differently, to operate with fewer resources and achieve a greater focus on performance management. Yet 37 per cent of HR managers reported that cultural change had 'not been that successful' (that figure rises to 44 per cent in the public sector). Many reported feeling overwhelmed by the amount of change, or disillusioned by its nature.

Leading organizations are turning this conventional wisdom on its head and recognizing culture as a specific driver of the organization and a key enabler of innovation. So in Google recruiting the 'right' people who 'fit' is a key strategic focus and other human resource practices are specifically designed to ensure that people with the right skills are able to thrive within the culture.

Edgar Schein argues that what leaders pay attention to is a primary embedding mechanism of culture change, since it teaches people what is valued.[25] So if leaders demonstrate short-termist attitudes, low emotional intelligence, unwillingness to confront poor practice or inability to generate trust, the organization's culture will reflect this. The simplest way to unlock growth is to manage and lead better. Yet relatively few managers receive leadership development and few businesses have a clear model of leadership that improves employee engagement, removes barriers to innovation and uncovers hidden strengths in people and the organization.

Neglecting the human aspects of change

Agility involves 'moving quickly, decisively, and effectively in anticipating, initiating and taking advantage of change'.[26] Yet leading the changes required to address what Heifetz and Laurie call 'adaptive' challenges can be difficult,[27] and symptoms of failed implementation are everywhere: teams who don't work well together, unclear goals, conflicting priorities and political behaviour make it difficult to execute strategy effectively.

Sometimes that is because change is targeted at the wrong level, for instance focusing only on short-term technical challenges such as automating routine transactional activities (the 'means') rather than on how to improve the higher-value-added information gathering and support of vital business activities (the 'ends'). Consequently change efforts often fail to hit the mark or make a difference to the productivity and nimbleness of the overall company.

More commonly, the main reasons why change fails relate to how change is managed and its impact on people. According to conventional, rational approaches to management, the authority figure is supposed to work out where the company is going and people are supposed to follow. Yet in practice, especially in times of complexity, ambiguity and paradox, many leaders struggle to set clear direction or gain employee commitment to change. Heifetz and Laurie argue that managers are often blind-sided by their technical orientation, which causes them to misread the nature of change required and to underestimate the challenge of mobilizing people throughout the organization in order to make the necessary changes.[28] So rather than involving the people who will be most affected by the change or guiding them through the transition, senior executives tend to use 'tell and sell' approaches to impose their own solution to a problem. Gaining 'buy-in' then becomes a problem. Indeed these authors argue that the prevailing notion of leadership – consisting of having a vision and aligning people with that vision – is bankrupt.

In the distribution company mentioned earlier, after reviewing why their previous change efforts had been unsuccessful, managers recognized that they had failed to articulate the benefits of the proposed change or get the right people on board at the outset, due to poor communication. Moreover, the strategic intent was not translated into operational objectives that people could understand. Lacking clear targets, people did not know what 'success' would look like, what would be required from them or when the change outcomes would be delivered. As a result, there was plenty of change activity but little real progress.

We return to the theme of what kinds of culture, leadership and management enable organizational agility throughout the book.

Agility at the expense of resilience

Agile organizations need resilient, flexible and competent staff who are engaged and productive, willing and able to adapt to continuous change. At an individual level, resilience is about the ability to thrive and perform despite ongoing change, uncertainty and confusion. Resilience is severely put to the test in today's work-intensive and insecure workplaces that tend to be dehumanizing and routinely destroy meaning for people.

Thanks to technology and 24/7 working environments, people are often left feeling that they can never quite get away from work and that the boundaries between work and leisure have dissolved. With demands for more for less, people are required to work harder, longer and in different ways. Thanks to advanced technology, many jobs are 'hollowed out' and people are left bearing the brunt of agility in terms of lost jobs, security and satisfaction, and increased stress.

Moreover, organizational agility is too often pursued through cutting core operating costs and embracing flexible workforce models that result in increased workloads, outsourcing, redundancy, short-term and zero-hours contracts, and reduced protection for employees. As discussed earlier, the balance in the employment relationship between employers and employees appears heavily tipped in favour of employers.

In a context of ongoing change, communication is often inadequate. Many employees don't understand or buy the need for 'new' that is being imposed, and struggle to identify the WIFM ('what's in it for me?') factors. More generally, when too much change is happening at the same time, the benefits of change fail to be realized or embedded. People become weary of change, lose track of what has been achieved and wait for the next wave of change to pass over their heads as they attempt to carry on with the 'day job'.

There are often mismatches between company values statements and actual practice, which lead to employee cynicism. Poor leadership and management compound the problem. If senior leaders fail to 'walk the talk' on values, then this inconsistency will be reflected in the culture. For instance, if health-care organizations espouse the rhetoric of being patient-centred when in reality only key performance indicator (KPI) box ticking is rewarded and the lowest quality patient care is tolerated, employee cynicism (and poor practice) can be expected. Similarly, the typically wide disparities between executive rewards and those of the rest of the workforce undermine a sense of common purpose and make a mockery of the message 'we're all in this together'. Many companies declare that employees are their 'greatest asset' yet a 2014 UK survey found that just 35 per cent of those employees surveyed feel valued by their employers and 39 per cent would change jobs tomorrow if they could.[29]

When such gaps occur between rhetoric and reality, the employment relationship between employers and employees becomes less trusting and more transactional – people become less willing to 'go the extra mile' for the organization unless there is some clear benefit for them to do so. And even when jobs are not at risk, demands for ongoing change may cause some staff to passively resist anything that challenges their work world. In such circumstances, speed, innovation and willingness to 'go the extra mile' become empty aspirations.

Talent shortages

Our world is rapidly evolving – not only economically and technologically but also socially and demographically. With an ageing workforce in the West and generation Y gradually becoming the largest component of international workforces, the skills and experience mix in many organizations is in a state of flux.

Talent is a scarce resource – even more than technology and capital – and skills shortages are set to increase as globalization and competitive pressures take hold across all sectors and industries and as improving economic conditions spur employees to seek new jobs. Today, major global skills shortages exist in a wide range of industries and sectors such as construction and utilities and pose a significant barrier to growth. In Germany, manufacturing companies have been hit by a lack of trained engineers, while Germany and France need more skilled IT workers. In the UK's IT sector there is a dearth of software engineers and data specialists.

In a 2014 global survey of chief executives by consultancy firm KPMG, the struggle to locate suitably skilled employees was ranked second in the major challenges facing business leaders, behind achieving profitable growth.[30] Because even with investments in new technology, if companies cannot access or grow the key talent they need, they are unlikely to be able to compete successfully. So in a business environment where, according to human-resources consulting firm Towers Watson, 59 per cent of companies have trouble finding critical-skill employees,[31] the ability to attract and retain skilled and talented people is a powerful competitive advantage.

The first so-called 'war for talent' at the end of the 1990s reflected the struggle of major consultancy firms to attract and retain high-potential or specialist talent who were their engine of growth. A new 'war for talent' is on the cards, but this time, as companies attempt to develop distinct talent strategies tailored to their business and its strategy – its products, markets and business goals – they are also aiming to grow their own people by addressing the development needs of all employees, not just the high potentials.

These new talent strategies must take account of what 'talent' itself wants. Scarce skilled and marketable 'talent' can dictate their own 'new deal' terms. New generations have different expectations of their careers and their employers from those of their parents. As a result, employers must also rapidly evolve in order to find new and more relevant ways to engage, inspire and motivate up to four different generations of staff within one workplace (the baby boomers, generation X, generation Y and 'gen edge'). When employees have power in the employment relationship, the rules of the game will be rewritten, whether employers like it or not. In a knowledge or service-based organization where people are the main factor of production, attempting to increase agility and resilience simply by tinkering with the more instrumental aspects of organization – while ignoring their potential impact on people and culture – is like rearranging the deckchairs on the RMS *Titanic*.

Conclusion

This challenging cocktail of ingredients represents a complex set of potential barriers to organizational agility. We have discussed how:

- *Fear (risk aversion) and lack of strategic sensitivity are real constraints*, though they can be overcome (as we shall discuss later in this book).
- *Command and control management styles* may increase efficiency in the short term but may undermine empowerment and innovation, key to resilience and agility.
- The challenge of *mobilizing people for change* is often underestimated.
- *Culture is as, or more, important than strategy* in determining an organization's fate – yet less attention is paid to it.
- *Talent shortages and changing employee expectations* will drive the need for a more open, win-win employment relationship with employees.
- *Agility* and *resilience* are essential 'soul mates'.

If the stakes were not so high, incremental improvements might be enough. But real change is needed and it is needed now. In today's context, organizations may need to reconfigure themselves many times in pursuit of greater agility, so reframing organizational design is now a necessity.

If a firm is too bound by conventional answers or precedent, it will have great difficulty conceiving a bold new path. So we need leaders who are brave enough to embrace a new way of leading that is fit for today's challenges.

The mindset that enables a firm to successfully move forward with agility is often a complex blend of expertise, opportunism, courage, creativity and decisiveness despite uncertainty. New approaches to strategic thinking, strategy making and strategy execution are required – and new routines such as continuously scanning the horizon, looking out for opportunities, actively embracing innovation, testing new ideas and learning from what works, working collaboratively across organizational boundaries, designing the organization for speed and flexibility.

Above all, organizational agility and resilience are only sustainable when the human as well as the instrumental aspects of organization are attended to, and kept in dynamic balance. So some of the 'ways we do business around here' may need to be challenged and some previous recipes for success may need to be unlearned.

What follows in the next chapter is an outline road map for leaders, managers, HR and OD specialists – indeed anyone who wants to help build more resiliently agile organizations. We look at the scope of the situation, the key actions required and, most importantly, what it will take to succeed in developing organizational agility and resilience, getting ahead of the curve and perhaps becoming a shaper of the track!

Checklist

How agile are you?

- Are you changing as fast as the world around you?

- Is your culture enabling you to be agile or impeding you?

- To what extent do your structures and routines support agility?

- Being agile requires the people, processes, strategy and technology of an enterprise to be inextricably linked so that there is a continual, dynamic response to change. Where are the weakest links in your organization's response to change?

- How effective is decision making at the top?

- How can you and your organization become more forward thinking?

- What has been the effect of the last major change in your organization? What did you learn from this change? How are these lessons being applied?

- What are the key factors that help your managers to learn? Are these factors primarily internal or external?

Notes

1 Economist Intelligence Unit (EIU) (2009) [accessed 19 January 2015] Organisational Agility: How Business Can Survive and Thrive in Turbulent Times, *Economist Intelligence Unit* [Online] http://www.emc.com/collateral/leadership/organisational-agility-230309.pdf.

2 Herriot, P and Pemberton, C (1995) *New Deals: The revolution in managerial careers,* Wiley, Chichester.

3 Feldman, MS (2003) A performative perspective on stability and change in organizational routines, *Industrial and Corporate Change*, **12** (4), pp 727–52.

4 Garicano, L (2000) Hierarchies and the organisation of knowledge in production, *Journal of Political Economy*, **108** (5), pp 874–904.

5 Chartered Institute of Personnel and Development (CIPD) and Healthcare People Management Association (HPMA) (2013) Employee Outlook: Focus on culture change and patient care in the NHS, London: CIPD.

6 Cohen, MD *et al* (1996) Routines and other recurrent action patterns of organizations: contemporary research issues, *Industrial and Corporate Change*, 5, pp 653–98.

7 March, JG and Simon, HA (1958) *Organizations*, John Wiley and Sons, New York.

8 Nelson RR and Winter SG (1982) *An Evolutionary Theory of Economic Change*, Harvard University Press: Cambridge, MA.

9 Feldman, MS and Rafaeli, A (2002) Organisational routines as sources of connection and understandings, *Journal of Management Studies*, 39, 309–32.

10 Finkelstein, S (2013) *Why Smart Executives Fail: And what you can learn from their mistakes*, Portfolio Penguin, New York, reprint edn, p1.

11 Kakabadse, A, in Cafolla, L (2013) [accessed 30 August 2014] Going Against Grey, Classified Post.com, published on 27 September [Online] http://www.classifiedpost.com/hk/article/going-against-grey.

12 Barton, D and Wiseman, M (2013) Focusing capital on the long term, McKinsey and Company.

13 Sources: Kantar Worldpanel, Retail Gazette, 31 July 2014 [Online] http://www.retailgazette.co.uk/kantar-worldpanel; and Straus, R (2014) End of the road for supermarket megastores? Retailers plan smaller sites as households ditch big weekly shop, *Daily Mail*, 4 August [Online] http://www.thisismoney.co.uk/money/news/article-2715679/Death-supermarket-megastore-Plans-new-sites-drop-lowest-level-financial-crisis-households-ditch-big-weekly-shop.html#ixzz39XXCDFAJ.

14 Petter, J (2014) EMC Leader Report 2020: Escaping 'analysis-paralysis', EMC.

15 Hoverstadt, P (2009) *The Fractal Organization: Creating sustainable organizations with the viable systems model*, John Wiley and Sons, Chichester, p61.

16 Heifetz, RA and Laurie, DL (2001) The work of leadership, *Harvard Business Review*, December.

17 Plsek, P (2003) Complexity and the Adoption of Innovation in Health Care, paper presented at Accelerating Quality Improvement in Health Care, a conference held in Washington, DC, 27–28 January.

18 Stacey, R (1996) *Strategic Management and Organizational Dynamics*, Pitman Publishing, London.

19 O'Connor, J (2010) *Leading with NLP*, HarperCollins, New York.

20 Bartram, A (2000) *Navigating Complexity: The essential guide to complexity theory*, Spiro Press, London.

21 Kotter, J (1996) *Leading Change*, Harvard Business School Press, Boston.

22 See cebglobal.com/transformation.

23 Bunting, M (2005) *Willing Slaves: How the overwork culture is ruling our lives*, Harper Perennial, London.

24 Lucy, D, Poorkavoos, M and Wellbelove, J (2014) *The Management Agenda*, Roffey Park, Horsham.

25 Schein, EH (2004) *Organizational Culture and Leadership*, 3rd edn, Jossey-Bass, San Francisco.

26 Jamrog J, Vickers, M and Bear, D (2006) Building and sustaining a culture that supports innovation, *Human Resource Planning*, **29** (3), pp 9–19.

27 Heifetz, RA and Laurie, DL (2001) The work of leadership, *Harvard Business Review*, December.

28 Ibid.

29 Lucy, D, Poorkavoos, M and Wellbelove, J (2014) *The Management Agenda*, Roffey Park, Horsham.

30 KPMG (2014) [accessed 30 August 2014] Business Instincts survey, *KPMG* [Online] http://www.kpmg.co.uk/email/06Jun14/OM016469A/PageTurner/index.html.

31 Towers Watson (2012) [accessed 30 August 2014] Global Talent Management and Rewards Survey [Online] http://www.towerswatson.com/en/Press/2012/09/companies-worldwide-struggle-to-attract-and-retain-critical-skill-and-high-potential-employees-tower.

The resiliently agile organization

In Chapters 1 and 2 we looked at some of the factors driving the need for agility and resilience and also considered some of the key aspects of organization that represent significant barriers. We have seen that agility's more recent roots are in software development and while the notion of the agile enterprise is a broader notion this is less well developed.

I have argued that agility – the search for speed and adaptability – must be accompanied by resilience or 'bouncebackability' at organizational, team and individual levels. One without the other is not sustainable. After all, many organizations are using lean tools and agile methods but are not changing the system as a whole, so things go on much as before without the significant shifts in culture required for sustainable change.

My goal in this chapter is to take a whole-system look at agility and resilience. We consider:

- the qualities and capabilities of agile firms;
- the resiliently agile model.

This model looks at organizational agility and resilience 'in the round'. This sets the tone for the rest of the book, since in later chapters we will explore in more detail what is involved in developing the key capabilities and routines that underpin the model and how these can be applied in practice.

Agility is a complex capability. It is not just one system but a set of structures, systems, processes and behaviours – and how these fit together – that make up agile capability. For organizations to become resiliently agile will require not simply shifts in the tangible aspects of organization – for instance in structures – but also in the intangible aspects:

- people's mindsets and skills;
- cultures;

- philosophies;
- capabilities;
- routines and habits.

Taken together these should enhance an organization's latent agility and resilience.

The qualities and capabilities of agile firms

The rare organizations that have agility and resilience embedded in their cultural DNA and have proved successful over time, such as WL Gore and Associates or the John Lewis Partnership, are thought to be best placed to succeed in a hyper-competitive environment. Such organizations have a strongly mutual ethic embracing the interests of employees as well as of the organization. As such examples make clear, being resiliently agile is not just what you *do*; it is what you *are*, or become; a state of being, the way your system works, which influences what you are capable of and what you do. So while agile tools and processes are useful, the real enabler of agility and resilience is embodied in the people and culture of organizations.

The traits of an agile business include rapid decision making and execution, a high-performance culture, flexibility of management practices and resources, and organizational structures that support collaboration. Moreover they are:

- Obsessed with providing customer value – prepared to put in significant effort to establish exactly what it is that their customers want, and then putting those things first.
- Continuously adaptive, able to change ways of working in order to deliver optimum value to customers and to do so at a moment's notice – they are *behaviourally* resilient.
- Dynamically networked – at the centre of a number of interacting networks that enable the organization to gather knowledge and use expertise quickly and effectively – they are *context* resilient.
- Rigorously focused on new learning and creating value through knowledge – they are *cognitively* resilient powerhouses of innovation.
- Ruthlessly decisive – they must be prepared to dispose of parts of the organization that no longer add value.

To unpack these ideas a little more, let us consider some of the different aspects of organizational resilience – context, cognitive and behavioural – and how these play out in different situations.

'Bouncebackability'

As an open system, any organization is of course embedded in wider societal, industrial and political systems that influence the pace and spread of innovation. Through dynamic networks, organizations can gather knowledge and use expertise quickly in order to respond to adverse conditions and recover from misfortune, damage or a destabilizing perturbation in the environment that would otherwise destroy them. If crisis cannot be prevented, resilient organizations can bounce back from what has happened and turn crises into a source of strategic opportunity, thanks to their increase in learning and resilience capacity.[1] So the firm can withstand anything that comes along and has the means available for recovery and renewal next time if needed.

In crisis situations strong crisis leadership and effective, speedy decision making are of the essence. At the US Hancock Bank, following the disaster of losing everything to Hurricane Katrina in 2005, the bank's leaders made some courageous decisions based on the bank's identity and purpose. Hancock reopened three days later, ahead of other banks, using IOUs – an extraordinary but effective solution to an extraordinary situation. Implicit therefore in the effective handling of crises is having the courage and the ability to evaluate strategies fast, make some tough calls and accelerate work programmes against organizational goals. The challenge for risk-averse leaders is to recognize when they have enough data to gain insight into possible ways forward, and to have the confidence to make decisions and take action.

Resilience is not just about getting through crises. Truly resilient organizations have the foresight and situation awareness to prevent potential crises emerging. They demonstrate *cognitive* resilience – the ability to notice shifts, work through unfamiliar situations and develop options on how to respond.

Learning as key to adaptation and innovation

Adaptive firms such as Apple, Google, 3M and Amazon are 'change-able'; they can adjust and learn better, faster and more economically than their peers, giving them an 'adaptive advantage'.[2] Pettigrew and colleagues used the phrase 'receptive context' to describe the degree to which a particular group or organization naturally takes on change and new ideas.[3] Organizations with a high receptive context are seen as 'ripe' for change; they quickly adopt innovative concepts in order to meet the challenges they experience. They focus rigorously on creating value through knowledge. Generative relationships between 'boundary workers', who act as environmental scanners, aid this process so ideas develop further and the observable outcomes are more than merely the sum of the parts. Change becomes a natural and inevitable part of organizational life so organizations can maintain effectiveness across a range of tasks, situations and conditions even while changing. Conversely, organizations with low receptive context might experience the same challenges and learn about the same innovations, but they lack the will or ability to implement the idea.

To build a receptive context Abrahamson recommends 'pacing' – interspersing major change efforts with small-scale changes at a more local level that key parts of the business are free to initiate where they add value.[4] This is not a pure agile methodology, stripping away procedure and hierarchy just before the point of chaos, but rather a hybrid of change techniques. The aim is to empower and let change happen at a local level where it strategically makes sense, while taking advantage of standardization and lean methodologies where these are more appropriate.

A learning climate

For cognitive resilience to flourish requires a learning climate where controlled experimentation and shared learning from successes and failures is encouraged. In common with 'learning organization' theories, resiliently agile organizations recognize that ideas and information can emerge from anyone, in any part of the system, at any time. Such organizations tend to have high levels of staff awareness and engagement and self-development opportunities for all. They look outside, embrace inter-company learning and are open to learning from others, including competitors. They also look inside, encouraging internal exchange so that departments see themselves as each others' customers. They have enabling structures, processes and patterns that support experimentation and allow great ideas to be turned into new products and services. For instance, IT is used for sharing knowledge and mutual awareness; reward approaches incentivize and reinforce learning.

In general, the most agile organizations tend to be entrepreneurial start-ups that initially act as powerhouses of innovation. Take any of the first mover success stories from the computer and software industry – such as Hewlett-Packard and Microsoft. In their early days the founders and employees demonstrated common purpose, great skill and highly effective knowledge-sharing practices. As market shapers and leaders they forged the way ahead for whole industries to follow. It was typically only as they grew into large corporations that these pioneers formalized their processes and became so market dominant that they perhaps lost sight of the competition and were unable to keep up with changing client expectations or with competitors' innovations. The story of how Microsoft initially dismissed the development of the tablet by Apple as unimportant is a timely reminder of how easy it is to miss or dismiss emergent signals. So while agility may be part of an organization's DNA at the outset, it is important to watch out for, and avoid the loss of learning, a precursor to rigidity.

Flexibility

Allied to adaptability is flexibility – the ability to employ multiple ways to succeed, craft a range of resource and capability alternatives and the capacity to move seamlessly between them.[5] This is about developing skills at aligning, realigning and mobilizing people and resources; taking resolute action and removing barriers to change; partnering and collaborating with others. To be flexible and responsive organizations need appropriately flexible roles, responsibilities and structures. In particular they need people with flexible mindsets and skill sets who are willing and able to adjust to what is now required of them.

Organizational agility and resilience depend largely on people's willingness to deploy their mental agility, skill sets, behaviours, resources and their discretionary efforts on behalf of the firm. Agile firms therefore need a strong employment relationship built on trust and reciprocation. As discussed in Chapter 2, today's 'white-collar' employment relationships tend to be based on the unitarist assumption that 'what is good for the business is good for the people'. Take flexible working arrangements, for instance – these should give employees choice about where and when they work. However, in some forms of flexible working post-recession, such as 'zero-hours' contracting, flexibility benefits only the employer, so workers lacking power in the employment relationship may find that what is good for the business is not so good for them. If the employment relationship becomes low-trust and employees become 'disengaged' from their organization, they are less likely to want to 'go the extra mile' to benefit the organization. What is needed is a more mutual employment relationship in which both the organization and its workforce can reap the rewards of agility.

Routines: standardization and innovation

Major companies have traditionally understood that efficiency comes from routinizing the non-routine so that people can develop useful habits that drive their behaviour and can fully deploy their resources under challenging conditions. Through practice they develop *behavioural* resilience – the routines that enable them to deal effectively with challenging situations. For example, the UK flying display team the Red Arrows practise their complex air manoeuvres daily until they become almost instinctual in response to any threat such as unexpected bad weather.

However, if organizational routines become set in stone, they keep the organization firmly anchored in the past. To gain adaptive advantage in a context of change requires a willingness to review and occasionally abandon the disciplines of conventional hierarchies and adopt new, more dynamic routines – a particular challenge in today's context of tighter governance, increased regulation and risk aversion.

So can routines be deliberately changed to increase agility? The answer is yes. In dynamically stable contexts (ie where stability and change are quite similar[6]), routines can evolve to contribute to the dynamic capability of firms.[7] They can also be consciously applied to improve:

- organizational adaptation;[8]
- evolution;[9]
- learning;[10]

- flexibility;[11]
- improvisation and innovation.[12]

A cohesive sense of what a company believes (the genuine core values that contribute to cognitive resilience) is the foundation for developing day-to-day behaviours that translate intended strategies into new useful habits that lead to beneficial actions. So if organizational values lead to habits of investigation rather than assumption, or routines of collaboration rather than antagonism, and traditions of flexibility rather than rigidity, people are more likely to intuitively behave in ways that open the system and generate resilient responses.

Similarly, standardizing routines that cause ideas to proliferate, such as the practised behaviours for innovative problem solving, leads to heightened levels of inventiveness – or 'learned resourcefulness',[13] what Coutu calls 'ritualized ingenuity'.[14] So if people are in the habit of continuously scanning the market and have processes to speedily convert effective ideas into new products and business opportunities, they are better able to use whatever resources and opportunities are at hand to move the firm forward. This can lead to timing advantages allowing the firm to capitalize on rapid response opportunities, to do more with less, and to use all of its assets to full advantage.

Collins and Hansen describe how the development of the iPod was less the result of one person's brilliant idea than of a multistep iterative process based upon empirical validation.[15] Paradoxically then, a system that supports innovation must both allow ideas to go forward in the absence of evidence, yet be steadfast in insisting on evidence of effectiveness for evaluation.[16] So the process of innovating becomes disciplined: 'The great task, rarely achieved, is to blend creative intensity with relentless discipline so as to amplify the creativity rather than destroy it. When you marry operating excellence with innovation, you multiply the value of your creativity.'[17]

Similarly leaders need to become clearer about when to control the innovation process 'tightly' and when they can be 'loose' so that people can exercise autonomy.[18] Loose elements allow for experimentation, essentially spreading the risk of change by simultaneous piloting of ideas or processes in different departments or geographic areas. However, this does mean that staff must be empowered to challenge and try new things and that they clearly understand their organization's purpose and the aim of initiative.

The Center for Effective Organizations identifies four routines in particular that distinguish the sustainably agile high-performing organizations from what they call the 'thrashers'. These agile companies have the ability to *strategize* in dynamic ways; accurately *perceive* changes in their external environment; *test* possible responses; and *implement* incremental and discontinuous changes in products, technology, operations, structures, systems and capabilities as a whole. To these I would add other key routines relating to how people will work together, such as *teaming* and *empowering*.

Clearly the appetite for new routines is there. For instance, an IBM study has found that executives are increasingly looking outside the organization to get new ideas rather than simply relying on internal formulae.[19] The deeper roots of the change towards 'open' innovation go back to the 1980s and 1990s when many global pharmaceutical companies began to look externally for product innovation. Today, almost half of the CEOs in the IBM study expect their organizations to source innovation from the outside – and are actively participating in open innovation networks. Seven out of ten CEOs of outperforming organizations are now intent on increasing their partner network in the pursuit of innovation.

Importantly, it is the whole system of routines, not the possession of one or two of them, which confers agility. It is this combination of qualities, capabilities and routines that underpin the resiliently agile model.

The resiliently agile model

The model shown in Figure 3.1 outlines the component activities of organizational agility and resilience, which we shall explore in more detail in later chapters. It outlines some of the inputs – capabilities, resources and enablers, activities or interventions – required to build agility and resilience. It also details some of the outputs and effects – more broadly measured outcomes such as speed and innovation or results that may include immediate, intermediate and longer-term outcomes such as sustainable financial performance, positive organizational reputation, healthy employment relationship and so on. At the heart of the model are people and culture which permeate all the quadrants.

Quadrant 1: strategizing

Conventional strategy assumes that the future can be predicted but, in contexts exposed to the challenge of speed and complexity, predictability is unattainable. Instead, organizations need to develop strategic agility, defined by Doz and Kosonen as:

> The ability to continuously adjust and adapt strategic direction in core activities, as a function of strategic ambitions and changing circumstances and create not just new products and services but also new business models and innovative ways to create value in complex and fast-changing conditions.[20]

What these authors call 'strategic sensitivity' allows firms to accurately perceive changes in their external environment. This describes leaders' sharpness of perception and the intensity of their awareness and attention. Leaders with high levels of cognitive resilience have the capacity for high quality 'intelligent' strategic thinking and dialogue that converts data into usable knowledge and are able to make and implement bold decisions fast. They demonstrate deep empathy with, and understanding of, customers and stakeholders.

FIGURE 3.1 Component activities of organizational agility and resilience

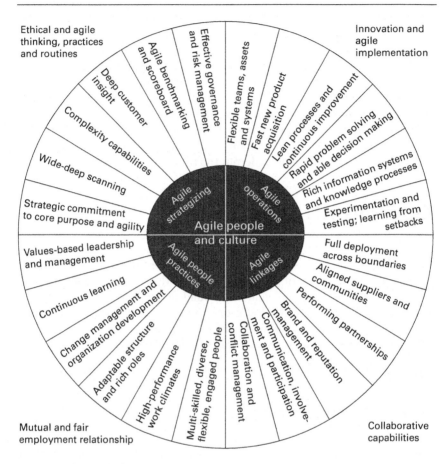

SOURCE © Linda Holbeche

The shift to strategizing

Strategy is usually developed by those at the top and implemented by everyone else. The conventional strategic management cycle – *plan, do, check* and *adapt* – often operates imperfectly and not surprisingly there is often a gap between strategic intent (planning) and implementation (doing). In contrast, agile strategizing is not confined to those at the top of organizations. Just as living systems learn from their experiences, resiliently agile organizations adopt a learning approach to strategy – where participation is encouraged at all levels and strategy creation is a continuous process, rather than a one-off going through the motions of developing an annual business plan then getting on with 'business as usual'.

So strategizing involves a wider group of people in thinking and acting strategically. Everyone needs to be externally aware and 'savvy' – sensing changes in the environment, coping with ambiguity and taking mitigating action to avoid problems or seizing latent opportunities, being willing to voice and being empowered to act on such knowledge. Given the dictum 'I own what I help to create', it makes sense to tap into the collective wisdom of employees and other stakeholders – to gather feedback and insight about customers and the changing marketplace, to develop ideas about what needs to change and explore the 'how' if not the 'what' of strategy. By being involved in collectively scanning the environment, people see the need for change and are usually more willing to play their part in making the changes required. Thus, unlike conventional approaches to strategy making, strategic agility becomes a shared, embedded capability and it becomes easier to close the conventional implementation gap, to some extent at least.

And there appears to be growing evidence that, thanks to the influence of information technology and social media, employees, especially generation Y, increasingly expect to be involved in strategic development.[21] These expectations are likely to lead to a democratization of business model innovation in which more decentralized ideas generation and handling inside organizations can be used to integrate elements of the value chain in more flexible, but also often disruptive, ways. The task for top leadership is to build an inclusive community of leaders that taps into the collective intelligence of the workforce. As ideas evolve, leaders must provide constructive sense making.

That's not to say that agile organizations lack strategic plans. Instead they focus planning on developing their core where they are the most strategically differentiated. The obsession is providing customer value; continually developing new capabilities as a source of competitive advantage; being prepared to put in significant effort to establish exactly what it is that their customers want, and then putting those things first (see Table 3.1). As Peters and Waterman observed about the way 'excellent companies' interact with customers,[22] the most striking and consistent feature of agile organizations is their obsession with quality and service. Rather than being driven by technology or by a desire to be a low-cost producer, these 'excellent' companies are driven by the customer. They use strategies of service, quality and reliability to increase customer loyalty, long-term revenue and growth, in contrast to the short-term sales-oriented approach we see so often in companies. By focusing on their core and by deliberately developing deep customer insight in the context of emerging trends, agile organizations are able to adapt plans as the marketplace shifts, tailoring what they do to what is needed to grow the business.

We explore the mindset and skill-set shifts required for strategic agility in Chapter 4.

But how can chaos be avoided? Leaders must also develop specific structures (also called system constraints) to serve as a counterbalance to randomness and anarchy. First, senior leaders need to create a strong identity

TABLE 3.1 The shift to agile (1)

Conventional strategy making	Agile strategizing
Annual process	Ongoing process
Focused on margin	Focused on customer
Innovate at the margins	Innovate at the core
Developed at the top	Top-down/bottom-up
Aim to increase productivity through controls	Aim to increase productivity collaboratively
Gap between strategy making and execution	Strategy making and execution are seamless

for the organization so that clarity over organizational purpose or vision can act as a strategic compass. Thus clear priorities can be set, which help people to focus on the things that matter, enabling manageable workloads. With respect to reward, recognition plays a key role in raising employee performance and engagement.[23] In addition to shared purpose these structures include shared operating platforms and reward systems.[24] Leaders must ensure that people can access high quality and timely data and support the development of a culture conducive to learning and experimentation. Ethics and reputation become the system constraints within which investment and other decisions are made. Risk management becomes a meaningful enabler of innovation rather than a bureaucratic hurdle to be overcome. Agile methodology can then be applied – not only to projects – to ensure that the implementation of strategy can keep pace with changing requirements (see Table 3.2).

Thus a virtuous circle of high performance ensues – people gain 'line of sight' to the strategy, are aligned and enabled to perform, are more willing to offer their discretionary effort, receive feedback and encouragement and contribute ideas that move the organization forward.

A unified top team

Top leadership – its role, capability and priorities – is one of the key factors influencing whether or not an organizational context is conducive to change. To keep the organization functioning optimally at the edge of chaos the top team must be unified and coherent, and able to make bold decisions

TABLE 3.2 The shift to agile (2)

Conventional strategy making	Resiliently agile strategizing
Based on forecasts	Based on wide-deep scanning and other (collective) intelligence
Pursuit of competitive advantage	Pursuit of multiple transient advantages
Commitment to shareholders	Commitment to stakeholders
Short term	Short and long term
Risk management restrains innovation	Risk management co-exists with innovation
Board scrutiny is light touch	Board scrutiny based on real understanding
Ethics occasionally sacrificed to commercial gain	Ethics always drives decision making

quickly without getting caught up in political power plays. Strategic agility therefore requires top team commitment to agility, cabinet responsibility and collaboration. As we have discussed, this can be difficult to achieve because many top teams struggle to deal with today's complex and paradoxical conditions, and boards too may be highly risk averse and unwilling to endorse the degree of experimentation that may be required in agile strategy. Yet without this commitment to agility at the top, the status quo will remain and agile methods will be suboptimized. As the 2013 IBM report suggests,[25] leaders therefore need to be bold, dare to be open, embrace disruption and build shared value.

Agile implementing

In agile there is little or no separation between strategy creation and implementation (as discussed above, and as we explore further in Chapters 4 and 5). That is largely because employees at all levels are aware of what the organization is aiming to do, what the challenges are and about the part they can play in securing their organization's success. Agile implementing has two key elements:

- Agile operations to deliver strategic intent in the most effective way possible (discussed in Chapter 5).
- The process of change, an inevitable aspect of executing strategic intent (explored in Chapter 10).

With respect to agile operations, the emphasis is on speed, efficiency and flexibility as well as on quality and innovation, with the customer as the central focus of all activity. Organizational assets and systems are designed to enhance flexibility, efficiency and speed so that there is resource fluidity,[26] or the internal capability to reconfigure business systems and redeploy resources rapidly. Continuous improvement, lean tools and agile project management methodology are applied across operations and become part of the organization's culture, enabling continuous feedback, iterative adjustment to changing customer requirements and speedy and effective delivery.

Agile innovation

In agile organizations 'business as usual' is always becoming 'business as new'. That is because they are learning organizations that are continually pushing back boundaries of knowledge and skill through experimentation and testing. Rather than a stereotypical blame culture when mistakes are made, in agile organizations there is a culture of active learning – from setbacks as well as successes. Rich information systems and knowledge processes enable people to access the information they need to do their jobs and also to share ideas for delivering improved customer value. Change efforts are targeted on creating meaningful information flows and having the right people in place to analyse and interpret them (Table 3.3).

High-performance work practices are conducive to innovation, employee engagement and high levels of bounded employee autonomy. These include people working in small, non-hierarchical teams with a limited number of

TABLE 3.3 Agile innovation

From	To
Innovation in limited 'pockets'	A culture of innovation
Individual ingenuity	Individual and group idea development
Risk averse	Open to risk
Haphazard implementation	Disciplined implementation
Reward for organization	Mutual benefits

clearly defined goals that are achievable within a short period. Employees are empowered in day-to-day working life and there are ongoing opportunities for them to initiate and lead improvement and innovation in products, services and processes. Rapid problem solving and decision making at the right level are enabled by workplace practices such as self-organized team working, porous boundaries between internal organizational divisions and also partner organizations, inclusive improvement and innovation teams, management–union partnerships, openness and transparency, and distributed leadership.

The link between culture and performance

One of the principal debates around the concept of culture has focused on its potential link with firm's performance. JB Barney in his resource-based view linked sustained superior financial performance to cultures that were valuable, rare and imperfectly imitable.[27] Kotter and Heskett observed that good performance was not only linked to the 'strength' of culture, but also with 'adaptability'.[28] Several authors have built in the idea of 'alignment',[29] or 'appropriateness' with its environment and competitive strategies.[30]

In organizational cultures that are supportive of high-performance working and agility, managers and leaders typically prioritize employee engagement. The highest-performing organizations in Bersin by Deloitte's top quartile on their Total Performance Index are inclusive and diverse;[31] they offer flexible, humanistic work environments, open offices and space to move.[32] Goals are reviewed monthly – in contrast to organizations in lower-performance quartiles, which do this once a year. Thus people learn quickly and can stop what is evidently not working and do something that does. Accountability and visibility result from agile practices such as daily 'scrum' meetings, iterative testing and adjustment of products, and after-action reviews and improvements (see Chapter 5). Feedback is constant and employees set high standards for themselves and others.

At Netflix, CEO Reed Hastings has created a corporate culture based on his motto 'We Seek Excellence', which appears to attract and retain loyal, engaged and high-performing employees. Like Google this company is highly selective about recruitment so as to ensure that new hires fit into its corporate culture. Employees are motivated to work there because they are treated with the utmost respect, paid good salaries and are given more responsibility and freedom for being valuable contributors to their team. Netflix management sets the expectations for employees to achieve results then trusts them to work the hours required to do the job. Management strives to create an environment where a key employee benefit is working with excellent colleagues; where every person is someone you can respect and learn from.

It is when all these practices come together within a system of mutually reinforcing practices that high performance becomes sustainable and the benefits for organizations and their stakeholders are really significant.

Agile linkages

Disruptive innovation is leading to new, more flexible and interactive organizational forms, cultures, working arrangements and workplaces. Agile organization structures are less 'fixed' and more horizontal than conventional 'siloed' vertical structures, with permeable boundaries between functions, units and departments that allow for cooperation patterns and strategic collaboration to get established. Work is typically organized to ensure efficiency and effectiveness with strong, robust operations, process improvement and team working as embedded norms and clear, delegated decision-making authority at all levels. Such structures require high levels of self-management, accountability and willingness by individuals to keep on learning, developing and applying new skills. Management styles, communications processes, employment and development opportunities, and reward structures reflect this. Relationships between the players involved are critically important to effective collaboration.

Agile structures have more permeable external boundaries too. Indeed, as we shall discuss in Chapter 6, the trend towards working collaboratively with partner organizations (often including competitors and outsourcers) is becoming widespread and may well accelerate as markets become ever more competitive. So organizations are dynamically connected externally via adaptable supply chains, open source, collaborative networks and strategic alliances. Consequently the resilience of organizations is also dependent on the health of partner organizations, the communities they serve and the individual resilience of their staff.

Within knowledge-intensive industries the networked organization is on the rise,[33] especially in mature industries such as pharmaceuticals where companies face the common challenge of building new markets as well as products. Partner relationships can also act as sensors for emergent environmental changes. Thus organizations can set out to exploit opportunities and build new markets with pooled resources and new working arrangements.

To enable organizational linkages within and between organizations to work effectively and without damage to brand requires collaborative capabilities, innovation in roles and supportive structures. It also requires healthy employee relations – at individual and collective levels – including between trades unions and employers' organizations. Employee communications can play a key role in helping to build a flexible leadership culture in which people are informed, engaged, responsible and accountable at all levels.

Collaborative linkages between organizations can also enable freer movement across organizational boundaries for people in search of enhanced career opportunities. Employers usually consider such talent fluidity as a bad thing yet there are potentially positives to be gained. In US Ivy League universities, for instance, rather than being viewed as 'failures', outgoing employees are treated as alumni and future clients – and therefore valuable assets.[34] Those who leave can look forward to highly successful careers with long-lasting collaborative relationships with their former colleagues. Arguably many other types of organization could learn something from this higher-education practice when they reflect on their own approach to talent management and career development.

Collaboration is also needed on a wider scale to address societal and other challenges. Within an organization's ecosystem, including society at large, suppliers and customer groups, there are increasing demands for flexible reactions from organizations to co-determine what happens in markets, cooperation networks and societies. In this interconnected and changing environment, no organization can stand apart from its communities any more.

Especially during and since the economic recession triggered in 2008, the nature, role and ethics of business itself have come into question. Consequently no organization really wishes to be seen as paying mere lip service to the notion of corporate social responsibility. Indeed, a firm's reputation has become a vital business asset that can be irretrievably damaged if the firm becomes known to be an environmental polluter, for example, or exploiter of disadvantaged communities. And, as many high-profile cases have demonstrated, firms' reputations can be put as much at risk by the ways in which their suppliers conduct their business, as by their own practices. Even apparently legal practices from an earlier era, such as the clever use of tax avoidance schemes to minimize payment of corporation tax in their countries of operation, have damaged the reputations of a number of global firms such as Starbucks and others in various markets.

Agile people practices

Both agility and resilience are needed if an organization is to have adaptive capacity or 'change-ability' in its cultural DNA.[35] It isn't just leadership competencies that will need to change to achieve change-ability; employee attitudes, behaviour and skills will also need to shift and stretch. Changeable staff are flexible and competent, multiskilled, 'engaged' and productive, willing and able to adapt to continuous change.

So in agile organizations people become centre stage – their passion, grasp, creativity, interactions and relationships shape the very future of our organizations. The importance of having the 'right' people, working in the 'right' ways, working on the 'right' things, is driving new emphases in human resource strategies. So to build a multiskilled workforce, instead of hiring new people with a narrow skill set to meet a temporary need, leading companies strengthen their existing employees with additional skills. They offer career and talent mobility, a modern learning environment where approaches to development are 'pull' rather than 'push'. Thus talent management strategy is a key tool in building a more agile and adaptable workforce capable of responding to new competitive threats and capitalizing on new opportunities.

Employee engagement is becoming a key area of focus and the link between high performance and employee engagement has some face validity at least. The Engaging for Success report highlights numerous studies that suggest that, when employees are engaged and empowered, they tend to be innovative, willing to share their ideas, more aligned around common objectives, more productive and accountable, more likely to be ambassadors and promoters of their employers' brands, and to have longer tenures than less engaged employees.[36] Therefore, by improving understanding of what drives employee engagement, organizations can be more effective at increasing it.

Management and leadership needed

A number of reports have identified the growing importance of leadership and management in securing the future growth, productivity and competitiveness of firms. UK analysis by the UK Commission for Employment and Skills (UKCES) has shown that management skills are crucial to ensuring high-performance working, and best-practice management development can result in a 23 per cent increase in organizational performance.[37] However, research conducted by the Chartered Management Institute (CMI) and Penna found that 43 per cent of UK managers rate their own line manager as ineffective; and 93 per cent of respondents in a survey of 750 companies carried out by the Institute of Leadership and Management (ILM) reported that low levels of management skills were impacting on their business. A report by Deloitte argues that the need to develop leaders at all levels is the number one issue facing organizations around the world, yet only 13 per cent of respondents believe that their organization does an excellent job at developing leaders at all levels.

So there is a renewed focus on helping managers and leaders develop the skills and abilities they need to create high-performance climates that are conducive to workplace innovation. Longer-term benefits accrue when managers support and enable staff, especially if staff members are more expert in their fields than their line managers. In particular, the leadership of networks demands new approaches to facilitation and empowerment practice that transcend earlier transactional and transformational theories of leadership.

Since agility inherently involves change, organizations need to be 'changeable', with the changing context reframed as 'dynamically stable'. Agile organizations learn to design and implement change programmes in such a way that change 'sticks' – for a while at least. But such a nirvana is not easily achieved within today's competitive contexts in which employees are often required to pay a high price for business success. So if organizations and their workforces are to thrive in changing times we must aim for a better balance between organizational and individual needs. We must seek to create work contexts characterized by trust, mutuality, growth and empowerment. That way, everyone wins.

Conclusion

The quest for business agility is driving changes to the ways firms are being managed and led and to the routines they must embrace if they wish to be resilient. The scale of change required will, of course, depend on the situation that an organization faces and its current capabilities. As we have discussed:

- Building an agile organization is not just about using agile tools and methodology – it involves a *whole systems approach* to enhancing the qualities, capabilities, routines, resources and relationships needed to produce outputs that customers want over time.

- Leading and working in agile organizations requires *context, cognitive and behavioural resilience* at all levels – this is likely to require some significant shifts in mindsets and skill sets.

- *Culture can be more influential than strategy* in determining an organization's fortunes – and should receive relevant executive attention accordingly.

- In today's marketplace, *people are the source of production* – they must be partners in the process of organizational evolution and treated as such.

- Agility and resilience can be enhanced by 'tinkering' at the edges, but to be sustainable must be built on *shared foundations of purpose, values and integrity*.

As this *tour d'horizon* of resilient agility suggests, some organizations may be able to gently evolve towards agile, while for others, nothing short of a revolution will be necessary. In the coming chapters we work through each of the framework quadrants in turn, spending more time, as seems fitting, on the people and culture aspects of organizations. In the next chapter we look at the first quadrant: agile strategizing.

Checklist

How much commitment is there to agile in your organization?
In your organization, which are the issues that attract most attention and where most management effort is made:

- Find new sources of income/funding?

- Attract new customers?

- Develop innovative products?

- Retain current customers?

- Enable bespoke responses?

- Avoid risks and enhance safety?

- Ensure compliance?

- Boost performance?

- Speed-up responses?

- Cut support costs?

- Collaborate effectively across boundaries?

- Increase flexibility for the business?

- Increase flexibility for people?

- Attract the people you need?

- Increase understanding and engagement?

- Make it easy for people to do difficult jobs?

- Support mobile activities, relocation and outsourcing?

- Reduce stress?

Are these the right areas to focus on? What might need to shift? How can this be achieved?

Notes

1 Lengnick-Hall, CA and Beck, TE (2005) Adaptive fit versus robust transformation: how organizations respond to environmental change, *Journal of Management*, **31**, pp 738–57.

2 McCann, J, Selsky, J and Lee, J (2004) Building agility, resilience and performance in turbulent times, *People & Strategy*, **32** (3), pp 45–51.

3 Pettigrew, A, Ferlie, E and McKee L (1992) Shaping strategic change – the case of the NHS in the 1980s, *Public Money & Management*, **12** (3), pp 27–31.

4 Abrahamson, E (1990) Change without pain, *Harvard Business Review*, July.

5 D'Aveni, R (1994) *Hypercompetition: The dynamics of strategic maneuvering*, Free Press, New York.

6 Teece, DG, Pisano, J and Shuen, A (1997) Dynamic capabilities and strategic management, *Strategic Management Journal*, **18**, pp 509–33.

7 Teece, DG and Pisano J (1994) The dynamic capabilities of firms, *Industrial and Corporate Change*, **3**, pp 537–56.

8   Cyert, RM and March, JG (1963) *A Behavioral Theory of the Firm,* Englewood Cliffs, New Jersey.

9   Miner, AS (1991) Organisational evolution and the social ecology of jobs, *American Sociological Review,* **56,** pp 772–85.

10 Feldman, MS (2000) Organisational routines as a source of continuous change, *Organization Science,* **11,** pp 611–29.

11 Adler, PS, Goldoftas, B and Levine, DI (1999) Flexibility versus efficiency? A case study of model change-overs in the Toyota production system, *Organization Science,* **10,** pp 43–68.

12 Miner, AS (1990) Structural evolution through idiosyncratic jobs, *Organization Science,* **1,** pp 195–210.

13 Rosenbaum M and Jaffe Y (1983) Learned helplessness: the role of individual differences in learned resourcefulness, *British Journal of Social Psychology,* **22,** pp 215–25.

14 Coutu, D (2002) How resiliency works, *Harvard Business Review,* **80** (5), pp 46–55.

15 Collins, J and Hansen, MT (2011) *Great By Choice: Uncertainty, chaos and luck – why some thrive despite them all,* HarperCollins, New York.

16 Plsek, P (2003) [accessed 14 July 2011] Complexity and the Adoption of Innovation in Health Care, conference on Strategies to Speed the Diffusion of Evidence-based Innovations, 27–28 January, Washington DC [Online] http://www.nihcm.org/pdf/Plsek.pdf.

17 Collins, J and Hansen, MT (2011) *Great By Choice: Uncertainty, chaos and luck – why some thrive despite them all,* HarperCollins, New York.

18 Lavie, D (2006) The competitive advantage of interconnected firms: an extension of the resource-based view, *Academy of Management Review,* **31,** pp 638–58.

19 IBM (2013) Reinventing the Rules of Engagement: CEO Insights from the Global C-suite Study, IBM Institute for Business Value.

20 Doz, Y and Kosonen, M (2007) *Fast Strategy,* Wharton School Publishing, Pennsylvania.

21 This view has been expressed by Booz Allen Hamilton, Boston Consulting Group and the McKinsey Global Institute.

22 Waterman, RH Jr and Peters, T (2004) *In Search of Excellence: Lessons from America's best-run companies,* Profile Books, London.

23 Source: High-Impact Performance Management: Five Best Practices to Make Recognition and Rewards Meaningful, Stacia Sherman Garr/Bersin & Associates, 2012.

24 Dyer, L and Ericksen, J (2009) Complexity-based agile enterprises: putting self-organizing emergence to work, in *The Sage Handbook of Human Resource Management,* ed A Wilkinson *et al,* Sage, London, pp 436–57.

25 IBM (2013) Reinventing the Rules of Engagement: CEO Insights from the Global C-suite Study, IBM Institute for Business Value.

26 Doz, Y and Kosonen, M (2007) *Fast Strategy,* Wharton School Publishing, Pennsylvania.

27 Barney, JB (1986) Organizational culture: can it be a source of sustained competitive advantage? *Academy of Management Review*, **11** (3), pp 656–65.

28 Kotter, JP and Heskett, L (1992) *Corporate Culture and Performance*, Free Press, New York.

29 Newman, KL and Nollen, SD (1996) Culture and congruence: the fit between management practices and national culture, *Journal of International Business Studies*, **27** (4), pp 735–79.

30 Goffee, R and Jones, G (2003) *The Character of a Corporation*, Profile Books, London.

31 Source: High-Impact Performance Management: Using Goals to Focus the 21st Century Workforce, Stacia Sherman Garr/Bersin by Deloitte, 2014.

32 Source: The Diversity & Inclusion Benchmarking Report, Bersin by Deloitte/ Stacia Sherman Garr, March 2014.

33 Dyer, J and Nobeoka, K (2000) Creating and managing a high-performance knowledge-sharing network: the Toyota case, *Strategic Management Journal*, **21**, pp 345–67.

34 Source: Kennie, T (2012) Disruptive Innovation and the Higher Education Ecosystem, The Leadership Foundation for Higher Education.

35 Holbeche, LS (2005) *The High Performance Organization*, Butterworth-Heinemann, Oxford.

36 MacLeod, D and Clarke, N (2009) [accessed 30 August 2014] Engaging for Success: Enhancing performance through employee engagement, London: BIS [Online] http://www.engageforsuccess.org/wp-content/uploads/2012/09/ file52215.pdf.

37 Shury, J *et al* (2012) UK Commission's Employer Perspectives Survey 2012: UK Results, UKCES Evidence Report 64.

Agile strategizing

I n this chapter we look at the first quadrant of the resiliently agile framework: strategizing. This is how top management teams establish an aspirational purpose, develop a widely shared strategy and manage the climate and commitment to execution. All decisions, including strategy, should flow from this purpose.[1]

In strategizing, the processes of strategy creation are no longer restricted to top management. To close the strategy implementation gap everyone needs to be aware of what the organization is aiming to achieve and have opportunities to play a part in shaping the future. Similarly everyone needs to be capable of what the Center for Effective Organizations (CEO) calls 'perceiving' – the process of broadly, deeply and continuously monitoring the environment to sense changes and rapidly communicate these perceptions to decision makers who interpret and formulate appropriate responses.[2]

Strategizing is also an experimental process for the agile enterprise, in which individuals repeatedly generate ideas (exploration), identify ways to capitalize on ideas (exploitation), nimbly respond to environmental feedback (adaptation) and move on to the next idea (exit).[3] So while top leadership clearly has a key role to play in strategizing and perceiving, so too do others.

In this chapter we look at:

- The scale of the strategizing challenge – and lessons from long-lived organizations.

- The role of top leadership in strategizing – and the skills involved.

- Getting others involved in the strategizing process.

The scale of the challenge

So fast is the pace of change today that, with shrinking product life cycles and success ever more fleeting, many companies are finding that the basis of their competitive advantage is rapidly eroding and their business models are soon obsolete. If organizations are to survive and thrive they must shift their business models – and their leadership skills – to become what Heifetz and Laurie call 'adaptive firms'.[4]

A business model describes the rationale of why and how an organization creates, delivers and captures value. It reflects the dominant performance logic that specifies how business is done, who the customers are and where the costs and profits are. This logic outlines how financial and non-financial resources flow through the organization, and the organizational capabilities required to achieve joined-up implementation of the business model. Innovation in the business model requires developments in the structure and/or the financial model of the business and so also includes strategic partnerships, shared services or alternative financing vehicles.[5]

Leaders need to be clear-sighted about where value is found and about the level of change required to enable the organization to survive and thrive in the new environment, since the scale of business model transformation required will vary according to the organization and its specific situation. Laurie and Lynch argue that there are three strategically different situations that companies face when building on their current success – retaining, refining or changing their business model.[6] Each situation determines where innovation is most needed and the broad approach to organization design. In the first two cases, innovation is focused on both process and product. In the latter case, the organization needs to innovate its overall value proposition to the market.

Rita Gunther McGrath goes further, arguing that in today's context it is unrealistic of company leaders to assume that their firms can achieve sustainable competitive advantage (SCA).[7] Instead, she proposes that organizations should focus on achieving a series of transient advantages (TA) by launching new strategic initiatives again and again, and creating a portfolio of advantages that can be built quickly and abandoned just as quickly. So rather than working to a fixed business model, the pursuit of TA implies the organization must be able to run potentially multiple, experimental business models concurrently and be prepared to dispose of parts of itself that no longer add value.

To be resilient, organizations need to be ambidextrous – able to manage today's business efficiently, while also adapting to changes in the environment so that they are still around tomorrow.[8] The demands on an organization in its immediate task environment are always to some degree in conflict with the longer term (eg investment in the here and now versus future projects; differentiation versus low-cost production) so trade-offs need to be made. While these trade-offs can never be entirely contained, the most successful organizations reconcile them to a large degree and in so doing enhance their long-term competitiveness.

Given this level of complexity, how can leaders create strategies that provide sufficient clarity and avoid chaos? Looking back at companies that have survived successfully over time may provide some clues.

Lessons from long-lived organizations

In a study of successful long-lived organizations which he defined as 'living companies', Arie de Geus draws a sharp distinction between the purpose of living companies – to fulfil their potential and perpetuate themselves as ongoing communities – and that of 'economic companies', which are in business solely to produce wealth for a small group of individuals.[9] Long-lived companies have four essential traits in common: they are sensitive to their environment in order to learn and adapt; cohesive, with a strong sense of identity; tolerant of unconventional thinking and experimentation; and conservative in financial policy in order to retain the resources that allow for flexibility.

Similarly, Jim Collins and Jerry Porras studied long-lived 'visionary' companies such as Hewlett-Packard, 3M, Motorola, Procter & Gamble, Disney and Wal-Mart.[10] They found that visionary companies had fewer charismatic visionary 'time teller' leaders and more 'clock builders' who focused on building a company that could prosper far beyond the tenure of any single leader and through multiple product life cycles. And in visionary companies, management tends to be home-grown, thus ensuring continuity and succession. Insiders maintain the core values and understand them in a way that outsiders usually cannot. Insiders also act as the most effective change agents who can stimulate change and progress.

Both studies emphasize the importance of being guided by a core ideology – a purpose beyond simply making money and strong values. This ideology provides a strong sense of identity and continuity that strengthens the organization in the face of change. Visionary leaders build a cult-like culture around their core ideologies. For instance, Walt Disney created an entire language to reinforce his company's ideology. Disneyland employees are 'cast members'. Similarly, the Johnson & Johnson credo still guides employee behaviour decades after it was first developed.

Both studies also identified that, alongside a passionately held core ideology that provides stability and cohesion, there is a relentless drive for progress that stimulates change, innovation and renewal. So continuity and change co-exist. As Jim Collins points out: 'By being clear about their core values and guiding purpose – about what should not change – companies can feel liberated to experiment with everything else.'[11]

And rather than seeing potential dilemmas and choices as problems to be solved, companies in both these studies recognized the importance of embracing a 'both-and' rather than an 'either/or' way of thinking.

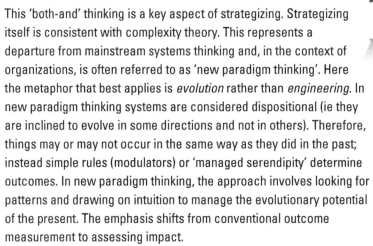

Strategizing and complexity

This 'both-and' thinking is a key aspect of strategizing. Strategizing itself is consistent with complexity theory. This represents a departure from mainstream systems thinking and, in the context of organizations, is often referred to as 'new paradigm thinking'. Here the metaphor that best applies is *evolution* rather than *engineering*. In new paradigm thinking systems are considered dispositional (ie they are inclined to evolve in some directions and not in others). Therefore, things may or may not occur in the same way as they did in the past; instead simple rules (modulators) or 'managed serendipity' determine outcomes. In new paradigm thinking, the approach involves looking for patterns and drawing on intuition to manage the evolutionary potential of the present. The emphasis shifts from conventional outcome measurement to assessing impact.

So rather than taking a technical, singular view – defining some idealized future state and then attempting to close the gap by adopting a conventional problem-solving approach, looking for root causes and potential solutions – new paradigm thinking is relational and takes a holistic view. In complexity both-and applies: order and chaos need each other; ambiguity and paradox are inevitable challenges to be coped with. Change can be revolutionary and dramatic; strategy can be emergent and opportunistic, and diversity provides competitive advantage.

Redefining 'value'

In the current context, an interesting shift appears to be under way – according to a study by IBM[12] – with regard to how some companies determine value. Most conventional companies have 'an almost single-minded focus on "capturing" value solely for the benefit of the individual organization'. In contrast, the most successful organizations in the IBM study are interested in innovation that drives enhanced value for the widest group of stakeholders possible – customers, employees, partners and shareholders alike. So the routine primacy given to shareholder value in many businesses is starting to be challenged by the shifts taking place in the broader context and a new 'both-and' is perhaps emerging.

In agile, the task of leaders is to lead the development of strategy and create a context and a process through which employees can be actively involved in strategizing. Before we look in more detail at what this entails, let us consider the implications of today's complex leadership challenges for the skills and mindsets of leaders.

Strategic leadership in complexity

Despite the complexity and uncertainty of today's global environment, senior leaders are still expected to provide strategic leadership, defined as 'the ability to anticipate, envision, maintain flexibility and empower others to create strategic change as necessary'.[13] The shift taking place in how some leaders do that reflects the move away from the conventional top-down linear *predict* and *plan* approaches promoted by business schools to *perceive* and *respond*.

As we have discussed previously, given the level of business complexity in 21st-century environments, leaders must be sensitive to what is shifting in the environment and develop greater ease in working with paradox and trusting their instincts. The ability to decide what information to heed, what to ignore, and how to organize and communicate that which we judge to be important is becoming a core competence for leaders, according to Gardner.[14]

To help their companies succeed in what Prahalad and Krishnan call the 'new age of innovation', effective leaders look beyond the accepted, the norm, the known and the popular to what is necessary to thrive.[15] They need to have a global perspective, understand their context and focus on critical volatilities and discontinuities. They need to do this with curiosity, courage, commitment, consummate attention, passion, resilience and dedication[16] – and still bring people with them:

> Outstanding leaders now focus on finding the pathways through the contradictions and tensions within the firm, balancing uncomfortable, unpopular but necessary decisions with winning hearts and minds.[17]

Complacency is one of the greatest dangers for any business and the challenge for leaders is to keep injecting urgency. Much depends on how good a CEO is at motivating his or her team and generating the sort of excitement that leads people to do things in different ways. According to Bob Johansen, VUCA leaders energize the workforce by countering complexity with clarity, and uncertainty with understanding.[18] They interpret current reality and shape collective visions of the future through creativity and the development of the overall business vision and direction, setting a common objective that everyone strives to achieve and driving action to seize emerging opportunities. They translate organizational goals into actionable deliverables and empower employees at all levels to make decisions, ensuring that each person on the front line knows exactly what to do to achieve the goal.[19]

Indeed Ireland and Hitt argue that a more appropriate concept of strategic leadership in the 21st century is to move from the 'Great Leader' to the 'Great Groups' view of strategic leadership.[20] This allows knowledge to be more readily shared and the results include outstanding financial performance, customer satisfaction, expanded knowledge bases, integrated communications with stakeholders, continuous process/people improvements and shared leadership.

So leaders are faced with seemingly contradictory requirements: to achieve both strategic clarity and consistency *and* also operational agility and resilience. Balancing conflicting demands requires a different management mindset, skill set and approach from what is required to deliver a relatively simple business model in relatively 'straightforward' scenarios. Some of the detectable shifts in management emphasis are detailed in Table 4.1.

Ability to counter complexity with clarity

Agile leaders counter complexity with clarity by developing a clear vision of where they want their organizations to be in three to five years time. They

TABLE 4.1 A shifting emphasis

From	To
Sensing and reacting	Anticipating, proacting, creating (eg new business models)
Business as usual	Agile business
Innovation in 'pockets'	System-wide innovation and continuous improvement
Customer service	Intense customer focus
Managing global supply chains	Managing global value creation
Efficiency	Efficiency and effectiveness
Employees as resources	Employees as partners
Engage and inspire	Enable and empower
Control of the agenda	Ride paradox and facilitate possibilities
Driving change	Building capability and capacity for change
Either/or	Both-and

help people to make sense of the volatility by working collaboratively and being excellent communicators who can connect with all levels of employees and ensure understanding. A report by the Center for Creative Leadership notes that today's VUCA business environment requires leaders to possess more strategic, complex and adaptive critical-thinking abilities.[21] This means that leaders must be comfortable with not knowing all the answers. In response to demands for enhanced transparency they must acknowledge their accountability for the performance of their businesses. Leaders need to be adaptable, open to change, and knowledgeable about their organization beyond their functional areas of expertise. They must develop deep self-insight into their strengths and weaknesses as leaders. Above all, leaders must be able to learn fast – because change is constant. These skills and abilities are very different from the more technical or function-specific skills and abilities required of leaders in the past.

As with all routines, these skills and competencies improve with experience and practice. For example, divergent thinking skills can be honed through brainstorming, devil's advocacy techniques and dialogue. Problem-solving techniques that rely on frequent iterations serve as catalysts for new ideas and increase the odds of success, simply because there are more options available for consideration. When applied routinely to solving problems, such techniques help leaders to know where to go 'tight', ie with management specifying the parameters of the project, including the 'non-negotiables' and making the final decisions; and where the process is 'loose' so that people know where their contribution is invited and can be made to best effect.

Of course not every leader can lead effectively in paradoxical and ambiguous settings. Today the most important leadership derailers include hesitancy to take necessary business risks, personal arrogance and insensitivity, controlling leadership style, and reluctance to tackle difficult people issues. So it is crucial for leaders to recognize their own strengths and limitations – and what their organization needs. When Google's founders, Sergey Brin and Larry Page, realized that Google was going to be a huge success they hired Silicon Valley veteran boss Eric Schmidt in 2001 to replace them as chief executive.[22] They recognized that just having a world-beating product and eager customers was not enough to secure sustainable success. They realized that even though they were brilliant at developing the product – the search engine – they lacked the ability to handle the business transformation required to take Google to the next level.

Schmidt had the skills to turn Google from a promising start-up into a global giant – and they were right. He was able to motivate workers, reshape departments and internal processes to ensure that Google could grow at a rapid pace. In other words, Schmidt had the rare skill to effect business transformation, to reshape the business and keep it performing while the company grew. It could be argued that every organization and CEO needs this mindset and skill set.

Ability to lead people through change

To provide the bold, sophisticated leadership that the 21st century demands, leaders must create a context for change, recognize and apply the new rules of the game, provide strategic clarity and build capacity to act. Yet they must remain flexible about how they get there. They also need a head for dealing with the risks that are an inherent part of innovation and change. Ideas such as 'control of the agenda' in the traditional sense must shift towards 'facilitating possibility'. Expressions such as 'driving change' must shift towards 'building capability and capacity for change'.

Above all, leaders need to be able to lead people through change and create convergence in contexts where the speed of change can be overwhelming. Relationships, integrity and the ability to build trust lie at the heart of this. As Charles Tilley, chief executive of CIMA, points out: 'Business value goes beyond the numbers. A focus on relationships, in the context of the business model and how it creates sustainable value helps support better integrated thinking and decision-making – leading to better governance, better performance management and better reporting: in short, better business.'[23] This requires an open strategy process, heightened strategic awareness all round thanks to high-quality internal dialogue, where the main challenge for leaders is to help with collective sense-making. Thus agility and resilience become intertwined in the process of direction setting.

This democratization of the workplace can be challenging for some leaders who have long been immersed in management hierarchies where important sounding titles and reporting structures indicate power and encourage ego-driven behaviour. Yet when employees participate in strategizing, the familiar gap between strategy making and implementation starts to close as people come to understand why change is needed, and have the chance to share collective intelligence and contribute their best ideas.

Leading the process of strategizing

A study by the Center for Effective Organizations (CEO) found that, in agile organizations, strategy has three explicit parts: a sense of shared purpose, a change-friendly identity that is nonetheless stable enough to ground the organization, and a robust strategic intent that clarifies how the firm differentiates itself.[24]

First leaders need to define their business and its purpose. Purpose involves answering the question 'why does this organization exist?' According to the late Peter Drucker, the only valid definition of business purpose is to create a customer by offering value that captures the fancy of someone who is willing to pay to obtain something valuable for it. Therefore the question 'what is our business?' can only be answered by looking from the outside – at the customer and market – starting with the customer's reality, values and expectations.

A sense of shared purpose

Firms foster a positive, constructive organizational identity through a strong sense of purpose, authentic core values and a genuine vision. Collective sense-making relies on the language of the organization (ie its words and images) to describe situations and construct meaning.[25] Agile leaders create the strategic narrative that provides the rationale for change and helps people to see what success looks like. They use stories to empower, champion and celebrate change agents in the organization. And when leaders use positive language that implies capability, influence, competence, consistent core values and a clear sense of direction, they set the stage for constructive sense-making.

A vision is a key element of this strategic narrative. The goal of a vision is to ensure that everyone is heading in the same direction to achieve the same outcome. Jim Collins and Jerry Porras in their 1994 book entitled *Built to Last: Successful habits of visionary companies* used the term 'Big Hairy Audacious Goal' (BHAG) to define visionary goals that are more strategic and emotionally compelling. It should be possible to visualize your organization achieving its vision but not so easy for your organization to reach out and take hold of the vision straight away. It should provide a meaningful stretch that gives employees a reason to come to work, generates enthusiasm for what they do, creates team spirit and a commitment to making it happen. For instance, NASA achieved their vision of 'landing a man on the moon and returning him safely to earth'.

It is about inspiring and engaging people, thinking about what motivates them and giving them the space to gain a higher sense of purpose, localizing the message for teams so that they can make sense of their contribution to the larger organization. So it is important to check:

- Is the definition of the future simple, clear and compelling? (Your future should be defined and vividly described in terms of beliefs, behaviours and results.)
- Does everyone understand how they contribute to achieving the vision? Make sure every member of your team knows how they connect to the big picture. Being productive in ways that do not contribute to achieving the future vision wastes precious time and resources.

Dialogue

Especially when change is needed, what matters is that dialogue takes place. This means leaders listening, understanding and acting upon what they hear. These capabilities enable information to flow more freely than ever throughout the organization as a human system. McKinsey has found that effective organizations seem to be transforming strategy development into an ongoing process of ad hoc, topic-specific leadership conversations and budget-reallocation meetings conducted periodically throughout the year.[26] Some organizations have instituted a more broadly democratic process that pulls in company-wide participation through social technology and game-based strategy development.

Many organizations bring together executives and graduate recruits to discuss business issues; recruits typically have energy and new ideas and may also have strong ideas about the values of the business. Some CEOs hold regional board meetings in different offices so that they can ask staff for feedback and discuss issues of concern. Organization Development (OD) specialists can help to facilitate large-scale gatherings that engage employees in dialogue about the organization's context challenges using methodologies such as Real-Time-Strategic-Change and Future-Search.

When conflict occurs it is important, as Nancy Kline recommends, to get protagonists listening to each other, restating key points from each other's point of view and outlining areas of agreement.[27] For instance, in the early 2000s, a major UK newspaper publisher recognized that the advent of the internet and digital would have significant impact on its business model of print journalism since consumers would expect to be able to download content on an ongoing basis and free of charge. The company wanted to get ahead of the curve and be seen as a market leader in this new way of providing information. Journalists were initially unconvinced and unwilling to embrace the new ways of working. Key to helping journalists see the need for change was getting them involved in discussion about the changing context and the adaptive challenge the firm was facing. A series of large-scale gatherings took place in which groups of journalists were provided with relevant context and business information and worked through the implications for the business. They identified a number of ways in which the new model could be made to work financially and became active partners with management in developing the new offering.

Some leaders may be concerned about opening up dialogue on all strategic matters for fear that this might slow down decision making. Here the rule of 'go slow to go fast' usually applies. However, there will be many situations where it is inappropriate to involve people in the decision-making process. In such cases, careful signposting can help to avoid confusion about why people are not being consulted about some matters while they are about others.

A robust strategic intent: focus on the core

The organization's core is the heart of its strategic intent. Hamel and Prahalad identified the concept of core competencies – the complex combinations of skills, processes, resources, technologies and structures that together distinguish a firm and give advantage in terms of the company's ability to design, make, market, sell and deliver products and services of particular quality into defined markets.[28]

In any industry, there are three primary paths to competitive advantage: differentiation, low cost or structural advantage.[29] In today's marketplaces, strategic differentiation, focus and client alignment have become significantly more important than low cost or structural advantage. Without differentiation, companies may end up being in what is often referred to as the 'squeezed middle'. In pursuing a differentiation strategy the key to success is truly understanding your unique core and then focusing resources on it to create value.

The consistently highest-performing institutions in the Fortune 500 focus on the core where they are strongly distinctive and from which they derive their identity. This is where they invest the most and generate the greatest returns. By contrast, areas that are not core may be sources of weakness. Focusing on the core allows organizations to change at short notice, to build real-time capacity and potentially rapidly reconfigure the business portfolio. So, by focusing on the core leaders organizations can build the characteristics that make their organizations stand out and set them ahead of the field.

Identifying the challenges ahead

To help their organizations stay ahead in such challenging and volatile times CEOs need to anticipate what is coming next and identify the 'adaptive challenges' their organizations are likely to face. Without a crystal ball, how can leaders gain insight into the challenges ahead? Heifetz and Laurie use the analogy of a football coach, who 'gets on the balcony' from where they can see the whole pitch and watch the game in progress.[30] As they seek to create a more differentiated and financially sustainable organization, leaders need to 'get on the balcony' to perceive what is around the corner, look for new opportunities, spot the adaptive challenges and make the right moves.

Wide-deep scanning

Getting on to the balcony requires wide-deep scanning of the changing business context, gathering intelligence from many sources to explore the 'big picture' issues facing the firm and its customers. How, then, do leaders 'get on the balcony'? Heifetz and Laurie describe how when the late Lord (then Colin) Marshall came to lead the loss-making British Airways in the 1980s, in looking into the nature of the threat posed by dissatisfied customers he and his team listened to the ideas and concerns of people inside and outside the organization.[31] They identified lack of trust by customers and employees as a key adaptive challenge for the organization, and recognized that competing values and norms were being played out on the executive team in dysfunctional ways that impaired the capacity of the rest of the company to collaborate. Marshall and his team held up a mirror to themselves, recognizing that they embodied the adaptive challenges facing the organization – and decided to address the situation. They created the vision of British Airways becoming the world's favourite airline. The leadership team set new standards for their own behaviour and started to model a new way of operating that built trust with employees and other stakeholders. They also held themselves to account.

Leaders should be asking themselves questions such as:

- Where do we see ourselves positioned today? Where would we like to be positioned in the future? How might we differentiate ourselves from other providers?
- What are we investing in, defending, innovating, personalizing? What are our inputs/outputs?
- How do we achieve international reach – multi-local or multinational?
- Is the core of our business strategy to respond quickly to change or are we about efficiency, driving down cost and eliminating waste wherever possible? Are we market following or shaping? (These different goals will bring different strategies, mindsets and cultures.)

Scenario planning is increasingly used to help firms develop and refine strategic options in the light of potential context changes. Once changes to the industry structure and the company's positioning are understood they can be assessed with respect to the organization's strategic intent, capabilities and risk appetite – as important or unimportant, opportunity or threat. Then more detailed mapping or modelling of strategic flows and processes can take place.

To build these practices into the fabric of their organization leaders need to work with staff to raise their situation awareness, to identify and unblock the systemic and practical barriers to great customer and business outcomes. In agile organizations employees should be involved in wide-deep scanning. Accordingly, information flows both ways in an unfiltered way. After all, it is not just the CEO and the executive team who have a perspective on what is crucial to the business – staff too should know what needs to be done to improve and grow the business and they will view it from a different angle. Moreover, what employees (especially generation Y or millennials) increasingly want from their workplace is to be included, for the goals of the company to be tied to a vision, greater flexibility in scheduling and tasks, feedback and recognition.

Staff should be encouraged to be vigilant about the organization, its performance and potential problems. Leaders need to listen and learn. Heifetz and Laurie argue that rather than protecting people from outside threats, leaders should expose them to some of the uncertainties and external pressures for change. Managers and employees can be expected to gather intelligence from customers, regulators and other stakeholders via multiple touch points, structures and practices. As they work in groups on some of the challenges facing their organization, employees come to recognize the need for change, share ideas about what and how to change and become more committed to changing.

At Ohio State University strategic planning engages all members of its community.[32] The goal of the university is to be consistently recognized among the top 10 public comprehensive research universities in the world. To achieve this goal, every college and support unit – in collaboration with its constituents – has developed a strategic plan to prioritize objectives and guide decision making. Since all the strategic plans are founded in the overarching principles of Ohio State's vision, mission and values, the plans thus support and sustain each other. Their integrated nature is evidence of the commitment of the colleges and support units to a 'one university' ethic.

Build creative participation

Conventionally, thought leadership is confined to specialist research and development (R&D) teams, yet in agile the creative contribution of a wider range of staff is tapped. To achieve transient advantages, and keep organizations fresh and ahead of the pack, a culture of innovation needs to be embedded throughout both top-down and bottom-up. Leaders need to invest in thought leadership, research and innovative models that also reduce risk, so it is important to bring together the right parties from the outset, including experts from around the business, communicating strategic intent and encouraging internal dialogue. Launching a good idea or concept for discussion can be a way of stimulating participation – employees can then help to shape and refine the initial idea. Simple processes such as the following can help:

- Engage a team in brainstorming specific improvements related to a top strategic priority, problem, challenge, or goal.
- Prioritize the top ideas as a team, without in-depth analysis.
- Every participant judging whether the best ideas are translated into the 'right' actions.
- Translate the top ideas into SMART (specific, measurable, achievable, realistic and timely) goals for ongoing tracking.
- Track progress as a management team, focusing intensely on supporting actions related to the goals and visibly recognizing the positive progress of the team.[33]

The key to building ownership is addressing the prioritization step as a group.

In some organizations, whole teams are charged with taking a refined idea further and developing an implementation blueprint; then sufficient resources are provided to aid implementation. In other cases teams are themselves charged with discovering, so employees themselves become the mainspring of new ideas. For instance, Oral-B wanted to find a way to create a unique selling proposition for its electric toothbrushes. The traditional approach is to brainstorm this in-house. Instead the firm took an unusual step and crowdsourced the challenge, using the eYeka platform.[34] In just 22 days Oral-B received 67 unique and innovative ideas from community members in 24 countries. Three won prizes. Using the e-Yeka community gave the firm the head start needed and helped them to anticipate some of the problems that needed to be considered in the development of the product; in particular, the importance of content, gamification, family interaction and socialization. Oral-B used the crowdsourced insights to develop an internet-connected brush that gathers data on the users' brushing techniques and notifies them when the head needs replacing.

Focus intensely on the customer

Customers are at the heart of any business model. Without (profitable) customers, no company can survive for long. Agile organizations remain strongly in touch with constantly changing customer needs; a customer-centric approach provides parameters for innovation, helps to create value and ensures flexibility.

Outside-in thinking

The strength of an organization's customer focus tends to reflect its stage in the organizational life cycle (ie entrepreneurial, growth, maturity, decline, exit). At the entrepreneurial stage the focus is intensely on the customer, yet each subsequent stage of the life cycle gets further removed from this outside-in thinking. In the growth stage organizations tend to get into problem-solving mode as they deal with the challenges arising from initial undercapitalization. Typically, as organizations mature they tend to develop inside-out thinking and lose touch with what customers really want.

Take the case of Kodak, a company founded in 1892 and that made photography available to the masses, but had failed to adapt its business model to the development of digital photography, even though it had invented the technology. Kodak filed for Chapter 11 bankruptcy protection in January 2012. In contrast, Fujifilm, a firm whose roots are also in photographic film – an industry that declined with the advent of digital photography – took a different course, choosing to reflect on how it might apply its expertise to new markets. In September 2007 the firm launched a line of skincare products called Astalift based on technology it had developed for film.[35]

And while the good news is that Kodak has recently emerged from bankruptcy protection – slimmer, and with a new business plan, focused on packaging, graphic communications and functional printing – if the company is to thrive in this highly competitive market, company leaders will need to lead cultural change and find fresh ways of making business faster, easier and less expensive for its customers.

So organizations need to develop outside-in thinking and work back from the needs of customer/end user when designing strategy, work and management processes. As Drucker pointed out, we must start with the customer's reality and expectations and understand what the customer thinks, fears, feels and hears. A key plank of Colin Marshall's turnaround plan for British Airways in the 1980s was to build a culture of genuine customer service in which the customer was central. He instigated a pioneering training programme called 'Putting People First', in which every employee was invited to spend a day learning the airline's new mantra – understanding what real service meant to the customer – and meeting the man responsible. One of his key messages was on service recovery: 'The customer doesn't expect everything will go right all of the time – the big test is what you do when things go wrong.' Within a short time British Airways was able to fulfil its brand promise of an outstanding customer experience and did indeed become the world's favourite airline for a long period.

Segmentation

In order to better understand and satisfy customers, companies usually group them into distinct segments with common needs, behaviours or other attributes. A business model may define one or several large or small customer segments and a conscious decision should be made about which segments to serve and which segments to ignore. Once this decision is made, a business model and specific customer value propositions can be carefully designed around a strong understanding of target customer needs.

Customer value propositions define why customers choose one company rather than another to meet a specific need. Each value proposition will consist of a selected bundle of products and/or services that provide benefits to a specific customer segment. Some value propositions may consist of existing products with modified or improved features; others will be innovative and represent a new or disruptive offer.

Design, brand, status, newness, performance, usability and price are just some of the cocktail of criteria influencing customer choice. The challenge is to determine for what value each customer segment is really willing to pay and the type of pricing mechanism chosen – fixed (predefined) or dynamic (where prices change according to market conditions such as buying airline or rail tickets) – can make a big difference in terms of revenues generated. Similarly, the nature of the customer relationship for each customer segment (eg self-service, automated services, online communities, dedicated personal service and so on) will strongly influence the overall customer experience and therefore sales and customer acquisition and retention.

Co-creation and intelligent products

In today's creative times, concepts of mass customization and customer co-creation have gained importance and open source innovation is becoming topical. Customers increasingly want a supplier relationship that gives them more individual choice and personalization. Companies such as Lego and

Procter & Gamble recognized some time ago that involving customers in some of the R&D work that was previously carried out only by technical specialists would allow for customized products and services, as well as economies of scale, so producing lasting benefits.

The desire for co-creation is a reflection of changing social tastes and ultimately will alter the nature and viability of industries. Thanks to the digital revolution, new industries such as digital publishing have transformed the dynamics of knowledge creation and print publishing. Whereas content was previously produced and edited by expert professionals, today content is produced and published directly through peer-to-peer networks via smartphones – no one edits the content; rather the audience democratically ranks and reviews in real time. The Apple iPod is an example of a product that taps into the growing desire of consumers to co-create their products and services. It essentially allows consumers to personalize their listening experiences by building playlists and assembling favourites, accessing them when and where they prefer. As a result, a whole generation of today's consumers now considers the fixed scheduling of mainstream television and radio channels as archaic.

This active involvement of the customer in the development process changes the innovation dynamic. It is no longer a matter of companies managing a supply chain; to be agile, companies now need to connect with an entire low-capital-intensive consumer-to-supplier ecosystem – an enhanced network of units, suppliers, partners and consumers.

Managing costs

Any organization needs to live within its means, concentrate on what matters most and transform itself for the future. To optimize a business model, leaders need to reduce the capital intensity of the business by managing costs and freeing up capital in non-core assets. Having a focused strategy allows you not only to define what you are going to invest in, but also to articulate clearly what you are not going to do, so that you can avoid waste and distraction. The costs involved in operating a business model are mainly likely to be found in its key resources, activities and partnerships.

Key resources

Key resources can be physical, financial, intellectual (for instance brands, customer databases etc) and can be owned or leased by the company or acquired from key partners. In knowledge-intensive and creative industries human beings are crucial 'resources'. Leaders therefore need to invest in the social architecture required to attract and mobilize global talent. As we shall discuss in Chapter 8, this is likely to include clear values; investment in skills, training and development; clarity about performance, measurement and reward; and building collaborative and integrative capacity.

Key activities and partnerships

Key activities are those required to create and offer a value proposition, reach markets, maintain customer relationships and earn revenues. These will vary according to the business model type. For instance, in a company producing fast-moving consumer goods, key activities will include supply chain management, production and problem solving. To enable these key activities, leaders need to ensure that the IT architecture is fit for purpose, with flexible systems, resilient business processes and focused measurement and analytics.

The challenge of keeping costs down can be addressed in many ways. In many cases, it may make little sense for a company to own all its resources or perform every activity by itself. Carrying out non-core activities through partnerships with suppliers or other third parties, for instance by outsourcing or sharing infrastructure, should provide economies of scale, reduce support and administrative costs, and increase flexibility by rapid scaling up/down. Organizations often embark on cost reduction by exploiting existing flexibilities and/or reducing workforce costs by delayering structures to remove unnecessary overhead. Some organizations seek productivity improvements by improving absence rates; modifying pay, including overtime and increments; and modifying terms and conditions, including changing working hours, leave arrangements, sick pay and redundancy policies. Efficiencies can be achieved through back-office consolidation, process improvement, automation, delayering, changing the skills mix, various HR practices and processes, and flexibility in staff time or numbers. However, greater cost savings can probably be achieved by reducing complexity (arising from too many activities under way at the same time), fragmentation (eg through having conflicting data centres), redundancy and unneeded hierarchy.

Focus on value

In managing costs it is important to be clear whether the business model's cost structures are primarily cost-driven or value-driven, since this will affect the nature and extent of investment as well as the cost management required. Focusing on value – creating great products that customers will want and appreciate – requires a value-orientation mindset. By accelerating the route to quality and being willing to release products sooner, the organization can do less and achieve more. So leaders should be asking themselves: what capabilities and what culture do we need in order to generate revenue faster? If the goal is to become only medium responsive then working with existing structures but aiming for continuous integration may be enough. However, moving to higher value-added – where responsiveness is key – may require significant investment and perhaps cultural and structural shifts: for instance, encouraging collaborative behaviours and developing team-based structures without silos.

Benchmarking for agility

Agile organizations actively benchmark their key processes and capabilities against other agile organizations, regardless of sector (see Figure 4.1). They learn from but do not slavishly adopt other company practices, unless they are directly relevant to their needs. Instead they are prepared to find answers to questions such as: how can we serve our customers better, without incurring extra costs? What routines and approaches do the 'best in class' use? What can we learn from them?

FIGURE 4.1 The benchmarking process

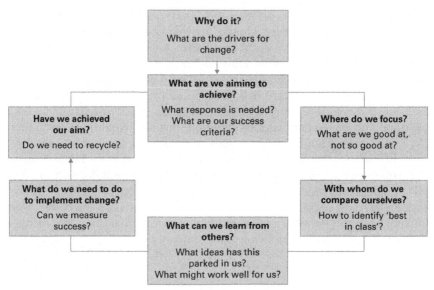

SOURCE © The Work Foundation

Areas to benchmark might include:

- specification and planning;
- infrastructure design and microsystems;
- measurement and oversight;
- self-study and managing knowledge.

CEOs in some sectors are increasingly undertaking accompanied benchmarking visits to peer companies elsewhere in order to learn from each other. Reviewing what has been learned helps to pinpoint where change is needed and helps to answer the question: *How do I translate the measures and metrics we use to report performance in a way that is meaningful to the whole organization and its stakeholders?*

Agile scoreboarding

The question of what constitutes success is under review following the financial crisis triggered in 2008, which exposed the systemic risks that were due to malpractice (eg in the banking sector). The challenge, of course, is that many standard data collection methods (eg employee surveys) can be very blunt instruments, partly because they are not context-sensitive or dynamic enough and are mostly too linear to embrace uncertainty. Consequently, many 'metrics' and forms of measurement are pursued at the expense of actual insight, and insight is not translated into meaningful behaviour.

In the context of agility and resilience, a new blend of organizational and individual 'indicators' is needed that takes account of the demands of a new generation of employees who want work to have more meaning and societal value. Such indicators could enable employees to better understand and manage their own personal development, rather than measurement purely for the purpose of organizational performance management.

CASE STUDY ING – strategic proof points[36]

With a new CEO and a new global strategy ING was keen to ensure that the strategy was both understood and being adopted at local level. Accordingly, the Internal Communications (IC) team worked as part of an integrated multidisciplinary team with Corporate Strategy, HR, Branding and External Communications with a shared goal to look beyond engagement with the strategy and to ensure adoption. IC led the co-creation of the CEO roadshow, which took place in many locations over an extended six-month period. This gave time for the team to adopt agile methodology – to pause and accelerate, to take time out to listen, learn and adapt as they went along.

At the roadshows the CEO was able to meet local staff. He outlined the new global strategy, then invited each local CEO to present how local plans would be affected by the global strategy. This acted symbolically and practically as a catalyst for adoption. The IC team were able to spot in advance where there was a lack of resonance or disconnect, since they had worked beforehand with local leaders to help them explore the implications of the global strategy for adoption in their context. Unlike in waterfall planning, where conflict usually becomes obvious only at the point of delivery, this pre-roadshow phase allowed potential conflict to be surfaced early and addressed quickly. By listening, watching and learning, the IC team were able to catch issues before they turned into crises.

IC was also able to quickly bring back to the international team valuable insights about what was happening on the ground – and these were fed back into the process as appropriate.

Rather than using traditional campaign metrics to gauge how well adoption was going, the team looked at regular intervals for 'proof points' – in the forms of anecdotes, stories and other 'soft' evidence. From these they were able to formulate more meaningful 'hard' metrics. The global ING Communications Network continues to be instrumental in collecting and contextualizing these proof points to inform shifts in strategy and approach.

A picture is worth a thousand words

Of course there are many ways to track progress towards a vision. The use of social media and other ways of capturing and analysing mass narratives via cloud technology may offer a way forward. Pictures are always more captivating than numbers or words – and a balanced scorecard,[37] modified to your company's needs, can help to articulate what you are aiming for and what return on agility looks like from a range of stakeholder perspectives. The balanced scorecard represented in Figure 4.2 highlights that this organization considers its responsibilities to its local communities alongside its other business drivers.

FIGURE 4.2 A balanced scorecard

Business Perspective
How do those to whom we are accountable view us?

Customer Perspective
How do our customers view us?

Strategic Perspective
How do we continue to improve our performance? What must we be good at?

Employee Perspective
How do our employees view us?

Community Perspective
How are we viewed by others?

SOURCE © The Work Foundation

One major US corporation measures what they call their corporate 'adaptive capacity' (AC).[38] They have worked with various researchers and consultants to build a way of monitoring and assessing their corporation's adaptive capacity at three levels – individual, team and organizational – along the lines of the balanced scorecard idea. They have termed this their 'AC dashboard'. In addition, they do an annual assessment of their industry's adaptive capacity, especially to gain a more precise idea of how their corporation can and will endure in a crisis situation in the event of various types of major disruptions.

They also use technology to track what is happening and to turn all this information into knowledge. That is part of what drives their AC dashboard. New data mining and artificial intelligence applications – derived from software originally created to find patterns in overwhelming amounts of scientific data – help them to make sense of all the information flowing through their organization. This allows them to respond to trends faster than most of their competitors, adding to their agility.

Effective governance and risk management

In the wake of various corporate scandals and higher levels of regulation and scrutiny, new forms of risk have been identified and higher levels of accountability demanded of business leaders. In a resilient organization, leadership achieves a balance between risk taking and risk containment in order to ensure ongoing innovation.[39]

Executives are increasingly required to offer stakeholders much greater insight into the strategic imperatives of their organization and of the value drivers underpinning business models. They need to demonstrate how strategy, governance, performance and prospects lead to the creation of value in the short, medium and long term. Increasingly, too, they are being held to account for the ways in which staff, customers and suppliers are treated, and also for the behaviours, values, standards, ethics and monitoring of their organization, its supply chain, its outputs and its impact on environmental and societal sustainability. Boards increasingly want to understand how critical 'resources' such as talent and future leaders are being sourced and developed, what the pipeline of intellectual property looks like and how this is being capitalized.

Boards also want to know what contingency plans are in place to ensure business continuity in the case of various forms of disruption or sabotage. For instance, in the US company described above, technology helps to build organizational resilience through what they call 'strategic boundary management', which sometimes means that they try to build smart firewalls where they need them. In the case of disasters, boards also want to know that the business has strong business recovery plans. Businesses that come through major crises and disasters best are those that have thought through in advance how their people, operations and systems might be disrupted by a crisis and carry out disaster recovery exercises and rehearsals, running through as many 'what if' scenarios as possible.

The danger is that boards can become so concerned about risk that the vital spark of innovation can be smothered by over-detailed and bureaucratic risk management procedures. For boards and management teams to avoid this, in their search for new ideas and opportunities they need to define how much innovation they really want, and the risks involved in achieving the objective. For instance, is the organization trying to become market leading in a new technology category that carries high levels of uncertainty, or is innovation needed to help the organization make small-scale incremental moves, or both? By reviewing what the aim is, it is easier for executives and boards to appreciate the implications for both risk and reward and to equip the organization to innovate. So leaders need to be asking themselves: how do we foster a climate that combines creativity *and* discipline – a culture in which sensible risk is encouraged? This theme is explored further in Chapter 11; in Chapter 12 we consider how to equip leaders for complexity.

Conclusion

In the current context there is no status quo. Stakeholders who believe that the need for change is a temporary phenomenon are in for an unpleasant surprise. Agility is defined by constant change, so the organization needs to have an appetite for change and the capability to enact it in a disciplined and structured way. So a key task for agile leaders is to build the organization's capacity to act – over the short, medium and long term:

- Closing the implementation gap requires *a strategizing approach*, building momentum for change by making decisions and *involving and enabling* the teams who will implement them.

- A *shared purpose* is key to providing clarity.

- In developing a shared competitive agenda and setting strategic priorities, focus on the core and on *desired outcomes for stakeholders* over the short and longer term.

- The ability to be *curious and inquiring* is crucial: fixing problems becomes secondary to better understanding of how to work with them so that adjustments in the organizational system are better attuned to both the internal and external context.

The scale of the challenges being addressed is too great and organizations are too complex for changes to be restricted to certain corners – change needs to be organization-wide. As new routines take root, instead of strategy making being formulaic and an occasional process, strategizing becomes continuous and involves a wider constituency of stakeholders in activities such as wide-deep scanning, data gathering and analysis, testing, developing feedback loops and innovating.

The case for workplace innovation is clear: it has a major impact on the organization's productivity, quality and competitiveness. To stimulate innovation we need stronger, more collaborative ways of working and a broad-based, systemic approach to generating and sharing insights and new ideas, including using internal and external networks. The onus for top management is on communication and sense making, on equipping employees with the tools to find, filter and focus the information they need. The idea here is that employees feel challenged to innovate, drive change and to be accountable for outcomes, not just outputs.

The question is how to achieve innovation as part of 'business as usual'. While consistent 'no surprises' execution would be ideal, given the pace of change and the need for experimentation, people will not always get things right first time. It is not only the increase in external scrutiny that will determine whether or not people are willing to risk experimenting (and potentially failing) but also how the organization deals with the consequences of mistakes. So a blame culture kills innovation and staff morale while a learning culture enables it. Recognizing this means that leaders can be proactive and provide a light-touch risk infrastructure to assist experimentation and decision making at the right levels.

In the next chapter we look at how the strategic implementation gap can be closed in practice in fast-changing contexts. In particular we consider the key processes of organizing and mobilizing people in the context of agile operations.[40]

Checklist

- Why does your company exist?

- Who are its customers?

- What are the key environmental factors that are likely to affect your organization in the medium and long term?

- What are the key drivers for change coming from within the business and organization?

- What possible future scenarios might result?

- What are the implications of these for your organization (factors to be capitalized/constrained)?

- How might this affect future demand for your products and services?

- How should you respond if you are to thrive or even just survive in this emerging reality?

- How are others (eg your competitors) responding?

- What is your vision for your organization's sector in 30 years?

- What will the most successful organizations be doing in 30 years that the others are not?

- In 15 years from now, what will have changed most in terms of your organization's (eg) context, customer base, production methods, supply chain, workforce...

- Which aspect of your strategy is most critical to ensuring the future success of your organization?

- What are the key decisions that your organization faces currently?

- What mechanisms does your organization have to identify to analyse emerging trends? For instance, how do you systematically collect 'external' intelligence from your workforce? Who are the custodians who regularly scan and manage environmental challenges that you face?

- How effectively are these trends acted upon and the necessary changes made?

- What are the disciplines or critical success factors for you to succeed?

- What are the core competencies needed to accomplish your strategy/ gain transient advantages?

- What culture do you need in order to accomplish your strategic goals?

- How much are employees involved in decision making? How much are their ideas invited, heard and responded to?

- How much are people expected to use their initiative to find customer-centred solutions?

- How much are good ideas/good practice disseminated?

- How well does your organization manage for diversity?

- Do people have clear parameters for experimentation? Do they know where innovation is needed?

- What are the key implications of this analysis for people at company and local level?

- What aspects of organization and culture need to change?

- What are your current areas of focus?

- What will need to become key priorities?

- How will you address these priorities? What will you need to do?

- How can you and your organization become more forward thinking?

Notes

1   Basu, R and Green, SG (1997) Leader-member exchange and transformational leadership: an empirical examination of innovative behaviors in leader-member dyads, *Journal of Applied Social Psychology*, 27, pp 477–99.

2   Worley, CG, Williams, TD and Lawler, EE (2014) *The Agility Factor: Building adaptable organizations for superior performance*, Jossey-Bass, San Francisco.

3   Ibid.

4   Heifetz, RA and Laurie, DL (2001) The work of leadership, *Harvard Business Review*, December.

5   Marsh, C *et al* (2009) Integrated Organisation Design: The New Strategic Priority for HR Directors, White Paper 09/01, January, Centre for Evidence-based HR, University of Lancaster.

6   Laurie, DL and Lynch, R (2007) Aligning HR to the CEO growth agenda, *Human Resource Planning*, 30 (4), pp 25–33.

7   Gunther McGrath, R (2013) *The End of Competitive Advantage: How to keep your strategy moving as fast as your business*, Harvard Business Review Press, Boston.

8   Tushman, ML and O'Reilly, CA (1996) Ambidextrous organisations: managing evolutionary and revolutionary change, *California Management Review*, 38 (4), pp 8–30.

9   De Geus, AP (2002) *The Living Company: Habits for survival in a turbulent business environment*, Harvard Business School Press, Boston.

10 Collins, J and Porras, J (2005) *Built to Last: Successful habits of visionary companies*, Random House Business, London.

11 Collins, J (1995) [accessed 30 August 2014] Building Companies to Last [Online] http://www.jimcollins.com/article_topics/articles/building-companies.html.

12 IBM (2013) Reinventing the Rules of Engagement: CEO Insights from the Global C-suite Study, IBM Institute for Business Value.

13 Hitt, MA *et al* (2002) Strategic entrepreneurship: integrating entrepreneurial and strategic management perspectives, in *Strategic Entrepreneurship: Creating a new mindset*: 1–16, ed MA Hitt *et al*, Blackwell Publishers, Oxford.

14 Gardner, H (2006) The synthesizing leader, HBR list: breakthrough ideas for 2006, *Harvard Business Review*, 84 (2), pp 35–67.

15 Prahalad, CK and Krishnan, MS (2008) *The New Age of Innovation: Driving co-created value through global networks*, McGraw-Hill Professional, New York.

16 Fisher, JR Jr (2006) Leadership as great ideas, *Leadership Excellence*, 23 (2), p 14.

17 Kakabadse, A (2014) The success formulae: the CEO's roadmap to value delivery, referred to in A Nation of Accidental Managers!, M Martin, 19 August 2014, 14:40 [Online] http://www.mmartin-associates.co.uk/index.php/our-blogs/work-issues/133-a-nation-of-accidental-managers.

18 Johansen, R (2009) *Leaders Make the Future: Ten new leadership skills for an uncertain world*, Berrett-Koehler, San Francisco.

19 Covey, S (2004) *The 8th Habit: From effectiveness to greatness*, Free Press, New York.

20 Ireland, RD and Hitt, MA (2005) Achieving and maintaining strategic competitiveness in the 21st century: the role of strategic leadership, *Academy of Management Executive*, **19** (4), pp 65–77.

21 Petrie, N (2011) Future Trends in Leadership Development, Center for Creative Leadership White Paper Series.

22 Source: Orton-Jones, C (2014) Growth, innovation and business transformation, *Raconteur*, 14 May, p3.

23 Commentary on the launch of: The Tomorrow's Relationships: Unlocking value report [accessed 30 August 2014] The Tomorrow Company in collaboration with the Chartered Institute of Management Accountants (CIMA), the Chartered Institute of Personnel and Development (CIPD), KPMG and Linklaters [Online] http://www.kpmg.com/uk/en/issuesandinsights/articlespublications/newsreleases/pages/unlocking-value-in-relationships-is-key-to-success-in-business.aspx.

24 Williams, T, Worley, CM and Lawler, EE (2013) [accessed 30 August 2014] The Agility Factor, Strategy + Business [Online] http://www.strategy-business.com/article/00188?pg=all.

25 Thomas, JB, Clark, SM and Gioia, DA (1993) Strategic sensemaking and organizational performance: linkages among scanning, interpretation, action, and outcomes, *Academy of Management Journal*, **36** (2), pp 239–70.

26 Bradley, C, Bryan, L and Smit, S (2012) Managing the strategy journey, *McKinsey Quarterly*, July.

27 Kline, N (2002) *Time to Think: Listening to ignite the human mind*, Cassell, London.

28 Prahalad, CK and Hamel, G (1990) The core competence of the corporation, *Harvard Business Review*, **68** (3) pp 79–91.

29 Porter, ME (1996) What is strategy? *Harvard Business Review*, **74** (6), pp 61–81.

30 Heifetz, RA and Laurie, DL (2001) The work of leadership, *Harvard Business Review*, December.

31 Ibid.

32 [Online] http://oaa.osu.edu/strategicplanning.html.

33 Source: Kuppler, T [accessed 30 August 2014] How to Build Culture Muscle and Improve Engagement, Ownership, and Results [Online] http://www.cultureuniversity.com/how-to-build-culture-muscle-and-improve-engagement-ownership-and-results/.

34 Source: Orton-Jones, C (2014) Growth, innovation and business transformation, *Raconteur*, 14 May, p3.

35 Glenn, M (2009) Organisational Agility: How business can survive and thrive in turbulent times, The Economist Intelligence Unit.

36 Kindly provided by Melcrum based on their research report The Agile IC Function, October 2014.

37 Kaplan, RS and Norton, DP (1996) *The Balanced Scorecard: Translating strategy into action*, Harvard Business School Press, Boston.

38 American Management Association (AMA) (2006) [accessed 17 January 2015] Agility and Resilience in the Face of Continuous Change: A global study of current trends and future possibilities 2006–2016 [Online] http://www.amanet. org/images/hri-agility06.pdf, p43.

39 Bell, MA (2002) [accessed 19 January 2015] The Five Principles of Organizational Resilience, *Gartner*, 7 January [Online] https://www.gartner. com/doc/351410/principles-organizational-resilience.

40 Dyer, L and Ericksen, J (2009) Complexity-based agile enterprises: putting self-organizing emergence to work, in *The Sage Handbook of Human Resource Management*, ed A. Wilkinson *et al*, Sage, London, pp 436–57.

Agile implementation

Managers are constantly striving to improve the performance of their organizations. Key to this in fast-moving times is the ability to quickly translate strategic intent into action. In Chapter 4 we looked at how the agile routines of strategizing and perceiving/sensing are part of the solution to closing the implementation gap. Operations are really where the 'rubber hits the road' with respect to the strategic implementation gap. Closing the gap will require new ways of operating, new disciplines and the adoption of new routines and working practices so that innovation and speed become embedded capabilities in the new, agile 'business as usual'.

In this chapter we focus on some of the processes involved in executing strategy and in creating new products and services at speed. Agile organizations need to be 'ambidextrous',[1] aligned and efficient in their management of today's business demands as well as adaptive to changes in their environment.[2] Ambidexterity in an organization is achieved by balancing the routines of exploration and exploitation, which allow the organization to be creative and adaptable, while also continuing to rely on more traditional, proven methods of business.[3] If the pace of change were slower, organizations would have time to evolve at a gentler pace. However, in today's highly competitive environment, innovation becomes the new 'business as usual'. In this chapter we look at how agile organizations *test* possible responses; and *implement* changes in their products, technology, operations, structures, systems and overall capabilities.

We therefore also consider some agile work practices and key features of a learning culture that is conducive to innovation:

- agile operating model;
- experimenting – the routines of exploration;
- project-based working;
- agile managers – from controller to coach.

By implication, strategic implementation also involves the organization's capacity to bring about changes, both incremental and radical. Agile implementation involves managers at all levels having delegated authority for managing change; it involves embedded change-ability in the organization's operating model, and clear and unambiguous performance goals and measures that support the business model.[4] We look further at the process of change from the people perspective in Chapter 10.

Operating models

An operating model describes the main pieces of organization required to support the business model – its business processes, technology approach, data, organizational structure, suppliers and partners, locations – and how they relate to each other. It represents the blueprint of standards and operating procedures that underpin the workings of the organization. To be agile these must be simplified, standardized and aligned in order to enable the firm to keep close to market changes, and to experiment and change tack as needed.

A target operating model is designed to deliver the strategy of the organization. This involves making specific choices about the priorities, working practices and enabling mechanisms to achieve product breakthroughs and productivity improvements in a given context. For example, increasingly business strategies call for innovation. Boudreau argues that strategic plans should always be accompanied by execution plans and organizational goals that translate into actionable deliverables across four interrelated aspects of performance: market, culture, leadership and talent.[5] So an innovation strategy should be developed through top-down and bottom-up processes and widely communicated throughout the organization. Innovation governance should ensure that there is a clear organizational structure for innovation, well-defined roles and responsibilities, effective decision-making processes and KPIs for innovation.[6]

Developing agile operations requires new approaches to what Kevin Kelly describes generically as 'clockware' and 'swarmware'.[7] 'Clockware' refers to what is involved in operating the core production processes of the organization in such a way that they are planned, rational, standardized and controllable. In contrast 'swarmware' describes those management processes that explore new possibilities through experimentation, testing, autonomy, intuition and working at the edge of knowledge and experience. Both are needed – it is a question of balancing reason and intuition, planning and implementing.

For the effective implementation of an operating model Dave Ulrich and colleagues propose that certain capabilities are essential – leadership, speed, learning, accountability and talent through leveraging human resources.[8] For an agile operating model I would add to this list: collaboration, customer responsiveness, strategic clarity, shared mindset/culture, efficiency and the attributes of robustness, resilience, responsiveness, flexibility, innovation and adaptation, identified by Alberts and Hayes.[9]

Agile operating model elements

Let us look now at some of the other elements of an agile operating model in support of a strategy of innovation.

People and organization

Perhaps the most important aspect of an agile operating model is the workforce. If the workforce is skilled and motivated, supported by the right processes and technology, appropriate HR policies and practices and effective management, it should generate high productivity. So employee engagement should be integral to day-to-day management practice, rather than a standalone strategy. Yet few businesses have a clear model of leadership that improves engagement, removes barriers to innovation, or uncovers hidden strengths in people and the organization.

We shall return to the question of what engages people in Chapter 9 but for now I propose that when people feel they are doing something that matters, they generally feel motivated and a sense of achievement. Similarly, it is important to provide opportunities for employees to develop their skills so that they can work more effectively and therefore achieve more. When employees are encouraged and enabled to connect with other people in their organizations they form communities of like-minded individuals, who are willing to collaborate towards purposes that they share. When that happens, organizations are healthier, employees more engaged and increased productivity should lead to better business performance.

A culture conducive to innovation

If an organization's strategic intent is to achieve multiple transient advantages, then strong leadership and a culture conducive to innovation are needed (ie where people share information, are open to other people's ideas and where the CEO is the 'owner' of the drive for innovation). Such a culture is customer-focused, entrepreneurial, productive and supportive of innovation. It is built on principles of organizational purpose, trust and accountability, a context in which staff are usually willing and empowered to experiment and innovate. It has a strong sense of purpose and shared identity that glues the organization together and aligns individual, work group and enterprise goals as a continuum. Because while creative thinking and adaptation are most obvious when an innovative idea is initially generated, further creative development and enhancement of the idea takes place during local implementation and as the idea spreads across the organization.[10]

For innovation to be socialized and become the 'way we do things around here', participative working and empowerment must become central features of the workplace. When this happens, anyone can generate ideas and emerging ideas are supported by disciplined processes. Workforce innovation describes those working practices that enable people at all levels of an organization to react faster than in traditional hierarchies, use and develop their skills, knowledge and creativity to the fullest possible extent.[11] They include self-organized team working, weak internal organizational divisions and demarcations, inclusive improvement and innovation teams, management–union partnership, openness and transparency, and distributed leadership.

It is about inculcating a vision and supporting it with operational processes to enable employees to take judicious risks. When people are fully aware of their company's high-level goals, individuals and organizational subunits can operate as communities of interest, sharing rather than hoarding data, self-scanning their actions, combining scarce resources peer to peer to provide coherent responses without going up the hierarchy. Then by applying lean or agile project management methods (see below) people can minimize non-value-adding activities and methods, make best use of available resources and maximize client value.

Technology

Technology should be a key plank of an innovation strategy. A study by Harvard Analytic Services found that leading users take a more strategic and systematic approach than others, and are aggressively making use of new technologies to pursue a very different, more growth-oriented set of priorities.[12] So they place a far higher priority on innovation and faster time to market, while limited users place a higher priority on increasing productivity/efficiency and profitability. Leading users consider that, to gain competitive advantage, it is essential to develop more flexible business processes and technology infrastructures and to build stronger, more fluid connections among employees and with customers and suppliers.

The potential of new technology to be the source of communication and speedy production is widely in evidence as cloud computing, mobile devices and applications and social networking support new working practices. In many companies the use of iPads and tablets in the field has lowered costs and enabled better sales and customer service; and many companies are driving their businesses online. Technology can help companies to access and share knowledge across geographies, partnerships, time zones and supply chains, enabling and optimizing business potential. Virtual meeting tools are supporting flexible and virtual business operations that cross functions, business units, geographies and time zones. Some leading organizations are making considerable investment in developing an open innovation (OI) culture to enhance their internal corporate innovation capabilities. Open innovation management seeks to optimize the innovation inflows and outflows across the boundary that exists between an organization and its external innovation ecosystem, identifying and using ideas, technologies or innovations from parties external to an organization in order to create value.

Rich information systems

As organizations co-evolve and collaborate with others they need both access to knowledge and the ability to marshal resources quickly. Alberts and Hayes in their book *Power to the Edge* propose that, to help individuals and organizational subunits make sense of fast-changing complex situations, there should be information 'pull' rather than broadcast information 'push', collaborative efforts rather than individual efforts, and information handled once rather than multiple times.[13]

Agile organizations are built on an infrastructure of company-wide connectivity and information robustness. Rich information systems are those that provide people with access to the information and working knowledge they need to do their jobs. Of course when combinations of legacy systems do not speak with each other, or when companies involved in strategic partnerships use different IT systems, this can make doing the job very difficult. Especially in the case of mergers and acquisitions a common platform is needed if the intended economies of scale are to be realized.

Lean execution processes

Operations typically use standardized processes and systems to achieve operational excellence and cost-efficiency. So for organizations aspiring to be agile, the challenge is to standardize flexibility: to develop flexible assets, processes and systems that will continue to provide operational excellence and cost-efficiency and also free up capacity for innovation.

Increasingly organizations are embracing *lean thinking*. The core idea is to maximize customer value while minimizing waste in all its forms. The ultimate goal is to provide perfect value to the customer through a perfect value-creation process that has zero waste. To accomplish this, the focus of management must shift from optimizing separate technologies towards an integrated approach, optimizing the flow of products and services through entire value streams that flow horizontally across technologies, assets and departments to customers. Continuous improvement involves eliminating waste along entire value streams, instead of at isolated points, creating processes that need less human effort, less space, less capital, and less time to make products and services at far less cost and with fewer defects, as compared with traditional business systems. 'Japanese' production strategies such as *just in time* (JIT) strive to reduce in-process inventory and associated carrying costs. To meet JIT objectives, the process relies on signals (or kanban) between different points in a given process, which tell production when to make the next part. Manufacturing firms such as Toyota that adopted these methods from the 1980s ended up raising productivity significantly (through the elimination of waste).

Thus companies are able to respond to changing customer desires with high variety and quality, low cost and very fast throughput times. Also, information management becomes much simpler and more accurate.

Experimenting – the routines of exploration

What the Center for Effective Organizations (CEO) calls *testing* and Plsek[14] refers to as experimentation and '*pruning*' is how an organization sets up, runs and learns from experiments. This requires some slack in resource capacity (people, time, money, etc) to allow space to experiment with new ideas.[15] In today's more fluid environments, business leaders of knowledge-intensive firms must harness and direct their firms' innovation potential by remaking their businesses from the outside-in. That means increasing the organization's ability to solve their clients' issues by finding out what clients think about the issues they are facing, and therefore how firms can best help them, rather than simply selling solutions based on the firm's current capabilities.

Agile problem analysis

Setting up problem solving as an experiment helps stakeholders to understand that, in attempting to solve problems of which a firm has no experience, solutions are unlikely to be generated until ideas have been tested. Related to lean, agile problem analysis allows for accurate identification of real problems for which solutions can then be sought.

To analyse business problems using an agile approach one of the hardest tasks in designing an experiment is working out exactly what question to ask; and when you are asking for help in solving a problem, how much detail to give. The quality of answers is usually related to the quality of the questions. When working with a team whose understanding of the problem ranges across a wide spectrum, it is useful to provide enough structure and detail so that the people who are unfamiliar with the issues can make a contribution. It is essential to get a well-expressed problem statement quickly – to understand what problem your potential solution solves – and then create a project charter. It is important to separate symptoms from the real problem. For instance, as Hoverstadt points out, when managers find they are repeatedly taking decisions about the same operational issues, it is usually a sign that some sort of coordination mechanism is missing, resulting in problems being passed up to management to resolve.[16]

First bring together a cross-functional team to distinguish between those issues that are real problems, from those that are mere symptoms of the problem.[17] For example, a symptom presenting itself as a problem might be: 'it takes 40 minutes to complete an application form' – while the real problem is that the company is losing good applicants as a result of a cumbersome applications process. The symptoms should be put on a list of irrelevant items and circulated, in case a real problem is lurking undetected. If the problem is beyond the authority of anyone to solve it, then it becomes beyond the scope of the project.

Agility depends on focusing on one problem at a time – removing solved or false problems from the list as you go until you have identified the real problem and can rewrite the problem statement that provides the scope for the project. Problem-solving techniques such as this, which rely on frequent iterations, serve as catalysts for new ideas and increase the odds of success simply because there are more options available for consideration. If successful, what the project delivers becomes the new 'business as usual' (BAU).

Opportunities for problem solving

Innovation leaders are faced with addressing complex problems with no obvious answers so it is essential that they have the opportunity to tap into the diverse views, ideas, knowledge and insights of their workforces. After all, in the Web 2.0 age, employees ought to understand their market, the firm's technologies and their clients – and people expect to be involved. Tools such as crowdsourcing can be helpful in galvanizing people to find solutions to business challenges and dramatically increase the innovation capabilities of the company. The process works something like this:

1 Stakeholders brainstorm to come up with challenge ideas for a problem.

2 A selected problem is launched company-wide as a challenge, often via a portal.

3 Staff, including experts, collaborate to find possible solutions.

4 The best contributions are awarded with small cash prizes, gift certificates and/or accolades such as letters of appreciation from the CEO or head of R&D.

For example, the French skincare company L'Oréal had a problem with its Active Cosmetics Division,[18] which was not performing as well in the UK as in other markets, due to cultural differences – for instance the British generally do not ask their pharmacists for skincare advice, nor do they generally visit dermatologists unless they have a serious problem. So the company was wondering how to improve matters. The company had commissioned research into the mindset of British workers. This suggested that while many were keen to be more entrepreneurial at work, and more than one-quarter claimed to be sitting on a good idea, nine out of ten employees felt that their boss was uninspiring and were likely to look elsewhere for advice.

L'Oréal realized that its workers would be keen to help resolve the problem so the firm took its own advice and asked staff to become consultants with respect to the business challenge. They created an internal competition called 'The Next Fund' in which they invited employees to submit ideas about the underperforming division. The entries were judged by a top-level panel and a prize of £100,000 showed that the company intended to take seriously the best ideas.

The ability to utilize the diversity inherent within multidisciplinary teams has long been recognized as a key ingredient in creating a learning culture. One firm, for example, identified six business problems and, for each of the challenges they identified, they formed an expert team to look at any solutions submitted. The teams were made up of combinations of people who were currently working on the business problem and people who were new to the organization. This blend of experience turned out to be critical. While the design of the experiment was carefully structured, there was still plenty of scope for learning on the job.

Agile work planning

Doing the right work starts with widespread ideas generation around business problems and potential innovations, focusing on desired outcomes for customers and organizational results. Risk and value-driven mechanisms should be used to decide which ideas to work on. Rather than defining success by output it must be defined in outcome-based terms, describing the difference the results will make to the intended recipient, striking a balance between daily activity and the long-range view. A structure of standards can be developed based on what is happening when the outcome is being successfully achieved.

At product level, clearly stated goals, objectives and performance indicators provide a focus for the team's work. These inform management decisions about ways to allocate resources and deliver services. Lean and agile programmes of work then ensure that initiatives are designed around planned business outcomes. There is ongoing measurement of how well the intended outcomes are being achieved, with feedback loops to inform decisions about when goals might need to be adjusted. Programme management is required to ensure that multiple streams of work deliver organizational benefits.

Continually reviewing current requirements with the future in mind enables a deeper understanding of the longer-term workforce requirements. The goal should be to pick optimal responsibilities for individuals based on their capabilities and current organizational needs.

Setting up agile teams

Agile organizations require a learning mindset in the mainstream business and underlying lean and agile processes to support innovation. Agile project teams are part of the overall mix alongside operations teams. The people who will thrive in agile teams may differ from those who enjoy traditional project working. For instance, stereotypically millennial workers will probably embrace agile more readily than the traditional approaches. Critical attributes for agile project teams include:

- flexibility;
- adaptability;
- focus;
- a strong sense of purpose;
- relevant structure;
- viable processes.

Teams will self-organize their work strategy, structure and collaboration paths to reflect the context. They may need guidance to do this well. Leaders of successful operations need to provide the right structures, processes, training and incentives to build a culture supportive of innovation and managed risk by, for example:

- establishing the set of values that underpin innovation efforts;
- making decisions that define expectations;
- setting goals that encourage and make it safe for others to innovate;
- making decisions on innovation budgets;
- adopting new measures of success and rewarding those who excel at them;
- defining innovation governance responsibilities;
- defining roles, key responsibilities of the main players and ways of working around the innovation process;
- defining decision power lines and commitments on innovation.

Leaders must accept that, as new opportunities are developed in the process of trial and error, there will be some setbacks. By bounding experiments with agreed-upon criteria, and capturing learning, leaders can ensure that there is effective risk management of new ideas and that the company's capabilities are continuously improved.

Innovation as everyone's job

Resiliently agile organizations tend to have high degrees of behavioural resilience. These include the practised actions, particular routines, resource configurations and interaction patterns that represent the firm's response to disruptive conditions. These behaviours are designed to both create and capitalize on a firm's flexibility.

As an example: two remarkable pilots of the Second World War and innovators in aviation history – Eric 'Winkle' Brown and Jimmy Doolittle – both survived the war despite carrying out extraordinary aviation feats and facing extreme danger on many occasions. Both shared the characteristic of thorough preparation before any flight, checking every detail of the plane, routes, etc, so that when faced with the hazardous reality they could focus specifically and uniquely on what needed to be done in that particular context. These disciplined approaches, perhaps best reflected in the phrase 'practice makes perfect', are increasingly recognized as the mainspring not only of skill, but also of innovation.

At Seattle-based Virginia Mason Medical Center innovation is everyone's job.[19] Each person in the organization – from the executives to the front-line staff – is encouraged to apply lean concepts and innovation to their day-to-day work. A true culture of innovation inspires staff to routinely try new things without fear of failure, because it is about trying many ideas to find the one that will work best. Leaders encourage teams to break out of their mental valleys – or established patterns of thinking – so they can look at solutions in a different way. Virginia Mason uses four approaches to foster daily innovation:

1 *Everyday lean ideas (ELIs) system*: ELIs are small, quick-to-implement improvements tackled by staff in a local work unit, focused on improving safety, reducing defects, organizing materials or information, and saving time and money. An ELI immediately delivers small improvements while embedding lean thinking into staff who are potential future leaders. Ideas are fully tested and proven before they are implemented.

2 *Moonshine lab*: in early Japanese lean organizations, workers often stayed after hours to build new tools and fixtures that were added to the production line the following day. A moonshine lab is based on the idea of 'working while the moon shines' and creating prototypes to solve tasks at hand.

3 *Informatics in clinical daily work*: Virginia Mason also supports a small group of individuals who are constantly looking to leverage informatics to improve care.

4 *Innovation grants*: while ELIs nurture small ideas, innovation grants support breakthrough ideas that can help Virginia Mason leapfrog important performance measures. Grants provide up to US $25,000 and ideas are expected to be tested within about 18 months.

Since 2002 Virginia Mason has made use of lean concepts such as 'jidoka' – or having the instructions and knowledge necessary to do one's job right first time – in order to mistake-proof primary care. One guiding principle has been to equip clinicians with vital patient information that they need in order to care for their patients at the point of care.

One team of staff used a lean process called '5S' to organize common areas, nursing stations and medication rooms. They sorted, simplified and standardized the areas so that everything is clean and in its proper location, so that clinicians can find what they need without delay. By arranging nursing zones into a U-shape, people have the shortest distance to walk; work enters and leaves at the same place; there is increased communication; and it is easier to balance the workload between people – they can flex between jobs and help each other.

It is often assumed that standardizing business processes acts as a restraint on innovation. At Virginia Mason the reverse is true. In practice, developing simple, standardized processes that are known, understood and effective has freed up staff to innovate and improve the service to be responsive to customers and the market. Therefore, innovation goes hand in hand with rigorous, repeatable and measurable processes that are known and available to everyone.

A framework for knowledge sharing

It helps to establish a clear framework for knowledge sharing in order to reduce the distance between executives and local staff. For instance, the CEOs of Atlassian, an Australian software company, have instilled an open information culture that includes people as well as systems.[20] Workers are encouraged to 'put *information* out there' for others to consume rather than hoarding it in their private stores. Early in its corporate life cycle the firm developed its own 'corporate wiki' that was given the name 'Confluence' to represent the coming-together of ideas. New staff members are instructed to use the wiki and, without the infrastructure for traditional 'document management', these staff members have little alternative but to 'buy into' the system. The very act of using a wiki, with its easy access to information and default 'open' nature of information, has led to a bottom-up democracy of information where information sharing is the norm and the wiki is a destination for lively discussion and debate.

A Cap Gemini study found that helpful practices include bringing together the most innovative employees into cross-functional innovation teams, in a new and different physical space, but without isolating them. It is important to establish performance measures, make things manageable and let the teams get on with it. Some companies prefer to ring-fence innovators in 'skunkworks', which describes a group within an organization given a high degree of autonomy and unhampered by bureaucracy, tasked with working on advanced projects. For example, in 2011 Wal-Mart established @WalmartLabs, an 'idea incubator', as part of its growing e-commerce division in Silicon Valley – far removed from the company's Bentonville, Arkansas headquarters.[21] The group's innovations, including a unified company-wide e-commerce platform, helped Wal-Mart to increase online revenues by 30 per cent in 2013, outpacing Amazon's rate of growth.

GSK is approaching open innovation from a multitude of directions that range from creating small, focused teams to soliciting ideas through their Innovation at GSK website. GSK's global Open Innovation team develops consumer health-care ideas and/or technology innovations from concept to delivery. Members include experts in R&D, marketing and business development located in R&D centres around the globe, innovation hubs that are open-space work environments that facilitate collaboration and foster creativity. As scientific peers, they act as liaison between the originator of the initial idea and the key individuals in GSK responsible for the assessment and development of the innovative idea or technology.

Project-based working

Project-based work is a growing feature of many workplaces, since in the world of transient advantages products and services need to be developed rapidly alongside business as usual. Project working is therefore a key plank of strategic execution, which can result in innovative breakthroughs, new products and services. New Agile disciplines from the world of IT are being applied to project working and more broadly becoming part of organizational culture or 'the way we do things around here'.

The evolution of project management approaches

The origins of traditional project management were in planning and tracking large complex projects in areas such as construction. Traditional project management reflects a systems engineering approach that involves centralized planning, monitoring and decentralized execution. Its methods are highly disciplined and methodical, favouring logic, reason and planning. Back in the 1950s, project management was applied to software development using the so-called 'Big Bang' approach, so-called because developers would be given a brief, develop a product, then have to wait until delivery to find out what might need amending or where the software failed to meet client expectations – an obviously risky and expensive process.

By the 1970s, a stage-based approach to software development was introduced known as the 'waterfall' model, so-called because as each phase was completed it would lead on to another, making backwards moves to make corrections very difficult. With the waterfall model, projects need executive buy-in and funding at the start, teams are lined up, client requirements are gathered and there is an attempt to completely understand the whole project from the outset. The aim is for a perfect product, with testing applied until there are no 'bugs' in the system, then finally the product is demonstrated to the client. This method typically leads to both scope creep (since business needs might change during a long project, and developers might be asked to squeeze in 'one more thing') and limited flexibility, since once requirements have been predefined at the start of the project there is little room for manoeuvre. Moreover, the relatively slow feedback cycle in a fast-moving context, and limited client involvement throughout, means that customers may end up rejecting the finished product if their needs have moved on in the meantime.

These approaches work best in relatively predictable conditions when technical expertise is required over long project cycles, and when the material factors are known in advance and a central authority is in a position to ensure that all necessary actions are taken by the appropriate parties. In recent times it has been recognized that in fast-moving contexts, under conditions of uncertainty, predetermined solutions to problems can neither be reliably ascertained nor easily implemented, so executing traditional projects can be difficult. There can be too many project sponsors with conflicting needs; specifications often change and projects run out of funds before they are delivered. Nevertheless, these approaches are still very much favoured by large organizations who train employees in Prince 2 and other project management-related methodologies and software.

The development of agile project management

Software developers came to realize that, with rapid change as a backdrop, long stages of project development without feedback were doomed to failure. They saw that once products and services are launched, they encounter competitors' products, regulators, suppliers, and customer responses that force costly revisions. Execution processes therefore must be both agile and lean. Thanks to the proliferation of web services, software is being developed in smaller units that are easier to map to business processes. These enable frequent product releases and provide flexibility to deal with changes required in real time. Of course they must also be cost-effective, eliminating non-value-adding processes and management overhead.

Agile as 'best of breed'

Agile itself is a philosophy and a best-of-breed collection of methodologies, such as 'lean' used to develop and maintain software, that is now being more broadly applied to projects of other kinds. Indeed, agile is being embraced by companies such as Phillips as a means through which to become more entrepreneurial. Lightweight methodologies include 'scrum': 'a flexible, holistic product development strategy where a development team works as a unit to reach a common goal'.[22] Although Deming's plan–do–check–act cycle is encompassed in this system, Agile challenges assumptions of the traditional, sequential approach to product development. It enables teams to self-organize by encouraging physical co-location or close online collaboration of all team members, as well as daily face-to-face communication among all team members and disciplines in the project. Essentially the team has control of the project. With shared goals and scalable processes, agile working enables teams to achieve lower defects, faster releases and sustainable activity without the team burning out.

In an agile project, the 'product owner' has a dual role, both as subject-matter expert and as liaison between clients and technical teams. They work with the client to agree the big picture needs, then translate these into units of work that are progressed in 'sprints'. 'Big picture' needs – such as 'as a division we want faster loan approvals so we can increase trading by 10 per cent rather than do safer loan approvals so we can lower defaults by 10 per cent' – are translated into a simple value story by the product owner with the client. Acceptance criteria are agreed and funding attached to the various units of work required. The larger the unit of measurement, the less accurate it will be, so the 'big picture' value story is broken down to the daily task level to make it easier for people to understand agreed-upon goals. This gives developers the right information to do the job and allows for traceability and accountability within the team.

Sprints have disciplined start and finish times of between one and four weeks and team members hold each other to account for completing the work during this time. At the start of each sprint, the product owner brings client information to the team's planning meeting. Using a big chart, and in daily short stand-up meetings, team members keep each other informed of progress and issues. Peer pressure forces delivery, as in weekly sessions the teams demonstrate their work to each other (and clients) and actively gather rapid feedback and ideas. Thus testing and integration are occurring simultaneously.

A series of sprints adds up to an 'iteration' at the end of which either a usable product is shipped to the customer or the next large milestone set. At the end of each iteration there is a quick retrospective to gather learning and assess what had worked well or otherwise. In one sense, nothing is ever completely 'finished' though products are launched; rather each iteration in the development cycle 'learns' from the previous iteration. Thus agile methodology is more flexible, efficient and team-oriented than any of the previous models.

Agile approach to identifying stakeholders

Stakeholder prioritization is one of the fundamental building blocks of a successful project or organizational change strategy. A stakeholder is any individual or group of people who have a direct impact on the success of the project, or are affected by it. In designing projects and deciding which approach to take, it is vital to identify and involve the right stakeholders. Too often though, project teams get the stakeholder prioritization step wrong. Common pitfalls include prioritizing stakeholders based on the wrong assessment criteria or based upon input from too few people.

To identify relevant stakeholders it is useful to start with the project sponsor (the person with the idea) who has the funding, a vision of what the project should achieve and the political clout to help you identify additional stakeholders. Early in the project the list of stakeholders is based on this vision and is usually vague. In finding out who other stakeholders might be, organization charts are often unhelpful if they are out of date, so it is better to create a current one using a flip chart. Then involve a wider pool of people likely to be involved in creating the solution – analysts, creators, testers, managers, etc – to brainstorm potential stakeholders. Special interest groups (SIGs) such as auditors, who have jurisdiction over what the project is allowed to change, should also be consulted. Most of all, end users (internal and external) should be involved. Circulating the stakeholder list to all the identified parties ensures that any important stakeholders missing from the list can be added. By identifying relevant stakeholders it is possible to get a good idea about what they want the project to deliver.

Combining traditional and agile approaches

A portfolio of business projects may require using a mix of agile approaches alongside a more traditional disciplined process. What type of discipline, and how much structure, adaptability and flexibility are required? The answer will depend on what makes sense according to the company's life cycle stage, its structure and culture, with many companies preferring to rely on classic project management approaches rather than on agile or lean approaches. Combining the two approaches is not easy and the challenge then is how to strike the right balance. A framework for determining whether or not a particular project should be agile could include:

- How well equipped is the organization's culture to deal with chaos and decentralized decision making? Or is it more attuned to top-down hierarchical planning?
- How complex is the project requirement? When there are a small number of complex major projects under way the discipline of traditional project management is a sensible choice. It allows for clarity about the work to be done, by whom and when.
- How stable are the requirements – how much will these change every month? The less stable the requirements, the more an agile approach will be useful.
- What are the consequences of project failure? The greater the consequences, the more plan-driven the project tends to become.
- How large is the team? A team of 10 can be agile whereas a team of 500 cannot.

- What skills are required? Essentially, agile involves managing people through a shared culture and having people with overlapping skill sets who are competent to make decisions themselves instead of through a hierarchy. Conversely, when teams are made up of specialists from different fields it can be more difficult to allocate work among the different disciplines.
- What are workers' skill levels? The lower the skills, the more supervision will be required and the less agile the team.
- What is the project's scope? The degree of decentralization will reflect the scope of the project – which might vary from short iterations to a deadline a year ahead.

When a hybrid of both traditional and agile approaches is required projects typically start off using traditional planned approaches before they become more agile. There can be tensions that are essentially reflective of different cultures. For instance, in large projects using traditional approaches, plans are broken down into chunks by centralized planners, predictable techniques used, progress monitored and deviations addressed. In contrast, agile projects eschew detailed planning and estimating – it is about being able to replan as you go. This raises challenges such as:

- how to allocate budget between those projects that have detailed plans and budgets and those that do not;
- how to use adaptive planning techniques while still providing accurate progress status to traditional project manager counterparts.

There need to be clear demarcations between agile and traditional approaches and the best of both applied. In traditional approaches, funding is allocated and increases over the project cycle. In hybrid approaches, funding is allocated within a series of sprints when results are already emerging. Similarly, major deadlines on large projects might be set centrally, while in stages between major deadlines teams can do the micro-scheduling themselves. Clear and frequent communications are needed within and between teams so that everyone knows what is going on and to build trust between users of agile and traditional methodologies.

The skill sets for managing traditional and agile projects differ; therefore different kinds of project manager may be needed to run different projects. A traditionally trained project manager, who typically needs to have oversight of and control of the whole project, probably will not feel comfortable delegating decision making to the team and taking on the role of coach/facilitator/clearer of roadblocks for the team. Senior managers too may dislike not knowing in detail what is going on in all the projects. If managers will not relinquish control to the team, agile will not work. HR can help managers to become 'bilingual' – to make the shift from top-down control approaches to more agile – so that managers and teams can be on same page.

Spreading the learning from agile

It is important to bring learning from this lean work into the wider context of the traditional organization and export agile practices – such as scrum, testing, rapid feedback and stand-up meetings – to create a gradual sea change in 'the way we do things around here'. For example, so fast is the pace of change in retailing that US retailer Gap has moved from a 'push' to a 'pull' model, listening intensely to what customers want and making all their processes lean to ensure rapid response. They and others are having to adjust and adapt their supply chains, building transparency into inventory systems, designing collaborative working within organizations and redesigning work processes.

Different functional groups, such as R&D departments and sales teams have their own cultures, which differ from each other. By working out where different subcultures intersect, it is possible to find parts of the organization that can tolerate both agile and disciplined approaches. Then it is about finding ways to break down silos, encouraging people to move between disciplines, providing training, sharing with people the reasons why different approaches are needed at different times and what these involve.

Unilever has deliberately embraced agile working practices encompassing virtual working and has found it to be a total culture change in how work gets done. The firm has achieved many benefits from agile working, such as 30 per cent greater space utilization, multi-award-winning offices, including Singapore and Hamburg, and 60 per cent less waste and energy. In particular, employees are more productive and engaged.

Agile managers – from controller to coach

Creating an agile environment has fundamental implications for managers and leaders, for the structuring of work and for the development of an increasingly self-managed team culture. Senior leaders must manage the tension between risk and mitigation; they must ensure that teams are clear as to what is expected of them and emphasize the outcomes that matter most to the organization's stakeholders – its shareholders, customers and others. They must ensure that staff have the delegated authority required to make decisions related to their work, especially where their specific knowledge adds significant value. They stimulate innovation and creativity by encouraging and rewarding staff for using their knowledge in new ways to solve existing or emerging problems. A commitment to communication, training and change management is fundamental to success.

While the idea of self-organizing teams has been around since the 1980s, the implications for the roles of line managers are slowly emerging. At the very least, managers need to be versatile, able both to take direct control when appropriate and be coach/facilitator when it is not. In 2014 the US apparel retailer Zappos adopted 'holacracy',[23] a trademarked programme that represents an organic, self-managing structure in which formal job titles, managers and traditional hierarchies are abolished. Work is instead organized into either separate or overlapping circles in which collections of individuals collaborate in order to get the job done. Staff are invited to join or leave according to their skill set. Staff lease their software, space and training from a budget they are given, then are left to get on with the job. That is not to say that leadership does not exist. Each project still has a leader who also acts as coach. Each circle has a project coordinator or lead who needs the key skills of a manager, ie good communication, the ability to inspire others and organizational skills. By implication, the nature of leadership required is less about managing people and more about visioning and empowering them to act. Leadership becomes a capability, not a person. Transparency is central to this way of operating, since staff are held to account by their peers. The model is thus based on trust and win-win outcomes.

Even if this way of organizing may be inappropriate in many contexts, nevertheless some of its facets – such as delegating power, joint decision making, staff being free to act and a shared sense of purpose – are key aspects of agility. As organizations become ever more decentralized, with more project-based people selling their skills, or working for more than one employer at a time, new models of organizing will continue to evolve, and the transformation of manager roles is likely to continue apace.

Conclusion: HR implications

Many of this chapter's messages about agile implementation apply to the HR function itself. The HR implications of agile implementation are counter-intuitive in some respects and there is no 'one size fits all' to HR strategies. HR needs to embrace the strategic agility agenda – anticipating emerging business needs and their talent and culture implications. Workplace innovation and employee participation go hand in hand, together with the limitless possibilities for creative and rewarding entrepreneurship that these afford. By making better use of workforce talent, workplace innovation has a profound effect on employees' learning and development, health and wellbeing.

To model the way forward, HR should embrace and champion agile methodology, utilizing experimentation and incremental change to build people management solutions geared to supporting current and future business needs. HR should therefore:

- Act as innovation hub – collaborate with other disciplines to share knowledge, work on change programmes, etc.
- Design HR strategies 'outside-in', ie working back from the needs of the client, and collaboratively.
- Support innovation hubs – design spaces, facilitate connections, provide training, etc.
- Simplify HR policies, especially performance management.

- Apply agile work practices and project management disciplines to HR delivery.
- Go mobile and social.
- Help to source and develop agile teams.
- Address key 'implementation gaps' – identify underpinning issues, remove barriers using agile problem analysis and team working.
- Develop reward and recognition schemes that reinforce innovation, teamwork and knowledge sharing.
- Recruit, develop and nurture agile managers/team leaders.

As we shall discuss in the next chapter, HR can help to build a change-able high-performance work climate. Those who get the process right will reap the benefits.

Checklist

How knowledge-rich and innovative is your organization?

- Do people have clear parameters for experimentation? Do they know where innovation is needed?

- How much are employees involved in decision making? How much are their ideas invited, heard and responded to?

- How much are people expected to use their initiative to find customer-centred solutions?

- How much are good ideas/good practice disseminated?

- How well does your organization manage for diversity?

- How does the current structure impede or facilitate work effectiveness/strategy accomplishment?

- To what extent do people's roles provide 'line of sight' to mission, purpose and strategy?

- How effective is teamwork? What can be done to strengthen it?

Notes

1 Raisch, S and Birkinshaw, J (2008) Organizational ambidexterity: antecedents, outcomes, and moderators, *Journal of Management*, **34**, pp 375–409.

2 Duncan, R (1976) The ambidextrous organization: designing dual structures for innovation, in *The Management of Organization*, ed RH Killman, LR Pondy and D Sleven, North Holland, New York, pp 167–88.

3 March, JG (1991) Exploration and exploitation in organizational learning, *Organization Science*, **2**, pp 71–87.

4 Worley, C, Williams, TD and Lawler, EE (2014) *The Agility Factor: Building adaptable organizations for superior performance description*, Jossey-Bass, San Francisco.

5 Boudreau, J (2014) From Now to Next, i4cp Executive Thinksheet, Institute for Corporate Productivity, October.

6 Cap Gemini Innovation Leadership Study (2012): Managing Innovation: An insider perspective, Cap Gemini.

7 Kelly, K (1995) *Out of Control: The new biology of machines, social systems, and the economic world*, Basic Books, New York.

8 Ulrich, D, Younger, J, Brockbank, W and Ulrich, M (2012) *HR from the Outside In: Six competencies for the future of human resources*, McGraw-Hill, New York.

9 Alberts, DS and Hayes, RE (2003) [accessed 16 January 2015] Power to the Edge: Command... Control... in the Information Age, *The Command and Control Research Program* [Online] http://www.dodccrp.org/files/Alberts_Power.pdf.

10 Rogers, EM (1995) *Diffusion of Innovations,* 4th edn, Free Press, New York.

11 Totterdill, P (2013) The Future We Want? Work and Organisation in 2020, a report by the Advisory Board of the UK Work Organisation Network.

12 Harvard Business Review Analytic Services (2014): The Reinvention of Business: New operating models for the next-generation enterprise, p 2.

13 Alberts, DS and Hayes, RE (2003) *Power to the Edge: Command and control in the information age*, CCRP publication series.

14 Plsek, P (2003) [accessed 14 July 2011] Complexity and the Adoption of Innovation in Health Care, Conference on Strategies to Speed the Diffusion of Evidence-based Innovations, 27–28 January, Washington DC [Online] http://www.nihcm.org/pdf/Plsek.pdf.

15 Worley, C (2014) *The Agility Factor: Building adaptable organizations for superior performance description*, Jossey-Bass, San Francisco.

16 Hoverstadt, P (2008) *The Fractal Organization: Creating sustainable organizations with the viable systems model*, John Wiley and Sons, Chichester.

17 Dijoux, C (posted 7 April 2014) [accessed 15 January 2015] Bug Fixing Vs. Problem Solving – From Agile to Lean [Online] http://www.infoq.com/articles/bug-fixing-problem-solving.

18 Orton-Jones, C (2014) Growth, innovation and business transformation, *Raconteur*, 14 May, p15.

19 Virginia Mason Institute [accessed 30 August 2014] Bringing Innovation to Daily Work, *Virginia Mason Institute* [Online] http://www.virginiamasoninstitute.org/workfiles/CS-Bringing-Innovation.pdf.

20 Rotenstein, J (2011) It's the culture, stupid! How Atlassian maintains an open information culture, *Management Information eXchange*, 15 June, 5.09 am [Online] http://www.managementexchange.com/story/its-culture-stupid-how-permeating-information-culture-leads-corporate-success.

21 Olanrewaju, T, Smaje, K and Willmott, P (2014) [accessed 30 August 2014] The Seven Traits of Effective Digital Enterprises, *McKinsey & Company* [Online] http://www.ksrinc.com/mckinseysurvey/the_seven_traits_of_successful_digital_businesses.pdf.

22 Takeuchi, H and Nonaka, I (1986) The new new product development, *Harvard Business Review*, January–February.

23 Crush, P (2014) Managing without managers, *Edge Magazine*, May/June pp 32–37.

HR's role in building a high-performance work climate

Companies are always striving for better results and improving productivity is the focus of many organizational change efforts. Productivity is broadly speaking the difference between the cost of input and the value of output. It is often assumed that productivity can be improved by having fewer people, getting them to work harder and produce 'more for less'. Improving productivity does not have to be about making people work harder. As we discussed in Chapter 2, this approach is likely to produce only short-term gains and may actually reduce productivity over time since it can undermine employees' health, wellbeing and engagement. In Chapter 5 we considered how operational improvements such as simplifying and improving processes, introducing new products and services, intelligent cost management, team-based work, increased cooperation and communication can make a difference to performance. The company may even benefit more in the long run thanks to the improved potential for innovation.

In this chapter we look at some of the high-performance work practices (HPWP) that should produce real improvements in business performance and therefore flow through to job design. These are defined as 'practices that can facilitate employee involvement, skill enhancement and motivation',[1] and as the sum of the processes, practices and policies put in place by employers to enable employees to perform to their full potential.[2] HR can make a real difference to the business by developing these practices. A 2014 CIPD survey found that many HR professionals focus attention on workforce planning (64 per cent) and training and development (54 per cent) to improve their organization's responsiveness to change.[3] However, less attention is given to creating organizational environments that enable the agile workforce to thrive.

So in this chapter we focus on some of the many ways in which the HR function can contribute to building a culture of high performance and innovation. For instance, HR can help to recruit and retain the best talent, develop the skills of the workforce and help people adapt to new ways of working. HR can design policies aimed at protecting employee health and wellbeing, such as work–life balance, flexible working and benefits policies. HR can help people to manage their own development by providing tools for self-assessment and career tracks. Training and development should be complemented by organizational structures and cultures that support flexible working, adaptable skill application and better leadership and ownership of tasks at all levels. HR can help improve line manager skills by training managers in high-performance methods and coaching.

We focus in particular on how HR strategies relating to development, flexible working, performance management, reward and benefits are changing to reflect context shifts and also specific organizational strategies:

- stimulating learning practices;
- working flexibly;
- performance management.

Stimulating learning practices

Willingness to learn and share good practice is a characteristic of an agile culture. HR processes, especially training, can help to accelerate the development of innovative cultures. Significant improvements in individual, team and corporate performance can often be achieved in terms of output, speed and productivity by aligning training and development activities with business strategy. Training and development, when well targeted, should help employees to develop the skills they need to be effective and, ultimately, lead to improved business performance. Such alignment requires a systematic analysis of the most important development needs, defining the gap between what exists and what is required in order to improve existing competencies. This evaluation needs some careful thinking.

Technology platforms can make sharing knowledge easy and quick. First, though, it is important to encourage learners to adopt the discipline of sharing knowledge. People need the chance to share knowledge in safe environments such as a training programme where they can reflect and engage in dialogue on issues that matter to them. Getting people talking about what they have learned is a good way to embed new routines and spread fresh ideas.

Reflecting the growing interest in the business relevance of learning, there is renewed investment in corporate universities which first appeared in the

1950s. These are often similar to a conventional learning and development function, but increasingly are seen as more specifically business-driven and technology-enabled. They send a clear message to employees that the organization wants to invest in their development. With a corporate university it should be easy for any employee to see online what training opportunities are available on the job and in a classroom.

Unipart's corporate university, Unipart U,[4] offers focused training and 'see–learn–do' problem-solving sessions in the work area of each business unit, rather than in traditional classrooms. Staff use Unipart U's database to work out what they need to know, learn it in the morning and apply it immediately. Engineering is a key specialism and some of Unipart U's programmes lead to national vocational qualifications. It is hoped that the corporate university will prove helpful when recruiting graduates.

Working flexibly

In the UK the extent of flexible working has increased significantly in recent years, much of it employer-driven. Technology is enabling new flexible working arrangements that can work to the advantage of the employee, the employer or both. A report by Chess Media Group found that 87 per cent of modern workers are using flexiwork arrangements.[5] New technology such as smartphones and tablets enable people to stay in touch through e-mails and blogs and has made it much easier for people to work remotely.

Many of the options available range from the informal, such as employees occasionally working from home, or 'hot-desking' in offices when their main work is in the field, to more formalized kinds of flexible working arrangement. For instance, the Chartered Institute of Personnel and Development (CIPD) has found that one in five employees works from home at least once a week, and one in ten spend most of their time at the location of a client or customer.[6]

These flexible options typically fall into the following categories:

- *Functional*: here labour is allocated across traditional functional boundaries – for instance, through multiskilling, cross-functional working, task flexibility.
- *Numerical*: where there is variation in the number of employees or workers deployed in order to cope with peaks of work or occasional demands for specialist work – for instance, in various types of temporary work, seasonal, casual, agency, fixed-term workers, outsourcing, sharing resources, using contingent, contract or consulting talent.
- *Temporal*: this represents variability of working hours, either in a regular or irregular pattern – for instance, part time, annual hours, shift, overtime, voluntary reduced hours, flexitime, zero-hours arrangements.

- *Locational*: this involves employees working outside the normal workplace, including transfers of work to back offices – for instance, working at home, mobile, tele-/outworkers. Various forms of virtual working, such as telecommuting and remote working, involve moving the work to the worker instead of the worker to work.

Although thanks to the changing nature of work and shifting employee expectations there is demand for a greater degree of flexibility in when, where and how people work, the CIPD research found that many organizations are struggling to embrace new ways of working.[7] Lack of trust, cost considerations and misdirected investments are key factors preventing organizations from effectively implementing agile working practices. For instance, during and following the economic crisis triggered in 2008 many employers adopted practices that increased their flexibility, such as 'zero-hours' contracts that were potentially disadvantageous to workers. So many businesses appear to be out of step with employee expectations.

Others employers maintained a positive employment relationship with employees and continued to offer 'family-friendly' and work–life balance initiatives. This support – and European legislation designed to give any worker the right to request to work flexibly – have increased the range and take-up of the options on offer. Despite this, women remain in the majority of workers who formally work on flexible arrangements. Research suggests that reasons why more men do not opt for these are partly to do with the stigma attached to, for instance, working part-time and partly because many people fear that opting to work flexibly will limit their career options and, in uncertain times, could make them expendable when budgets are being cut.

However, trends suggest that people will increasingly opt for flexible working as a lifestyle choice. While a decade ago the priority for most working people was career advancement, which meant doing what was necessary to move up the corporate ladder, today the priority is pursuing a better work–life balance. A US study by EY (formerly Ernst and Young) found that people are choosing job opportunities where employers offer flexible working arrangements.[8] Over one-third of employees in the CIPD survey said they would like to change their working arrangements and, of those, the majority (43 per cent) would most like to change the start or finish time of their day. Just under half (45 per cent) of employees take phone calls or respond to e-mails outside of their working hours (with over one-third choosing to stay contactable rather than being pressured to do so).

By enabling employees to have greater flexibility, organizations have a greater chance of employee engagement, a more productive workforce and stronger organizational performance. To achieve this, though, organizations must question assumptions about people management practices and processes, and establish working solutions that are of value both to individuals and to the business. Given the ending of default retirement age and the rise of the multigenerational workforce, especially in Europe, flexible working is likely to become increasingly employee-driven to accommodate the needs of individuals and groups at different stages of their lives.

Performance management

HR can help to reinforce agility and resilience by redesigning performance management systems to reflect today's changing context. After all, when the old control-oriented and often derided appraisal systems first started to be rebranded as 'performance management' a few years back, the aim was for a much more positive, strategic, organizational performance-related and employee engagement-oriented agenda. Performance management is intended to align organization strategy, personal objectives and action and so maximize individual performances.

By implication, performance management should be a means whereby people receive the recognition, reward and development investment they deserve if they really are a firm's 'greatest assets'. By linking together many of the disparate strands of HR policy – such as goal setting, appraisal, training and development, talent management, reward and diversity – a performance management system (PMS) should reinforce employee motivation, drive continuous improvement and meet business needs. It should also ensure that employees feel fairly treated and that their development needs are met; and from the firm's perspective it should provide concrete evidence on which talent spotting, promotions or separation decisions can be based. All great, positive intentions.

The problem is that these positive intentions are hard to realize in practice. While the impact of performance management practices stands out as highly significant in most research studies on high-performance working,[9] all too often performance management systems seem designed to catch out the underperformer rather than to identify potential or reward great contribution. Implementation is often poor, with performance management reduced to a complex, bureaucratic HR process, mechanistic data collection and non-existent follow-up and only a vague connection to short-term business strategy. Prevalent since the 1980s has been Jack Welch's General Electric (GE) system of not only rating employees on individual attributes or performance measures but ranking employees against each other – commonly known as the 'rank and yank'. At GE managers were required to divide talent into three groups – a top 20 per cent, a middle 70 per cent and a bottom 10 per cent. People in the bottom 10 per cent were likely to be shown the door.[10]

Add to that the often formulaic, low-quality conversations with line managers who may consider performance management a burdensome addition to their real 'day job' and it is easy to see how performance management can actually reduce employee engagement and performance in the long term; many employees, far from feeling like 'assets' are left feeling like disposable commodities. And in today's fast-moving and highly pressurized climate it is easy to understand why something better is needed.

Indeed, in a Forbes blog article (9 July 2012), author Kevin Kruse calls the performance appraisal a 'workplace evil that must be destroyed like a blood sucking vampire'.[11] Kruse claims that firing people/being fired and doing performance reviews are the things most hated by managers and employees alike. He cites as key evils the vagueness and subjectivity of the standards and scales, along with the link to pay and the systemic avoidance of giving feedback to employees for a full year.

Towards more agile performance management

So how can organizations avoid these traps and produce truly meaningful and valuable performance management practice? Let's be clear – this is not about HR designing yet another sophisticated competency framework to add to an existing process. Instead HR can co-create simple and effective performance management processes and equitable reward systems that ensure people are fairly treated. By so doing, HR has the opportunity to shift culture by working with both primary cultural-embedding mechanisms (ie criteria for rewards) and secondary reinforcement mechanisms (ie organizational systems and procedures).

To achieve managerial objectives and also improve employee job satisfaction a performance management system should be designed to enhance overall performance and be about the development of potential, not just control. It should be company-wide, flow from the business plan, with senior managers having a clear idea of their own goals and modelling the process. Above all, if people really are the 'company's greatest asset' as so many company values state, a performance management system should be the articulation of a fair deal for employees as well as for the organization.

It is about going back to fundamentals, taking a broader look at what's needed to stimulate and sustain high performance. The underpinning principles on which effective performance management systems are based are as follows:

- Effective performance results from a partnership between the job holder and the organization.
- The employee has adequate skills for the job.
- The employee knows his/her role in the process.
- The employee's responsibilities match her/his accountabilities.
- The employee has access to the information needed, at the right time.

To develop more agile performance management:

Strengthen the link between organizational purpose, strategy and people's work Wherever employees work, they need to know what successful outcomes look like and what their part is in delivering the company's vision. This is about making sure people can have 'line of sight' to company purpose in their day job. Start with the strategic drivers and what you are trying to achieve overall in your business, short term and longer term. A broad scorecard of performance can be far more useful than a disparate set of KPIs since it is possible to define clear performance measures that really add value and link to business outcomes. Establish quality standards to ensure your people make real-time decisions that are consistent with your common purpose. Then support your quality standards with behavioural guidelines to shape your desired customer experience and enable your staff to measure, coach, recognize and reward one another in their day-to-day work.

At Carphone Warehouse, a leading telecoms retailer and provider, the company have used their Compass scorecard of five sets of criteria to drive a major culture change and higher financial performance.[12] In their retail stores this represents a shift from the short-termist view of achieving quick sales towards driving profit through giving brilliant service. The performance management process – and bonuses – drives the strategy down into everyone's performance management goals and rewards. Leading indicators are as important as short-term financial metrics and there is a wide range of tools and guidance available to managers and staff. The strategy has also led to a rethink of the company's reward strategy as a result of which basic wages in store have been increased, and the variable pay element is more team-based and geared to rewarding excellent customer service.

Design the PMS to continuously improve rather than just to prevent performance failure Instead of the system encouraging people to work ever harder, use it to help them work smarter. Work with line managers to identify and remove bottlenecks that prevent smooth workflow or create unmanageable workloads; the emphasis should be on the quality of output rather than input or hours worked. Netflix, an American provider of on-demand internet-streaming media, is careful to hire people who will put the company's interests first: they believe that 97 per cent of employees will do the right thing. Trust is the basis of Netflix's willingness to treat people as adults. A simple performance management and grading system provides people with clarity about how to succeed.

How well people perform can be as much a function of how they have been treated as what they are capable of The challenge for managers is to produce the conditions in which people are doing – and believe they are doing – 'good work', for which they willingly release their discretionary effort and achieve satisfaction from a job well done. So HR can help managers to create a high-performance climate in which people are trusted and expected to do what is needed – and have the resources, including information, and the authority they need to be truly empowered. Employees usually thrive in roles that give them scope to use their initiative and a chance to develop – so work with line managers to design jobs that will make the best use of the talents of employees, deliver business value and also provide employees with real stretch, growth and job satisfaction.

Developing leaders and managers to be able to create a high-performance climate becomes a priority. KPMG extensively trained more than 300 performance management leaders across their business to act as the vanguard of a movement to build continuous, ongoing performance feedback and review throughout the organization.[13] As a result, the proportion of staff who feel they have clear goals related to the organization's strategy – and that their reward is linked to their performance – has improved significantly.

Appraisals often tend to be process-driven whereas effective performance management is primarily relationship-based

So it is important to get line managers involved in redesigning the appraisal process to make it more stimulating, relevant and useful. Concentrate on improving the quality of the conversation. A strengths-based approach to performance conversations and reviews can bring many benefits since it builds on employee's strengths and energy levels, rather than diminishing and demotivating them. Some organizations are now replacing formal annual appraisals with informal and regular conversations between the individual and someone senior in their team, with the individual typically having gathered feedback from other stakeholders first.[14] One example is Netflix, where formal performance reviews have been replaced by getting managers and employees engaged in conversations about performance as an 'organic part of their work'.[15]

US apparel retailer Gap uses performance management in a transformational way to increase speed and flexibility. Their GPS (grow, perform, succeed) system involves managers and employees resetting objectives monthly, in an iterative way – with the ultimate outcome for Gap being satisfied customers and shareholders as their 'north star'. They discuss how people are progressing against goals and how these need to be adjusted for the next few weeks. It is all about building a mindset of accountability. There are no ratings or reviews; this is more about working together collaboratively.

Another approach known as ROWE, or results only work environment, is increasingly used in virtual working environments and has been implemented at Gap. Employees are paid for results (output) rather than the number of hours worked. ROWE helps managers to let go of old-fashioned performance management practices and begin the process of defining objective, measurable goals that can be clearly met or unmet by the individual contributors working for that manager, and holding people accountable for meeting only those that can be met. The process frees up people to work as they wish to, as long as the work gets done, and avoids managers having to focus on the minute details of employee daily routine.

In most contexts today, especially firms whose output is creative, business success is not based on individual brilliance alone

So it is essential that you have people working collaboratively.

High-performing teams are characterized more by the communication and knowledge-sharing that goes on between them than by individual excellence, so the old individualistic performance management models made famous by Jack Welch and others are not so useful when it comes to encouraging teamwork. In 2013 Microsoft changed its forced ranking from one that rated its top people as individuals to one that assessed teams. In traditional projects an individual's contribution to the team's success is evaluated by their boss. In agile, team members are accountable to each other. They are selected and assessed democratically and socially by their peers. Typically, 360-degree performance evaluations help individuals and teams to work out who will fit in and make a contribution. Those who don't are ejected by the team and must go elsewhere.

In one UK financial service organization that aspires to differentiate itself in a crowded marketplace on the grounds of its customer-centricity, the performance management system was getting in the way since it did not reflect the nature of the work required. Some of the PMS shortcomings were:

- It was focused on individual rather than on group performance – it should be about the collective.
- It favoured only new customer acquisition – not keeping and delighting existing customers.
- It fragmented performance – it focused on task not contribution; was geared to punishing mistakes etc.
- It did not help to retain, manage and develop high performers.

A group of high-potential managers worked with HR to redesign the performance management process 'bottom-up' along the lines of their recommendations as follows:

- The processes, ie development discussions/opportunities, should be separated out from review of performance/bonus.
- Competencies should be used by managers and employees as a tool throughout the year to aid dialogue and performance evaluation – managers at all levels to embrace the performance agreement, sponsored by general managers.
- A 'slick' feedback mechanism should feed into the development agreement on an ongoing basis.
- Reinforce the development and use of skills relating to providing customer value.
- Hold people to account for their contribution to customer outcomes.

- Reward needs to link to this – build collaboration into individual objectives or go for a company-wide flat-rate bonus scheme that shows 'we're all in this together'.
- Develop managers to distinguish between rewarding core job versus exceptional performance.
- Give line managers some discretion – a bonus pot so they can exercise judgement.

Really successful performance management is about achieving a better balance of employer and employee needs – and is more about building the trust, performance and capacity needed to drive the organization forward in the years to come. Any redesign should therefore be built on foundations of trust, respect and support. There are enough examples out there of firms making the high-engagement/high-performance connection to demonstrate that there is a direct link to productivity.

One such example is Adobe.[16] Like many others companies Adobe used to conduct annual performance appraisals between line managers and employees. Adobe has now scrapped these completely. The annual performance approach and stack ranking was prohibitive of innovation and contributed to lower engagement scores. People were merely justifying a rating. Managers too were overwhelmed by the process – with each appraisal taking up to eight hours per employee and an average headcount of five per manager, the process was very time consuming. A Pulse survey confirmed this suspicion.

A crowdsourced campaign came up with an alternative process designed and owned by staff. This 'check in' system sets development goals via an ongoing conversation. An employee can ask to check in at any time to discuss their aspirations and areas where they want to grow. The new system is going back to basics and building the foundations of real-time feedback. It's a different way of approaching how you train and equip your employee and management base. HR provides workshops for managers on how to give effective feedback, as well as tools and materials such as videos, webinars and online sessions. The statistics indicate that the new approach is working, with the culture that employees are creating leading to low voluntary attrition rates.

Recognition

It is important to avoid turning to reward as a lever for commitment and using financial gain as a way to alleviate staff discontent. Often the motivator for hard work and loyalty is not money: a simple thank you or recognition for good work can offer as much, if not more than financial reward. For example, at Cambridge Consultants, which develops products such as the artificial pancreas, employees can nominate co-workers for a 'Nobel' prize for a job well done.[17] There is a small cash prize but, more importantly, the prize highlights the employee's talent and dedication. Annual reviews in which employees can gather feedback from anyone they choose (including the chief executive), plus a company magazine, quarterly 'togetherness' meetings, a free restaurant and tailor-made career plans are among the reasons why Cambridge Consultants enjoys a low staff turnover rate of 6 per cent coupled with 10 per cent year-on-year growth.

Reward strategy

Reward strategy is where employer and employee needs may be at opposite ends of a spectrum. While it may be true to say that money does not motivate everyone, nevertheless people need to feel that they have had a fair deal. Particularly when reward and performance management processes are being changed, people are likely to be suspicious that they will actually be worse off as a result, and in some cases this may prove to be the case.

Motivation for reward strategies

Reward strategy should flow directly from business strategy. Its nature will therefore reflect the motivation of the business. For instance, some business strategies view people as costs to be cut. In contrast, other strategies recognize that 'people are the source of innovation and renewal, especially in knowledge-based organizations, and that the development of new markets, customers and revenue streams depends on the wise use of a firm's human assets'.[18] Therefore it is important to understand how employees perceive rewards, how these perceptions may vary by workforce segments and generations, how rewards affect behaviour and how behavioural changes affect business performance.

In the case of an innovation-led strategy, the reward emphasis must be strategic – looking at least to the medium term to grow the skills and approaches that should be rewarded. Reward should be integrated with other HR policies so that the 'right' employee behaviours are encouraged. (See Table 6.1.)

TABLE 6.1 Strategy: innovation-led

Employee role/ behaviour	Reward policy thrust	Other HR policies
Creativity: seeking new solutions	Mix of individual and collective rewards	Broadly defined job roles
Risk-taking behaviour	Use of 'soft' performance measures, periodically monitored	Cross-functional career paths to encourage the development of a broad range of skills

(Continued)

TABLE 6.1 (*Continued*)

Employee role/ behaviour	Reward policy thrust	Other HR policies
Medium-term focus	Emphasis on medium-term performance	Appraisal focusing on medium term and collective achievement
Collaborative and cooperative behaviour	Use of learning and personal growth opportunities as a 'soft' reward	High investment in learning and development
Concern for quality and continuous improvement	Broad-banded and flexible pay structure	Frequent use of teamworking
Equal concern for process and outcomes	High relative market pay	Promotion criteria reflect this
High tolerance of ambiguity and unpredictability	Strong element of basic pay and variable pay reflects own, team and organizational performance	Effective external and internal communications
Encouragement for learning and environmental scanning	Bonus reflects improved capability and contribution; managers rewarded for team and individual development	Self-nomination for learning events; open-access online learning materials; scenario-planning workshops

SOURCE Professor Stephen Bevan

I am very grateful to Jon Sparkes, former HR Director of The Generics Group, for the following case study, which describes how reward strategy was developed in support of an explicitly innovation-led business strategy and how it also served as a recruitment, retention and culture-change vehicle.

CASE STUDY   Generics Group AG

Formed in 1986, Generics Group AG floated on the London Stock
Exchange in 2000 at a valuation of £226 million; it employs approximately

500 staff in Cambridge (UK), Stockholm, Zurich, Baltimore and Boston. Th
of the business is the development and commercialization of technology, w.
it does through consulting in business and technology, licensing technology to
partner companies, creating new 'spin out' companies and investing in other
companies. In other words, this company's core product is innovation.

For example, a lift manufacturer needed lifts to stop with greater accuracy so
a Generics expert invented a new position-sensing technology. The intellectual
property rights were determined and the technology was licensed in the North
American automotive industry. Then a spin-out was created – Absolute Sensors
Ltd (ASL) – to exploit the business opportunity. The Generics Group supported
ASL for one year before selling its shares to Synaptics.

At the time of flotation the challenges for the business were to double
consulting revenue in four years and increase innovation in order to generate
greater license revenues and business incubation returns. The firm wanted
to increase the rate of business incubation and spin out to produce growth in
the investment portfolio. At the same time it wanted to maintain its creative/
entrepreneurial culture and develop a prestigious reputation as the first port of
call for business/technology solutions.

For the then HR Director Jon Sparkes, the challenge was to nearly double the
headcount with no compromise on calibre. This was a difficult task since the
firm's employees tend to be leading experts in their own fields and such people
are regularly sought after by other high-technology businesses, so there is stiff
competition for people with such skills. The strategy was to grow organically
achieving 15–20 per cent growth through recruitment and retention each year,
and also to acquire people through managing the integration of acquisitions.
From the outset the firm had a flexible culture, with an open management style
and the recruitment of entrepreneurial people. At the same time, post-2000 the
firm had responsibilities as a listed company. The challenge was to reward
employees for developing spin-outs and producing innovations, and to maintain
the culture.

In its response HR had to recognize the firm's competitive market position.
In East Anglia where it is based there was the highest salary inflation in the UK
and house prices were increasing at the highest rate in the UK. The principles on
which the reward strategy was based were:

- Rewarding individual excellence *and* team performance.

- Rewarding innovators and entrepreneurs.

- Sharing in the capital growth of the business.

- Recognizing work–life balance and promoting the wellbeing of employees and
their families.

- Promoting international culture.

An integrated reward strategy

With respect to salary, individual salaries were market-tested quarterly and bonuses were based on company and team performance. Specific individual performance was incentivized with rewards for innovators and targeted sales incentives. There was also a recruitment bounty for those who helped to bring in new talent. Employees were able to share in capital growth since the share option scheme covers all employees and there are share offers for 5 per cent of each spin-out company.

Maintaining culture

With respect to maintaining the flexible culture, various work–life balance initiatives were developed such as flexible working patterns, childcare information service membership, sabbaticals and extended leave. There was also a group personal pension scheme that was personal and portable, and access to an independent financial adviser. Various forms of private health-care insurances were available and employees enjoyed enhanced maternity and paternity benefits.

To promote an international culture, on-site language training was available for all – German, Spanish, French, Swedish and English. There was a positive approach to recruiting outside the UK (there are generally staff of 20+ nationalities) and placements and assignments available outside the UK.

To stimulate innovation and new business incubation, staff were flexibly deployed on a continuum from 100 per cent consulting to 100 per cent exploitation – although a combination of the two was considered desirable as the consulting work kept the individual close to the market and helped in the development of relevant and valuable intellectual property.

Employees were encouraged to bring forward ideas to a peer review body. The firm provided assistance in building the business proposition and protecting the innovation. A £2 million internal fund was set up to ensure the integration of operating and innovating metrics. Staff could share in the profit from licensing or options in the spin out – for example, a group of innovators inventing a technology that went on to generate licensing revenue would share in 10 per cent of the profit made from that intellectual property. If the exploitation route was a spin-out company then the innovators would share 10 per cent of the initial shares of the business (while their shareholding would later become diluted, they would benefit from the growth in the value of the business).

Over the years, many staff benefited from their participation in innovation. A small number went on to be founders and directors of spin-out companies in their own right, with one or two of those returning to Generics and building value for the company and themselves all over again.

Recruitment and retention

To attract and retain these stellar staff, Jon Sparkes carried out analysis of the career development paths of successful people and an assessment of the psychometric profile of proven innovators. He used this when recruiting staff in the UK and internationally, making no compromise on calibre. This allowed him to distinguish between generalists with wide breadth of skill, specialists with depth of skill in one area and polymaths who had deep skills in several areas – this last group being recognized as driving innovation. By 2000 the company was recruiting in 20 countries to identify and attract the right calibre and mix of people.

In summary, there was no distinction between HR and the business. In nailing the fundamentals of recruitment, recognition and reward, Jon was clear about the challenge and looked for solutions both from inside and outside of the textbook. The focus was on the culture, recognizing that culture is as much a consequence as cause of the strategies you put into effect.

Conclusion

As HR professionals adapt their own PMS and reward strategies to today's context and to their organization's needs, it is right to focus effort on improving the things that matter in the short term. After all, it's tough out there, with increasing economic pressures on employers and employees in many cases. However, it is important to avoid the temptation of simply going for the quick win by tightening up the PMS to get 'more for less' out of the workforce, squeezing the lemon until the pips squeak. As the cases in this chapter demonstrate, really successful performance management is about achieving a better balance of employer and employee needs – and is about building trust, performance and capacity to drive the organization forward in the years to come.

We have considered:

- Work practices and reward strategies can *enable or inhibit high performance*.
- *Workforce strategies should flow from the business strategy* – and take employee needs and context into account too.
- Reward should be *integrated* with other HR policies so that the 'right' employee behaviours are encouraged, developed and rewarded.
- Recruitment and other strategies must be geared specifically to the target audience – and *must be delivered if they are to retain people*.
- Strategies *influence not only individual behaviour but also company culture* – so it is important to recognize the effects of what you propose.

There are enough examples out there of firms making the high-engagement/ high-performance connection to demonstrate that the real task for HR is to ensure a brighter future by equipping line managers with the tools and ambition to develop talent and build sustainable high performance through employee engagement. A positive goal that is really worth going for!

In the next chapter we look at the third quadrant of the resiliently agile reference model – agile linkages.

Checklist

How is performance managed in your organization?

- How empowered are people?

- Are managers trained to delegate, coach and provide feedback?

- Are organizational/customer/employee needs in balance?

- How constructively is conflict dealt with?

- How clear are standards? And are employees involved in raising the bar?

- Are roles appropriately designed to provide stretch, yet be doable?

- How much are people provided with the skills, time and resource to do the job for which they are responsible?

- How much do systems help or hinder people in doing their jobs? How simple can procedures become while maintaining safeguards?

- How clear is everyone's line of sight to the customer?

- Do managers keep finger on the pulse, create shared sense of direction, clearly communicate expectations?

- How well do managers recognize and reward individuals and teams?

- Do managers regularly review workloads to ensure they are manageable?

- Do managers encourage others and practise work–life balance?

Notes

1 Applebaum, E, Bailey, T and Berg, P (2000) *Manufacturing Advantage: Why high performance work systems pay off*, Cornell University Press, New York.

2 Combs, J, Liu, Y and Hall, A (2006) How much do high-performance work practices matter? A meta-analysis of their effects on organizational performance, *Personnel Psychology*, **59** (3), Autumn, pp 501–28.

3 CIPD (2014) [accessed 30 August 2014] HR: Getting Smart About Agile Working [Online] http://www.cipd.co.uk/hr-resources/research/hr-smart-agile-working.aspx.

4 Chynoweth, C (2014) Learn at 10 and do at 11 – that's the Unipart Way, Business Section, *The Sunday Times*, 27 July, p 10.

5 The Future of Work: Reshaping the workplace today, building for tomorrow, 2014, Chess Media Group.

6 CIPD (2014) [accessed 30 August 2014] HR: Getting Smart About Agile Working, [Online] http://www.cipd.co.uk/hr-resources/research/hr-smart-agile-working.aspx.

7 Ibid.

8 Ernst & Young [accessed 19 January 2015] The Manager's Guide to Leading Teams Under Flexible Work Arrangements (2014) [Online] http://www.cio.co.uk/whitepapers/leadership/the-managers-guide-to-leading-teams/.

9 See Combs, J *et al* (2006) How much do high performance work practices matter? A meta-analysis of their effects on organisational performance, *Personnel Psychology*, **59** (3), Autumn, pp 501–28.

10 Business Week [accessed 19 January 2015] The Struggle to Measure Performance [Online] http://www.businessweek.com/stories/2006-01-08/the-struggle-to-measure-performance.

11 Kruse, K [accessed 19 January 2015] The Performance Appraisal: A Workplace Evil That Must Be Destroyed Like a Blood Sucking Vampire, *Forbes* [Online] http://www.forbes.com/sites/kevinkruse/2012/07/09/performance-appraisal/.

12 In *Performance Management*, Institute for Employment Studies (forthcoming).

13 Ibid.

14 Suddath, C (7 November 2013) [accessed 30 August 2014] Performance Reviews: Why Bother? (2014) *Bloomberg Business Week* [Online] http://www.bloomberg.com/bw/articles/2013-11-07/the-annual-performance-review-worthless-corporate-ritual

15 Mendoza, M (2014) Breaking Better, *Work*, **1**, June, CIPD.

16 Smedley, T (2014) Send in the cloud, *People Management*, May, pp 42–44.

17 Orton-Jones, C (2014) Growth, innovation and business transformation, *Raconteur*, 14 May, p 3.

18 Cascio, W (2002) Strategies for responsible restructuring, *Academy of Management Perspectives*, 1 August, **16** (8), pp 80–91.

Agile linkages

In Chapters 5 and 6 we looked at the nature of agile implementation and considered how managers, leaders and HR all have roles to play in stimulating an organizational culture conducive to open innovation, learning and democratic knowledge practices.

In this chapter we explore some of the types of internal and external linkages being forged by organizations in pursuit of organizational agility, flexibility and resilience, and their consequence for organizational forms. These flexible forms of organization cross multiple formerly fixed external and internal boundaries. The growing interdependence of firms is evident in the myriad forms of collaborative arrangements between partner organizations, including many with competitors. As firms move from being vertically integrated to becoming more specialized they are contracting out non-core functions to outsourcers. So strategic alliances – some 'tight' linkages, some 'loose' – are transforming the business landscape. Combined, these factors necessitate proactive, innovative and flexible workforce management strategies.

We shall look at what working and managing in some of these more flexible arrangements means for the people involved. People working within such alliances have to learn sophisticated skills relating to trust, relationship and team building, risk management and the ability to manage complexity. In particular we consider how to ensure that flexibility works for both the organization and its employees, and how collaborative capabilities, so essential to the success of these key linkages, can be built.

We look at:

- more flexible organizational forms;
- the rise of virtual working and implications for managers;
- working in strategic alliances;
- building an alliance culture.

The pursuit of flexibility

The term 'flexibility' applies to the ways that organizations adjust their employment practices in reaction to changes in business circumstances, and also to the ways that individuals organize their time, location and style of working. It also applies to the ways in which organizations structure themselves.

More flexible organizational forms

Inside firms the classic pyramid-shaped organization structure is giving way to more decentralized forms of internal organization that are generally flatter, leaner, less hierarchical and more flexible in nature than the traditional bureaucratic forms. For managers and employees the challenge is to develop effectively the mindsets, skill sets and practices – collaboration, empowerment and accountability – required to make these more flexible structures and cross-organization linkages work.

The lateral organization

Lateral structural arrangements are on the increase. These consist of a decentralized structure in which groups and departments work together at the same organizational level to achieve a common goal, such as managing an entire customer process, rather than operating as separate and distinct entities. Lateral structural arrangements are typically incorporated into existing vertical reporting structures. This type of arrangement depends on having collaborative and informal relations between the groups involved and requires coordination and consultation, often achieved via a matrix. In today's digital economy a growing trend is towards a technology-enabled team-based lateral organizational structure, similar to a traditional lateral structure, though carrying less management overhead. Without the need to climb a lengthy chain of command to receive approval for ideas or changes to the business model, teams can make the necessary changes to respond rapidly to different market conditions.

Lateral structures offer a number of advantages. For example, they foster a team mentality in which workers share information, which in turn creates a well-informed workforce capable of making quick decisions. They encourage open communication between workers in different departments and help to break down the barriers commonly associated with centralized organizational structures. However, amongst the disadvantages, complex matrix structures adopted by many global businesses often fail because they give too little consideration to how work is really done and they become unworkable in practice. For example, workers may experience conflicting loyalties when forced to report to managers from other departments; there may be duplication of activity and lack of oversight.

One of the most important factors to consider when developing a lateral structural arrangement is who will manage and plan interdepartmental interactions. Organization design expert Jay Galbraith advised that integration roles such as project managers, programme managers or product managers are vital to creating effective lateral relationships.[1] Effective governance procedures are needed, together with a simple performance measure that acts as a superordinate goal for the unit and assists in cross-functional trade-off decisions. As the lateral organization becomes more important, the role of the corporate centre becomes less about top-down control and more about making connections and defining the values and strong sense of purpose that can unite far-flung parts of the organization.

The front-back organization

The front-back hybrid model adopted for instance by IBM addresses the need to develop a customer-centric unit and integrate it into the existing organization. Here the 'back' of the organization – including operations, R&D and supply chain – is structured for efficiency and operational excellence and the 'front end' for customer intimacy, responsiveness, customization and revenue growth.

The ambidextrous organization

As discussed in Chapters 4 and 5, the 'ambidextrous organization' involves establishing separate operating units for exploratory activities, such as developing new business models and ensuring that the needs of innovative businesses are not neglected in favour of feeding the core business. Ambidextrous units can develop their own distinctive cultures and operating practices while having access to corporate resources. They manage organizational separation and linkages across units through a tightly integrated senior team.

Integrated teams

Many of today's challenges are beyond the skills of any single disciplinary team to address effectively. Consequently there is an increasing appetite for individuals and groups from different disciplines to work together on major projects, especially those involving strategic change, in order to produce more coherent outcomes. However, since until recently these expert communities may have operated in silos, people from different disciplines may not have worked together before, or share the same approach to innovation or speak the same language, so may lack a common way to describe, negotiate and act on the issue in hand.

There are many cultural, structural and conceptual reasons for this, such as the different 'discourses' (ie language, artefacts, habits and conventions) of disciplines and functions such as HR, finance, management – which, while all sharing commonalities, have some important differences. In particular, the discourse of finance seems far more powerful and dominant in organizations than that of 'people' and HR. This may have hindered the development of an integrated understanding of how people are central to value creation and how, in turn, work organizations should be central to developing people.

An open innovation challenge or experiment can help to overcome these barriers to progress by bringing together people from different but relevant disciplines in a shared online space, to undertake a co-discovery process with those interested in the problem.

The mobile office

Developing the 'flexible workplace' is usually driven both by the need to get employees out into the marketplace building business relationships – and winning business – and also to reduce costs of office accommodation. With mobile technology and the need for constant connections the requirement for costly travel and permanent real estate is coming into question. Satellite offices are an alternative form of flexible workplace. Such offices break up large, centralized facilities into a network of smaller workplaces that are often located closer to customers.

Small firms in particular are increasingly making use of 'hotelling' or shared-office options in which 'hotel' work spaces are furnished, equipped and supported with typical office services that can be hired by the hour, day or week instead of being permanently assigned. People using such facilities are typically supplied with mobile cabinets for personal storage; and a computer system routes phone calls and e-mail as necessary. Hotels are often ideal places to meet with clients, collaborate and build relationships. They are also increasingly places for focused, intense work. Thus, hotels have become important 'third places', locations outside the home and office where people choose to get work done.

Global teams

As never before, business success requires a global presence so organizations must communicate across cultures, continents and time zones in order to meet the demands of global customers who want just-in-time delivery and 24-hour customer service. Thanks to a vast and sophisticated communication network, business, projects, tasks and jobs are being transferred to where knowledge is to be found in different locations. Globally distributed development, production, sales, logistics and management functions are now commonplace. Virtual working too is on the increase amongst international teams as travel budgets shrink or become non-existent in these tough economic times. Above all, though, companies want access to professional skills and foreign resources.

Global companies in particular seek to build diverse, multicultural and geographically dispersed teams to reflect their markets and customers, to achieve lower fixed and variable costs abroad, to move development closer to the site of production or to establish development activities at local subsidiaries. So managers and HR must source, connect with and coordinate a multicultural global workforce, often virtually.

The ability to share knowledge is vital to leveraging the benefits of cross-border innovation projects, and online communications should enable a swift response to the demands of the global market. The global workforce must be able to operate as a single, seamless team to service customers and maximize revenue streams, so managers and employees need to be capable of what Amy Edmondson calls *teaming* – the ability to coordinate and collaborate without the benefit of stable team structures.[2] However, driving development activities and managing innovation processes across national borders is not always easy and there are many reasons why synergy is difficult to achieve. A Cap Gemini study found that typical challenges include poor leadership of cross-cultural innovation projects and a lack of communication or sharing of knowledge across national boundaries.[3] We shall consider later in this chapter how managing effectively at a distance can be achieved (see 'Managing a virtual team').

Spanning leadership

To support groups working across systems and developing engaging and collaborative ways of working requires spanning leadership, which is concerned with acquiring and disseminating resources external to a group. Leaders need to be able to think systemically and understand how the system itself works. They must look long term, and be able to understand and work with different goals, cultures and business priorities from those of their own organization. They need to develop middle managers who act at the system interfaces.

In today's global economy many workforces are multicultural. While there may not be a 'one size fits all' with respect to cultural leadership, embracing diversity in all its many forms is increasingly recognized as key to innovation and social justice. Cultural engagement is often the least developed dimension in intercultural encounters and at the same time it holds the key to how much people invest in improving the outcome of a situation. By working with the emotional dimension leaders can overcome the stumbling blocks and create business results outside of their comfort zones.

This may require a mindset shift for many leaders. Tarun Khanna argues that global companies will not succeed in unfamiliar markets unless they adapt – or even rebuild – their operating models and cultural assumptions.[4] In a global organization, mental models that are rooted in the HQ culture may lead to simplistic assumptions about how things work in different cultural contexts. The concept of 'contextual intelligence' is vital in developing talent. A culturally intelligent global leader lets go of habitual stereotyping, sees people as nuanced individuals and finds ways to focus on the business potential in the many differences in a diverse team. Therefore, being alert to what is needed, really listening and being prepared to adjust are key to stimulating real dialogue and mutual understanding.

The rise of virtual working

Virtual or remote working may be a feature of all the organization forms described above. At one level, virtual working is simply a flexible working option. Employees benefit – they save on commuting costs – and employers retain experienced employees who find the flexibility to work from home especially attractive. Amongst the business benefits, various studies suggest that virtual employees are usually more productive than their traditional counterparts because they learn how to minimize downtime by performing routine tasks during the short pockets of time between other commitments throughout the day. Virtual teams reduce the scope for discrimination since, with visual stimuli removed, people focus more on output and less on the person generating it.[5] In many cases virtual working is introduced to save costs on real estate. In BT Retail, for instance, almost everyone at all levels of the hierarchy works from home.

More generally, a virtual team – also known as a geographically dispersed team – is a group of individuals who collaborate across time, organizational and geographical boundaries. Other potential benefits of virtual working, identified by Cascio,[6] include:

- savings in time, travel and expenses;
- greater and quicker access to subject experts;
- opportunities to form teams without the need for physical proximity – therefore avoiding lengthy meetings and downtime;
- expansion of potential labour markets.

Virtual teams can be nimble and dynamic, shifting team membership to suit project needs with employees assigned to multiple, concurrent teams. Virtual teams can shorten cycle time and increase innovation.[7] They tend to be more creative and can leverage learning better than conventional teams.

The challenges

The challenges faced by virtual managers are somewhat different from their non-virtual counterparts. With matrix working, a virtual manager may not only be leading their own team but also a resource for teams led by others. Perhaps the greatest challenge is building trust – a critical factor for effective virtual working yet harder to build when people don't meet physically. Because virtual managers cannot see their team members, some struggle to trust that people are working and may try to catch them out by phoning at different times of day to see if the person is available to speak to them. As a result they undermine trust and working relationships.

Virtual workers can become literally and psychologically distanced from their organization, so managers must deal with the team's feelings of isolation and communication difficulties. BT Retail has learned that virtual or teleworking does not suit everyone so the company also provides opportunities for teams to meet physically in different locations in order that both social and business needs can be met (see 'The mobile office' above).

One UK public body reduced the number of its offices from 100 to 40 across England over four years, moving 1,500 out of 1,900 staff to be fully flexible. The organization provided all its social workers with 4G laptops, Blackberry devices and fully electronic case management systems. They ensured that online support and learning was also in place to reinforce the 'shift in culture'. In particular they paid attention to the social side of work, ensuring everyone attended the monthly team meeting, regardless of where they worked during the week. Agreements were made with partner organizations to have touchdown bases so that staff could meet with service users. They also introduced the Robertson Cooper 'Health & Wellbeing' tools so that they could fully analyse the factors in high performance and pick up any issues with individuals who prefer working in 'offices'.

Managing a virtual team

Roffey Park research looked into the nature of virtual working, including both the role of the virtual manager and that of global teams.[8] The following observations derive from this research.

Effective virtual managers are primarily builders of a collaborative culture that focuses on outcomes, supports worker autonomy and values diversity. Cultural barriers and differences can usually be addressed through proper team building and cultural assimilation exercises. Team members knowing and understanding each other leads to less conflict, better anticipation and a sense of belonging, thus increasing the effectiveness and productivity of the team. Clear rules, procedures and decision-making processes are needed to empower team members and speed up information sharing by defining the boundaries within which team members can operate. Effective virtual managers have a facilitative leadership style, are not micromanagers and are able to delegate effectively.

Building trust

For virtual managers, not having the benefit of being co-located with their team members they must be able to build relationships and trust – both remotely and face to face. When visiting regional offices, for example, a virtual manager could make a point of bringing together and spending extra time with remote teams, getting to know them individually and collectively, rather than simply getting on with their 'day job'.

Communication

Communication is vital for any team but can be twice as difficult when it is done by e-mail, telephone, skype etc. Virtual managers need to be disciplined about making time for regular exchange between parties. This is about keeping in touch with the team, not just for formal work or personal development communications, but for everyday work issues. At the same time they need to watch out for signs of potential burn-out, being sensitive to reading between the lines. Effective managers understand their team members' communication preferences and use appropriate methods and channels accordingly, for instance picking up the phone for a chat instead of sending only instruction e-mails.

Results-oriented

Similarly, effective virtual managers are focused and results-oriented. They tend to be good at planning, coordinating and organizing tasks and are able to multitask. They are skilled at managing performance from a distance, setting clear objectives and performance measures and, importantly, focusing on the outcomes and not the actual hours spent doing them. In assessing performance from a distance, without the usual non-verbal clues, they are still able to provide appropriate and timely feedback because they have regular planning and monitoring conversations where updating and reviewing progress takes place. They celebrate and acknowledge good performance. They also have good links within the wider organization, both in terms of understanding the organization's goals and having 'strategic vision' and in linking into the organization's political network. Thus they act as 'boundary-spanners' and ambassadors for their teams. And whilst many of these skills and attributes are desirable for most managers, they are essential for virtual managers.

Working in alliances

Increasingly organizations are looking beyond their own boundaries and working with third parties and partner organizations in strategic alliances to be able to:

- scale up and down rapidly by tapping into external resource networks;
- achieve economies of scale in 'back office' operations while maintaining customer intimacy and responsiveness in the 'front office';

- grow without being constrained by bureaucracy;
- access key skills.

Thus motivations for alliances fall broadly into the categories of achieving cost savings and/or going for growth and innovation. The organization's purpose in establishing alliances will determine the nature of form selected, how it operates and who benefits.

What is a strategic alliance?

Strategic alliances come in all shapes and sizes that share some of the following distinguishing features identified in Roffey Park's research:[9]

- They are *strategic*, with partnering organizations bound together by a set of strategic intentions or goals for their alliance activity.
- The partnering organizations *exchange or share resources and assets*: these may take the form of physical assets such as shared facilities or less tangible assets such as marketing expertise, brand management, technical knowledge or process expertise.
- They result in some form of *joint activity*, where personnel from the partnering organizations interact and collaborate.

Strategic alliances are not just about major companies forming 'tight' connections through joint ventures (JVs). Collaboration can also occur through a variety of 'loose' forms, ranging from interactions between key individuals or joint teams through to a shared corporate entity. Joint activities may be precisely defined and highly structured, or they might be ad hoc and opportunistic.

A strategic alliance is widely understood to have the following common traits:

- Cooperation: two or more legally defined partners working together within a mutually defined area.
- Each partner aims to attain key strategic objectives through the alliance.
- Each partner has the option to withdraw if the alliance is not generating its expected benefits.

Most alliances fit somewhere along the continuum set out in Figure 7.1.

At the informal end of the spectrum, the growth of small firms is leading to numerous new networks for doing business. Self-employed people and 'micro firms' may lack many of the resources of a larger entity so join networks of like-minded peers to share business development opportunities, resources and learning opportunities. Similarly, consultants and clients are increasingly working collaboratively to solve the client's problem, share resources (including intellectual property) and do joint marketing of the (successful) outcome.

FIGURE 7.1 Alliances: a spectrum of integration

Loose	Tight		Tight-loose
Informal	Contractual	Shared Entity	Entwined
Helping/learning	Outsourcing/supplier	Joint venture	Multiple links
Allied eg cross-selling	Franchising/ licensing	Shared services	'Networked organization'

◄─────────────────── Virtual teams ───────────────────►

SOURCE Based on the Roffey Park study 'Strategic Alliances: Getting the people bit right'

Contractual arrangements with third parties include franchising, licensing, outsourcing and offshoring and may ultimately include mergers and acquisitions. In between lie various alternative alliance arrangements such as partial ownership, relationships with preferred and trusted suppliers, multiple vendor contracts, joint ventures, consortia and shared services. For instance, in the UK public sector, institutions are increasingly developing pooled shared service operations for HR and IT support as part of their new delivery models.

Many employees will therefore experience working in alliances, some of which may be short-lived while others may last for many years.

Outsourcing and offshoring

Outsourcing involves redeploying a firm's own personnel and organization assets to a third-party supplier to carry out 'non-core' work previously carried out by the organization. This form of subcontracting is often entered into on the assumption that efficiencies can be gained. Typical targets for outsourcing include catering, security, cleaning and facilities management, ICT, car park, payroll/HR services, warehousing and distribution, marketing, call centres (complaint handling, after-sales services), finance and accounting. The average manufacturer now outsources 70–80 per cent of its finished product.[10] Some outsourcing contracts are short term and transactional, intended to enable flexibility, while in other cases long-term contracts and even a full merger takes place.

Offshoring involves outsourcing assets and work processes to economies where the costs of labour are significantly lower than in developed economies. These are examples of what Swart, Purcell and Kinnie call the 'farming out model',[11] which is more of a reconfiguration of skills than a true integration of complementary skill sets.[12] These arrangements (or at least their contracts) are usually 'tightly' managed, and administering outsourced relationships effectively becomes a core competence in itself. Many companies that are lured by low-cost labour markets make decisions that satisfy short-term budget requirements but may face problems if they know little about domestic outsourcing, and even less about offshore outsourcing.

This gives rise to the question: which assets are core and which are non-core? The answer is not always easy to give. For instance, many firms have outsourced to external agencies aspects of their HR processes such as recruitment only to recognize later that recruitment is a strategic process so have taken back responsibility in-house (in-sourced). Sometimes outsourced arrangements become more costly than the previously integrated models. Other typical problems include unsatisfactory delivery of services, unco-operative vendor behaviour and/or the competitive advantage to be gained from outsourcing no longer exists.[13]

Workforce implications

When outsourcing decisions are being made, the needs of employees are often low down the pecking order of considerations. From a company view-point, if outsourcing brings financial benefits it is a logical move. However, for outsourced employees the deal may not be so good. Former employees of the firm may end up carrying out the same work as before but on reduced terms and conditions. They may find themselves competing for their jobs against employees from emerging markets, creating an environment of inse-curity and limited commitment to the workplace.[14]

In such circumstances there no longer exists a supportive social contract between employer and employee. Many displaced employees end up feeling betrayal, anger at loss of benefits and changing working conditions, and anxiety about changes at the new company. As they experience stress and uncertainty, many enter states of intellectual paralysis that result in pro-ductivity loss. The resulting emotional scars can even impact on those who are not outsourced, whose loyalty may decrease sharply as they wonder whether they will be next to be 'sold off'. Thus outsourcing can easily end up having a negative effect on motivation and on human performance and can result in intangible costs such as the loss of valuable knowledge.

On the other hand, outsourcing can also have a positive effect on some people. If the outsourced employees were previously ignored in their old firm, they may find that their skills are now considered valuable and there may be opportunity for career expansion and promotion. They may also have contact with a wider group of employees than before and have the chance to develop new skills. As Wayne Cascio points out, in contrast to a restructuring strategy that regards people as costs to be cut, a more respon-sible strategy focuses on people as assets to be developed.[15]

Strategic alliances – the innovation model

The second main motivation for entering strategic alliances is to enable growth and innovation. Here investment is made in combining unique skill sets in order to gain competitive advantage. Included in this category are 'tight' joint ventures to exploit a potential opportunity and the 'tight-loose' 'networked organization'.

The 'networked organization'

Within knowledge-intensive industries a growing trend is towards the so-called 'networked organization', a loosely coupled configuration geared to building value for the network. Such networks are often dominated by resource-rich firms. If the central firm's purpose is innovation it will connect with firms or other entities with diverse skill sets and engage with them in knowledge sharing and collaborative product development. In a network culture the shift that occurs is from 'my information is power' to one in which 'sharing is power'.

For example, both Unilever and GlaxoSmithKline now have open innovation elements in over half of their R&D projects and are actively developing their open innovation processes to enable them to compete in complex global marketplaces. For Unilever, partnerships have become vital to delivery of what they call their 'three big targets' – ie to help 1 billion people improve their health and wellbeing, to halve the environmental footprint of their products and to source 100 per cent of their agricultural products sustainably. The R&D strategy focuses efforts in innovation ecosystems led from Unilever's hubs. These include a science grid around the hubs (universities, etc), the wider science and technology community, strategic commercial partners (private), and ports in hotspots (public and private). Partnerships are already bearing fruit in terms of innovation and profitability and are considered indispensable for building future winning capabilities.

In 2007 GSK opened their 'Innovation at GSK' website that invites people to submit their technologies or innovations to the company for review. They call their process the 'Want – Find – Get' model. They 'want' innovations that will contribute to their growth. They 'find' these 'wants' by building networks with innovators, then work with innovators to 'get' the technologies. Partnering with the UK government and Wellcome Trust provides another avenue to open innovation. Scientists from around the world are now based at a GSK campus in Stevenage (UK) to create a global hub for the life-sciences industry, while benefiting from GSK's resources and facilities.

Working in alliances – key features and challenges

Whatever their nature, the managerial and people challenges thrown up by strategic alliances are immense. At the heart of alliances is a willingness to dissolve boundaries, both between organizations and within people's minds, and to explore and learn from partners with different skills and ways of working.

Ambiguity

Alliances operate on the basis of shared ownership/governance and involve ambiguous and complex lines of control and accountabilities. Unlike mergers, where ownership is clear and the 'new order' has been legally ratified and formally structured in the guise of a new corporate entity and management structure, alliances are more fluid, temporary and often more complex. They are therefore vulnerable and susceptible to problems, with employees often working under greater uncertainty than in more fixed organizational forms.

Alliances require an extra degree of commitment and cooperation from a wide range of individuals and groups of employees. An integral aspect of alliance governance, therefore, is constant bargaining, managing expectations, handling conflict and building consensus. Such a task requires business people to balance control with cooperation, to have a sense of where they should tightly manage an alliance and where they should retain only a light hold and allow synergies to emerge.

Power dynamics

While the business drivers of a specific alliance may be clear, the power dynamics may be less apparent. Is this a partnership of equals, or is one partner really driving the alliance? How do people within the partner organizations feel? Are they comfortable/uncomfortable or are there disagreements between partners? Whatever the rationale for the alliance, it is likely that there will be a battle for hearts and minds, even at the stage of strategy formation and partner selection. In many cases, alliances emerge from strong relationships between key individuals and often continue even when their original purpose has been served – if the same individuals are involved. Conversely, alliances often fail, despite strong business drivers for collaboration, if one of the key individuals moves on or there is a falling out amongst the alliance champions.

Alliance partners inevitably have their own longer-term strategic goals and so a degree of conflict is inherent in the relationship. Partners are understandably often coy about the 'hidden' benefits they hope for. For example, they may be planning to steal expertise from their partner, or potentially acquire the partner. Rather than hoping such conflict can be avoided, the aim should be to build the alliance around common ground and have good processes for resolving differences. The challenge is to build trust and cohesive ties, foster cooperation and innovation.

Critical success factors

No matter how effective the relationship between the deal makers, trust is usually underscored by clear contractual arrangements and role specifications. Johnson and Scholes identified the following critical success factors for joint ventures:[16]

- proactive attitudes to commitment, trust and cultural sensitivity;
- clear organizational arrangements;
- the desire of all partners to achieve organizational learning from the alliance, rather than using partners to substitute for their lack of competences;
- allowing the alliance to evolve and change rather than prescribing it too parochially from the outset;
- efforts by partners to achieve strong interpersonal relationships, including bonding and flexibility to changing circumstances;
- decentralization of decision making and sufficient autonomy from both corporate parents.

Needs, aims, expectations, goals and outcomes should be explicitly expressed and agreed with the partner. Areas of mutual competition also need to be made explicit so that agreed-upon ground rules can be developed about how to handle potential conflicts of interest, including the importance of sharing information and knowledge. When the rules are clear, and there is joint commitment to them, the risk of misunderstanding diminishes.

Relationships

The relationships between alliance partners are fundamental to the very concept of an 'alliance'. The trouble is that organizations do not have relationships with each other, only individuals do. So alliances are largely interpersonal phenomena, and effective personal relationships are central to the success or failure of an alliance.[17] If alliances fizzle out, it is often because key people have moved on and no one else forms a new, close relationship with the alliance partner.

Because alliance relationships can be full of uncertainty and tension, it seems doubly important that those involved in alliances form good and trusting relationships with each other as people. The more open-ended or informal the alliance, the more important the relationships, as there is no formal contract that binds the partners together. Both at the organizational and personal level, alliance players have to work hard at establishing cooperation and rapport, yet always remain mindful that an alliance is, at its core, a temporary business agreement between two separate commercial ventures with their own interests and priorities. It is as though the personal nature of the relationship allows people to deal better with the ambiguous and uncertain nature of the alliance.

Alliances present organizations and individuals with a new axis of collaboration and competition. As they move along this line, people will need to shed old certainties and embrace new ambiguities. Traditional control mechanisms, both formal and informal (reporting structures, pay systems, cultural norms) may be absent in alliances, requiring individuals and teams to exercise their own judgement and discretion about how to achieve the goals of the alliance. Cementing the alliance together, and filling the gaps where processes and structures do not exist, requires the personal commitment of individuals to make the alliance work. In alliances, people occupy central stage.

Alliance partners need to understand each other's objectives and pursue 'win-win' solutions, which often involve compromise. If clear objectives have been set, alliance partners should then have criteria by which they will measure success. These high-level objectives need to be translated into clear short-term goals at team and individual level. A balance needs to be struck between formal management processes and the emerging 'spirit' of the alliance. Too much bureaucracy at an early stage signals lack of trust and stifles innovation. Unexpected synergy can occur if people remain open to new opportunities.

Key roles

There are many key roles in alliances but two of the most important are the *champion* and the '*alliance manager*'. Senior champions are vital at an early stage but also in sustaining corporate commitment to the alliance. The role of the alliance manager, which may appear under various titles, is a pivotal one in providing the 'glue' for the alliance. S/he is operationally responsible, working between partners and representing all interests.

The relationship with parent companies can be difficult to manage. Some parents are more controlling than others. In some cases the alliance manager has to spend more time reconciling parental differences than taking care of alliance business. One manager described the ideal alliance manager as someone who genuinely understands a 'win-win' solution. The 'looser' the alliance, the less direct authority one has over the other partners – so influencing, negotiating and persuading without direct control are essential skills.

Are effective alliance managers born or made? Spekman *et al* suggest that highly successful line managers do not automatically make good alliance managers because they must 'wear a number of different hats... they must be facile with operational, strategic and policy level concerns and be able to move easily between these levels since each affects the alliance at one or more stages in its life cycle'.[18] They conclude that some skills can be taught, such as functional and managerial skills; others can be earned, such as credibility and respect, personal networks and even interpersonal skills such as tact, sensitivity and cross-cultural awareness. However, certain key competencies, such as 'virtual thinking, creativity, pragmatism, questioning, appear to be unteachable and are more to do with the fact that they think and see the world differently'.

Another key alliance role is that of the 'microbargainer'.[19] All kinds of microbargains are struck between employees on different sides of an alliance during their regular day-to-day and week-by-week interactions. These deal makers play an important role in facilitating the process of collaborative exchange; in protecting and preventing key skills from migrating to partners; and fully exploiting any learning opportunities.

'Gate keepers', on the other hand, monitor all kinds of knowledge transfers and have sole responsibility for granting partners access to the organization and its people and processes. Lang describes the important role of the boundary spanner who 'helps to create and recreate the patterning of behaviours which themselves become the norms of the relationship'.[20] Individuals in these roles create and protect alliance boundaries and ensure that conversations take place between partners.

Building an alliance culture

Alliances need to evolve their own cultures, which are often different from either of the parent cultures. In human terms, alliances involve cooperation, interdependence, mutual though different benefits and complexity. Some people who work in multiple alliances suggest that a more generic 'alliance culture' is evolving. This involves certain patterns of behaviour from a kind of cultural repertoire that alliance workers will use in different situations such as unusually strong attention to positive relationships with others, manifest in careful manners: personal acts of kindness or generosity and attempts to solve problems amicably. Second, the 'culture' of the alliance is expressed on a day-to-day basis through the operating procedures used in the shared business activity, through attention to business goals and priorities, manifest in efficient use of meetings and goal setting.

Behavioural ground rules

The concept of 'culture' can seem very abstract so how can this understanding of alliance relationships be converted into something people can work with? As with virtual working, the simplest solution is to translate strategies for mediating difference and conflict and establishing trust into some behavioural form, for instance by establishing behavioural 'ground rules', which may be a more tangible device for discussing and agreeing how people will work together.

Senior managers have a key role to play in encouraging two-way communication. They need to be involved with the day-to-day operation to the point that they can keep their finger on the pulse of what is going on. Typically, at the start of an alliance, communication is top-down. Ideally, greater participation should be encouraged and bottom-up processes should be nurtured as soon as possible.

Processes for decision making are different in each alliance and are often difficult because of complex reporting lines and the need to achieve consensus between partners. The process for decision making must be agreed before the alliance is formalized. In a joint venture this may be easier where there is a major shareholder. Initially, decision making may be slow as too many people are involved in the process and it may take some time for sufficient trust to be built. Clarification is needed at the outset on which decisions need to be referred to the parents and which can be handled locally by the alliance manager. Decision-making processes themselves can be a source of competitive advantage and organizations can learn a lot about their partners by understanding their approach to problem solving.

Conflict and trust building

Interorganizational conflict is built into most alliances because the organizations have different strategic and long-term goals. Moreover, trust is slow to grow and quick to be destroyed. Alliance partners can trust too much or too little for their own good.[21] The sharing of relevant information is critical to partners' ability to deliver their part of the alliance. Yet in high-tech and some of the more complex international manufacturing alliances, controlling competitive information becomes a very difficult area. Sensitive marketing information can be gleaned from local specification changes and, for organizations determined to learn, all information can be used to acquire intimate knowledge of a potential competitor's capabilities and markets. Changes to a more open culture are sometimes difficult to achieve for this reason and leave a residual suspicion. So absolute trust is not the ultimate goal but an environment is needed in which partners trust enough to avoid checking up on each other the whole time.

Establishing and maintaining trust at a personal level is the key means of resolving potential conflicts. Exchange of information comes to symbolize the degree of trust between the partners. The more information is shared, the higher the level of trust. However, people also need to be clear as to which information they need to protect. Parkhe proposes some practical recipes for trust building such as avoiding surprises, open communication and frequent positive interactions between key people, followed by performance reviews to check behaviour.[22] Similarly, Axelrod emphasizes 'being nice' through playing fair and forgoing short-term gains in the interest of long-term benefits.[23] Lewis also suggests 'issue spotting', where alliance partners proactively raise potential issues, thereby reducing surprises and helping to build confidence that each partner is looking out for the other's interests.[24]

Key skills and behaviours for effective alliance working

Alliances could be said to represent agile working at its most fluid and ambiguous. Therefore, the skills required of employees and managers to make these organizational linkages work should equip all concerned to make a success of agile working. They include the following:

Setting an open style of leadership (especially those in senior positions) Alliance working seems to require a more informal and open personal style of leadership than the conventional model in large, hierarchical organizations. This is one way of showing that problems will not be hidden and that individuals are encouraged to use their own initiative to act. The open management style advocated for alliances is in line with a more general shift away from the 'command and control' behaviours, which are too slow to operate effectively, and towards those supportive of empowerment.

Understanding your partner's needs To work with another organization you have to really understand where they are coming from and show that you understand. Without this level of business and cultural understanding, negotiation and problem resolution are virtually impossible, so cultural agility is essential – sensitivity to other people's behaviour and the ability to modify one's own behaviour patterns when appropriate. Friendliness – the ability to develop warm interpersonal relationships quickly – is especially important.

Goal focus Each partner needs a clear view of what the alliance is for and how much resource it is worth. Because alliances can be ambiguous, people need to work harder to identify shared interim goals. They need broad business understanding – of their own and the partner's business and also the ability to see the alliance in a broad context. This may push strategic business understanding lower down the organizational hierarchy than is usually required.

Managing differences and negotiating for success Your needs and those of your partner will probably conflict. Alliance workers and managers need a repertoire of skills for managing conflicts large and small. By driving too hard a bargain you can make the alliance fail. The most successful alliance workers know when to stand firm and when to concede. This calls for patience and sometimes creativity as well as classic negotiating skills – the ability to solve difficult conflicts without damaging relationships.

Differences and tensions are bound to arise. Successful alliance working requires that these be raised and resolved with the minimum of damage to the underlying relationships. Keeping differences out in the open where they can be dealt with is better than letting trouble fester.

Operational effectiveness Work needs to be clearly managed and processes are needed to ensure delivery within a complex and shifting environment. Good day-to-day work process is even more important in an alliance than in a conventional business. In building the skills of alliance workers, general teamwork processes and disciplines are useful, particularly for people working in project teams and cross-functional teams with divided loyalties. Adopting the disciplines of project management can be extremely helpful in bridging cultural differences and getting everyone to sign up to shared objectives, timescales, responsibilities and the need for regular progress review. It is often in the most informal alliances that such project management approaches increase effectiveness.

Communication and information Communication – both formal and informal – is critical in avoiding misunderstandings and in reinforcing trust. Communication needs to be open and honest, but alliance partners also need to judge what information they will share.

Tolerance of ambiguity Managing complexity – dealing with many issues and much information, especially for managers of alliance relationships, can be testing of both business and personal identity and allegiance. In particular, alliance workers require a high level of emotional resilience. They can feel they are giving a lot of emotional energy to the alliance, which their own organization may or may not see. It is about being patient and nice to everyone while driving for output uses a lot of personal energy. People need to find strategies for keeping themselves going, for getting support from others and not taking personally any periods of failure.

Skills for alliances, or for life?

These skills and behaviours have some striking similarities to what is being said more generally about skill change at work. The skills of cultural sensitivity and negotiation apply just as much across countries, workgroups, functions and divisions as they do between alliance partners. Perhaps we should see alliance workers as the skill trendsetters of today. Employees should also see the chance of working in an alliance as an opportunity to learn ways of working that will stand them in good stead.

Individuals involved in alliances learn from their experience about how to take a wider view of business and how to deal with more complex personal relationships, although this is often a private experience, little discussed with others in their organization. Individual learning could be enhanced by building learning goals into alliance working for individuals and discussing learning more in performance reviews and team meetings. So attention should be given to building in processes for learning, sharing and protecting information.

Conclusion

Far more than in conventional structures with intact teams and command and control management styles, these more flexible organizational forms and working arrangements illustrate how agility can be made to work for both organizations and employees. They share many common challenges, not least building trust and managing ambiguity and conflict. At the same time they are a fertile proving ground for new approaches and rapid skills development – and the opportunities they present to embrace new approaches should be grasped:

- The development of a shared vision and processes to share knowledge are vital, as are *processes to handle conflict and deal with ambiguity.*

- More flexible forms of organization call for more *sophisticated 'people' relationship skills* and working practices.

- Trust – or lack of it – is a vital component to the success of these arrangements. *Trust can be built* through honesty and providing the right support.

- Employees act as a bridge between organizations; *they need to be empowered* to make decisions at local level.

Given the growth of these cross-boundary alliances, and the similarity of skills required for virtual and alliance teamworking, organizations might consider whether such skills – perhaps called 'working with partners' – should be mainstreamed into training and development for the majority of staff. Organizational learning can flow from more formal evaluations of the success of a business alliance, particularly when evaluating the achievement of original targets by tracking business measures or key indicators, and also improved by more thorough evaluation and documentation of learning experiences.

In the next chapter we start to look at the fourth quadrant of the resiliently agile model: *people practices.* In particular we look at what 'agile people' means and consider how people-related processes such as talent management are becoming more agile.

Checklist

How well do your linkages work?

- To what extent does the current structure facilitate or impede flexible management of work processes/capabilities, functions, products, programmes, customers, geographies or partners?

- How much commitment is there to alliance working at the highest level?

- Where do your established HR practices facilitate or impede collaboration and integration?

- Are team members educated at the outset regarding possible cultural differences and barriers in communication?

- What are the processes for surfacing and handling conflict?

- How well are differences of approach managed?

- How effective is communication between parties?

- How much help do people receive in learning new skills and approaches?

- What is being learned from partnership working? How is this applied?

Notes

1 Galbraith, JR (1992) *The Business Unit of the Future*, CEO Publication G 92–3 (206), University of Southern California.

2 Christensen, K (2013) [accessed 30 August 2014] Thought leader interview: Amy Edmondson, *Rotman Magazine*, Winter, pp 10–15 [Online] http://www-2.rotman.utoronto.ca/rotmanmag/ThoughtLeader_Edmondson.pdf.

3 Miller, P *et al* (2012) [accessed 30 August 2014] Innovation Leadership Study: Managing innovation – an insider perspective, CapGemini Consulting [Online] http://www.capgemini.com/resources/innovation-leadership-study--managing-innovation-an-insider-perspective.

4 Khanna, T (2014) Contextual intelligence, *Harvard Business Review*, 92 (9), September, pp 58–68.

5 Wilmore, J (2000) Managing virtual teams, *Training Journal*, February, pp 18–19.

6   Cascio, WF (2000) Managing a virtual workplace, *The Academy of Management Executive*, August, **14** (3), p 81.

7   Lipnack, J and Stamps, J (2000) *Virtual Teams: People working across boundaries with technology*, John Wiley and Sons, Chichester.

8   Smith, A and Sinclair, A (2003) *What Makes an Excellent Virtual Manager?*, Roffey Park, Horsham.

9   Garrow, V *et al* (2000) *Strategic Alliances: Getting the people bit right*, Roffey Park, Horsham.

10   Corbett, MF (2004) *The Outsourcing Revolution: Why it makes sense and how to do it right*, Dearborn, Chicago.

11   Swart, J, Purcell, J and Kinnie, N (2005) Knowledge Work and New Organisational Forms: the HRM challenge, Working Paper Series 205.06, University of Bath.

12   Dyer, J and Nobeoka, K (2000) Creating and managing a high-performance knowledge-sharing network: the Toyota case, *Strategic Management Journal*, **21**, pp 345–67.

13   Moran, J (1999) Outsourcing successful if bottom line improves, *Computing Canada* **25** (34), pp 27–28.

14   Kakabadse, AP and Kakabadse, N (2000) Outsourcing: a paradigm shift, *Journal of Management Development* **19** (8), pp 668–778.

15   Cascio, WF (2002) Strategies for responsible restructuring, *Academy of Management Perspectives*, 1 August, **16** (3) pp 80–91.

16   Johnson, G and Scholes, K (1999) *Exploring Corporate Strategy*, 5th edn, Prentice Hall, Harlow.

17   Spekman, R *et al* (1996) Creating strategic alliances which endure, *Long Range Planning*, **29** (3) pp 346–57.

18   Ibid.

19   Hamel, G and Doz, Y (1998) *Alliance Advantage: The art of creating value through partnering*, Harvard Business School Press, Boston.

20   Lang JW (1996) Strategic alliances between large and small high-tech firms (the small firm licensing option). *International Journal of Technology Management*, **12** (7/8), pp 796–807.

21   Parkhe, A (1998) Understanding trust in international alliances, *Journal of World Business*, **33** (3), pp 219–40.

22   Parkhe, A (1998) Building trust in international alliances, *Journal of World Business*, **33** (4), Winter, pp 417–37.

23   Axelrod, R (1984) *The Evolution of Cooperation*, Basic Books, New York.

24   Lewis, J (1989) *Partnerships for Profit*, Free Press, New York.

Agile people processes

In the last few chapters we have considered the 'what', why' and 'how' of resilient agility by looking at ways that organizations can strategize, implement strategy and create collaborative connections with delivery partners and other key stakeholders. We have considered some of the capabilities and routines that enable organizations to adapt and try new things. We have also seen how performance management should shift from short-term to longer-term approaches. Running through the first three quadrants of the resiliently agile model is the focus of the fourth – the 'who' of agility: people.

While the organizational capabilities we have discussed so far are all important, equipping the organization for growth goes beyond simply investing in new IT and fancy kit or developing new project management practices. In knowledge-intensive and service-intensive work *people* are the source of production. It is people who are ultimately responsible for delivering the vision, ideas, products, services and day-to-day work that make a company successful. Having the right people focused on the right things is key to business success.

Over the next few chapters we explore what 'agile' means when applied to people and culture. For instance, we look at what is involved in creating a context conducive to high performance in fast change – in other words, how organizational cultures and climates can become 'change-able' without destroying the vital enabler of agility – people's engagement with the work they do and the organization they work for.

In this chapter we look at some of the challenges of attracting and developing a flexible workforce – in particular those deemed to be 'talent'. We look at how people are changing their expectations about what they want from employers. All too often these people challenges are addressed piecemeal, with separate, short-term solutions where the temptation is to rush straight into action to 'fix' the problem. A more strategic approach based on facts is required in order to equip organizations with the people they need now and for the future. We look at the field of talent management and consider how processes such as strategic workforce planning and succession planning are becoming more agile to reflect the changing context:

- a diverse workforce;
- strategic workforce planning;
- talent management;
- finding the right people in the right place with the right skills;
- build strategies – growing the talent pool;
- agile succession planning.

So a very different set of HR, talent management and culture practices will be required, which are better suited to a highly volatile, global and knowledge-oriented age.

Let's begin by considering what the term 'agile people' means.

Agile people

Resiliently agile people are the lifeblood of high performance and an organization's true source of competitive advantage. At the same time, an agile organization requires flexibility to be built in to the resourcing model. Thus an agile workforce tends to be multiskilled; people are able and willing to adjust to new ways of working and to acquire new skills. Such workers can rightly be described as 'talented'.

A diverse workforce

Today's talent market is increasingly global and, as the talent map loses its borders, workforces become highly diverse. In Europe the workforce is ageing and UK employees can now anticipate longer working lives due in part to demographics and also to changes in pension arrangements and the ending of the default retirement age of 65 for men and 60 for women. By 2020 it is projected that the UK workforce aged 20–40 will decrease by 16 million and those aged 45–65 will increase by 17 million. This is giving rise to the extended workforce in Europe (the '4G' workforce, in which there can be four generations of workforce employed simultaneously).[1] People who might once have retired at or before 60 will want new development opportunities rather than to retire, and may need to move to other roles to allow younger workers to progress.

Some in the HR community consider age diversity to be a problem.[2] They are concerned about how to create opportunities for career development for younger workers. They are also concerned that, with no obligation for people to leave their employer when they reach the previous retirement age, tougher performance management and severances may replace previously honourable exits at retirement for those no longer able to perform at former levels.

On the other hand, many companies see the rise of a multigenerational workforce as a bonus and as a potential source of innovation. For instance, DIY retailer B&Q considers that an age-diverse workforce brings a wealth of skills and experience. In 2015 B&Q has operated without a default retirement age for nearly 20 years, and aims to provide age-neutral benefits for its 32,000 employees. Its oldest employee is 96 and works on the checkouts. With 28 per cent of its workforce over the age of 50, it has many employees who are semi-retired. The firm recognizes that an ageing population comes with some physical restrictions, for example injuries, bad backs and people becoming more frail, so it offers adjustments to utilize these people as well as it can.

Changing expectations

These days, with longer working lives, today's employees might expect at least five career changes during their working lives. Unlike the baby boomers (born 1943–60) and their predecessor generations who might have hoped to make their career in one organization, generation X (born 1961–81), generation Y or 'millennials' (born roughly 1982–1995) and certainly their successors, the 'Re-Generation' will have different aspirations and exacting expectations of their future employers.[3]

The large influx of millennials into the workforce has significant implication for workforce dynamics. The size of this group gives them not only a large 'vote' in the aggregate 'voice of the employee' but also significant influence on other generations about non-negotiable expectations in a work environment (eg flexibility, rapid career movement, learning, transparency).[4] Stereotypically, millennials want to make the world a better place, to improve the environment in a broader sense, and are not driven by purely materialistic values. They are natural clients – they have intuition and they want to have impact. They have low tolerance for bureaucracy, hierarchies, process.

In the graduate recruitment sector many major brand-leading companies, including international consultancies, are already finding that where once they would have had their pick of graduate recruits, they now struggle to attract potential candidates who may prefer bigger jobs in smaller, more fleet-of-foot organizations where they can rapidly acquire skills and experience. In particular, upcoming generations of workers appear more interested in community, environmental and social endeavours and careers such as teaching that offer the chance to do something worthwhile for others and the possibility of personal satisfaction.

Of course things may change as time moves on and there is already some evidence that record numbers of millennials are gravitating back towards large institutions and government agencies, seeking teamwork, protection against risk and solid work–life balance.[5] There is a new focus on upbeat messages and conventional big brands. However, if organizations are to retain these recruits, they may need to consider how to capture that vocation and develop strongly value-driven employer brands that deliver their promise.

Strategic workforce planning

Given the confusing landscape, how can organizations predict what their workforce will look like in months or years to come? After all, the future is uncertain, workforce systems are complex, resources are limited, making mistakes can be costly and decisions have to be taken and justified. Talent management is built upon talent intelligence – the understanding that businesses have the skills, expertise and qualities of their people. It is the basis of every people decision that companies make and, without it, they would be reduced to pure guesswork.

Therefore, strategic workforce planning is becoming once again a key tool to enable organizations to get to grips with their future workforce requirements and to develop and implement agile workforce design. This follows a period when the old-style top-down 'manpower planning' approaches, which used detailed modelling and assumed a slowly changing context, fell by the wayside in the light of frequent changes and radical restructurings such as mergers and acquisitions, which made previous forecasts irrelevant.

The aim of agile workforce planning is not to create an exact picture of the future workforce but instead to enable the organization to build capability and capacity for improvement, innovation, leadership, spread, scale-up and sustainability. Technology is a vital tool in getting to grips with the data you gather and already have in order to better understand your talent needs and recruitment, retention and deployment challenges. Conventional spreadsheet-based approaches to workforce planning and productivity measurement are too operational and short term for use in identifying future workforce needs. Indeed many HR teams struggle to carry out strategic workforce planning. Research by the Society for Human Resource Management (SHRM) found that 66 per cent of US employers have no planning for their talent needs and only 13 per cent of organizations are good at predicting future skills.[6] The biggest barriers to workforce planning are a lack of a methodology and tools. So HR may need to upgrade its capabilities in workforce analytics and business intelligence, including predictive modelling, or employ the services of relevant analysts.

Future-focused

Agile approaches to workforce planning assume that the future is inherently unpredictable, so planning should be scenario-based and take into account longer-term megatrends and current trends. A megatrend is a large, technological, economic, environmental, political, social or ethical change that is slow to form, such as population growth and ageing population. These are the underlying forces that drive trends possibly for decades. A trend is an emerging pattern of change likely to impact business and organizations and requires a response.

In forecasting future workforce needs it is important to take a longer-term view, as far out as the next 10–20 years, identifying where gaps are likely to emerge and putting plans in place to deal with these before they become problematic. For instance, utility company National Grid takes a 10-year time frame that is revisited annually, with the focus kept on 'critical job families' that are core to the business.[7]

Segmentation

To gain a better understanding of where the critical gaps might be, it is important to identify critical workforce segments – certain groups of workers who may be more crucial to delivering the future business strategy than others. These may be high-potential future leaders or hard-to-replace specialists or even part of the core workforce. By segmenting the workforce data you can give special attention to those who are most critical. That does not mean you can ignore the other segments, as different elements of the workforce deliver value in different ways. Some can help to upgrade core capabilities, while others have more potential to drive competitive differentiation. Choosing between improving core solutions and investing in innovation may not be necessary, as both may be needed.

Risk

Even the use of good data may not result in accurate predictions so a degree of risk is inherent in strategic workforce planning. In many organizations, senior management and other key staff from the baby boomer generation may be considering leaving the organization in the near future, or taking flexible retirement. It is important to find out not only who might be about to leave but also what vital knowledge they might take with them. Every effort must be made to transfer that knowledge quickly enough to avoid adverse impact on the organization. It is important to identify what levels of risk are acceptable and draw up a desired risk profile. At the same time, planning needs to be tactical; for instance, what would happen if entire teams were unable to make it to the office because of a public transport strike?

Once you have established insights into your current and future workforce needs and assessed the risks, it is then a question of articulating the message confidently to relevant stakeholders, and building a rigorous business case for any investment in talent. Once agreement has been reached about what needs to happen next, it is vital to act on these insights. After all, the surest way to increase the probability that the organization is able to attract and retain the talent it needs is to manage people in such a way that they want to stay and give of their best.

Measurement for improvement and whole system dashboard

Setting the right measures is important: if a talent shortage looms, for example, why are you measuring absenteeism? In aligning HR metrics with business goals it is important to get sponsorship from the top – the board needs to know what you are measuring and why. As the guardian of workforce data HR needs to be able to spell out the implications of what the data is saying with respect to the organization's capability to deliver its business strategy and meet its obligations to its shareholders. As Peter Cheese, CIPD chief executive, puts it: 'We (in HR) have to make the intangible tangible so we can demonstrate the value and importance of investing in people for the future success of organizations.'[8]

So HR needs to bridge between business objectives and the data by being able to answer questions such as:

- Are we losing our best talent?
- How many have we left?
- Are we improving month after month?
- How many of our top performers have we promoted from within?
- What openings have been filled from within?

Organizations also need to be able to track their return on talent investment continually, so having the right measures and (access to) analytical capability is essential. Analytics can also be used to provide an evidence base for workforce productivity and bonus structures can be designed to reflect this. Some of the enablers of employee productivity include:

- better people management by managers;
- appropriate HR policies and practices;
- employee engagement;
- improved resourcing and training;
- good job design – autonomy and flexibility;
- more effective communication and staff involvement;
- leadership of change and role modelling;
- knowledge sharing.

In selecting the right measures, a balanced scorecard can be helpful, working back from the desired outcomes of strategy to identify the talent 'lead' measures that matter. Specifically, HR needs to measure the organization's capabilites relating to leadership, culture, alignment, and learning.[9]

As with all aspects of workforce strategy, strategic workforce planning does not sit in isolation from other strategies. Unilever has put data analytics at the heart of its global HR strategy. The firm can now correlate employee engagement with attrition or career progression and identify factors that affect its talent pipeline. While responsibility for guiding the process might lie with HR, it must involve other stakeholders as it has potential implications for other aspects of organization.

Talent management

As we discussed in Chapter 2, there are chronic underlying talent shortages in many industries. Therefore talent – finding it, developing it, making the most of it – becomes a strategic priority, especially for those organizations aspiring to build sustainable high performance.

The term 'talent management' dates roughly from the late 1990s, when McKinsey published 'The War for Talent' to highlight the underlying chronic shortages of what they called 'talent' in professional service firms and other highly skilled knowledge work.[10] They emphasized the need for employers to adopt new and more employee-centric means to attract and retain the 'talent' needed for success. They argued that talent management is about identifying talented people, finding out what they want and giving it to them – if not, your competitors will. This followed a period of 'anti-planning' with respect to the workforce and 'do-it-yourself' approaches to career management.

From this time onwards, talent management was increasingly recognized as a distinct aspect of strategic HR capability, competitive advantage and a driver of sustainable organizational performance. When the international financial crisis began in 2008, talent management went into the doldrums and many companies ceased to pay attention to their high-potential talent, mistakenly assuming that people would remain with their current employer due to the scarcity of good jobs. Those assumptions proved unfounded, leading to a mismatch between supply and demand. After all, the boundary-less careers that were predicted years ago are now a reality and these are 'the opposite of organizational careers – careers that unfold in a single employment setting'.[11]

A new 'war for talent'

Today the advent of the digital economy and underlying shortages of certain types of talent are leading to a new 'war for talent'. As the baby boomer generation continues to depart the workplace they are replaced by generation Y (or 'millennials'), who may be the best-educated generation in history but are also the least experienced in the workplace. As global competition for employees and customers intensifies, employers in many industries will increasingly have to compete hard not just for market share but also to attract and source the best talent. When highly skilled talent is in short supply and employees have choice, 'key talent' can pick and choose who they work for. In the West only 18 per cent of firms say they have enough talent in place to meet future business needs,[12] and more than half report that their business is already being held back by a lack of leadership talent.[13]

Consequently there is a renewed focus on talent management and its related processes. Organizations try to develop enticing employer brands to differentiate themselves from the competition in order to attract the best. They offer 'onboarding' experiences to help new recruits quickly to become productive – and then hope to retain them. However, as the labour market for knowledge and service work becomes more buoyant, and with loyalty to employers a thing of the past, retention is becoming a major challenge – hence the plethora of employee engagement and reward initiatives.

Talent management: a debated topic

Definitions of the term 'talent management' and its component elements continue to evolve, and a plethora of strategic perspectives exist. The emphasis in most is on the systematic effort to integrate the ways to attract, develop, deploy and retain the most productive and promotable people the organization needs, both now and in the future. The term 'talent' is usually applied to an exclusive cadre of high-potential employees who are groomed for future senior (leadership) roles and considered most valuable to organizations: 'Talent management is the systematic attraction, identification, development, engagement, retention and deployment of those individuals who are of particular value to an organization, either in view of their "high potential" for the future or because they are fulfilling business/operation-critical roles.'[14]

Increasingly this exclusive approach to talent is being called into question and many organizations are adopting 'a very broad definition of talent management, taking a systems and strategic HRM viewpoint'.[15] This embraces the whole workforce – often called an 'inclusive' view of talent management. Partly that is because in today's fast-moving context it can be difficult to predict the organization's future workforce needs in the light of changing business models, so identifying which people and which roles will be most valuable becomes guesswork.

Talent management processes are often grouped according to *buy* or *build* talent strategies. 'Buy' activities include attracting, sourcing, assessing, hiring and 'onboarding' new recruits; 'build' processes include talent identification, engagement and retention, progression and development. Creating talent pools and career pathways are just some of the elements of a 'build' talent strategy.

Debates still rage as to where the emphasis should be put – on people or positions. Collings and Mellahi argue that strategic talent management involves 'the systematic identification of *key positions* which differentially contribute to the organization's sustainable competitive advantage, the development of a talent pool of high potential and high performing incumbents to fill these roles, and... filling these positions with competent incumbents and to ensure their continued commitment to the organization'.[16]

In contrast, Cappelli argues that 'it is more effective to develop talent within the broader context of the organization, rather than with a particular succession role in mind. This prevents developing employees to fit narrow, specialized roles but rather, once developed employees can be developed with broader competencies which would fit a range of roles.'[17] GlaxoSmithKline (GSK) uses the term 'talent' to cover both high potentials (those individuals who have the potential to move into broad leadership roles in the future) and high performers (those individuals who consistently deliver exceptional results). The high-performing category ensures that expert scientists are seen as key to the business as well as leaders.

Who 'owns' talent management?

Given the importance of talent to business success, ultimate responsibility for talent should lie with the CEO while HR is responsible for managing the related processes. So HR should work with business leaders to confirm their strategic priorities and what these mean in terms of the critical talent required. In a context of talent scarcity, with the potential for loss of knowledge, lack of innovation and decreasing shareholder value due to uncertainty, HR should help leaders to identify the talent gaps they are facing and explore options for closing them. Then HR can drive the overall process to add value, including carrying out talent risk assessments, monitoring turnover data and drawing inferences, creating and implementing talent strategies to alleviate risk.

Fresh approaches to talent management are needed

So talent management approaches should no longer be restricted to the favoured few or simply follow the tired old formulas of 'fast-track' development and conventional succession planning. Understanding the needs, aspirations and motivations of key employee segments will be critical to managing talent. Strategies such as building and embedding the employer brand, and tailoring packages, including development, will increasingly be used both to source scarce talent and to create win-win more broadly for individuals and organizations. Engaging employees' discretionary effort – finding new ways to motivate people, unblocking barriers to employee motivation, providing fair reward and recognition – are just some of the underpinnings of a resiliently agile talent management strategy.

Many talent processes continue to reflect the assumption underpinning the old-style 'psychological contract' or 'old deal' – that the organization has the whip hand in the employment relationship. As we discussed in Chapter 2, the slow erosion of the 'old deal' has left today's employees with few illusions about remaining with their employer for life and, often, little loyalty. Today employees must look after their own careers. Organizations are not in the driving seat when it comes to retaining talented individuals, who self-manage their careers and development and tend to have less loyalty to one employer. Consequently, even the best-laid plans for succession may be undermined by the sudden departure of a highly valued employee.

More broadly, today's fast-changing context requires systemic and open source approaches to talent. They are relational and personalized in nature, so one size does not fit all. Such approaches recognize that informal networks can be more effective than formal talent management processes and that an emerging 'new deal' needs to be 'co-created' with employees the organization wants to attract and retain.

This means that innovations in talent strategies and solutions should have the potential to span the needs of multiple segments of your workforce – no matter where they are in the world. It is also important when designing employer brands to bear in mind the things that matter to people of all generations: recognition and respect; flexibility and choices; meaningful work; and balance – with life and with community. At the same time, you will have to keep the differences in mind, too, and be prepared to flex the 'deal' to accommodate people's changing needs at different life stages and circumstances. Greater workforce diversity also has significant implications for how work will be delivered, and what future leaders look like.

So who will tomorrow's leaders be? How will they be identified and developed? For instance, there are now more women than men in the UK workforce yet in most sectors women remain significantly under-represented in executive roles or on boards. Women also make up the majority of people in the UK workforce working flexibly. More flexible ways of working, combined with a growth in the virtual workplace and the growing priority given by individuals to work–life balance, mean that new models of management are needed in order to make the most of the talents of individuals not working in full-time roles. This is producing a shift in emphasis to the 'output' or quality of contribution made while working, rather than to the 'input' or the hours spent at work.

Finding the right people in the right place with the right skills

Developing an agile workforce strategy is a holistic process and involves looking at how talent works throughout the organization. If the kinds of talent gap you are trying to close change in nature, you may need to change your employer branding or recruitment processes and reward strategies in order to continue to attract the 'right' people.

Sourcing talent

Talent today is already moving across international borders – engineering students from India, for instance.[18] Companies such as Google, Tata and Microsoft source talent globally, using intelligence sources to gain knowledge of where the best talent is to be found. Many organizations that need a steady stream of entry-level talent establish partnerships with universities that have high numbers of foreign nationals or a growing base of young people who thrive on international opportunities. For global sourcing of talent, employers will need a strong global technology platform that can be adapted to individual country needs. That means it has to be both scalable and flexible. Successful overseas candidates may need help to obtain the visas they need. Companies may have to support critical talent who want to work remotely – whether from home or elsewhere – so they will need to provide the communications technology, the collaboration tools and the systems to make work flow.

Recruitment

Potential recruits increasingly look for jobs online. A survey by Webrecruit (2014) found that 88 per cent of job searches now begin via Google, and 80 per cent of tablet users research job opportunities via their tablet at home after work.[19] Candidates tend to look at:

- First – job boards.
- Second – company careers sites.
- Third – recruitment agencies.

Conversely only 20 per cent of talent acquirers have a careers site – an area on a company's website dedicated to recruitment that is mobile optimized. So organizations that seek to recruit using only conventional means, such as job advertisements in print media, may be missing out on pools of potential recruits. The latest generation of jobseekers have been engaging via social platforms for several years and are likely to continue to do so. So it is important to use social interaction via a firm's careers site to help build relationships with candidates, adding a personal element to your recruitment process.

Increasingly, too, employers are using big data analytics and other new methods to help make the fraught process of hiring more scientific.

Employer brands

Many companies today develop employee value propositions (EVPs) or employer brands to describe their commitments to workers – just as they use the power of their brands to communicate their value to customers.[20] Employer brands are intended to both communicate the deal on offer and make your company desirable to candidates, providing a strong competitive advantage to the recruiting company.

It is also important that the company brand and other recruitment messaging signal the kinds of behaviours (and culture) the company wants to encourage. Thus potential recruits are clear about what to expect and about the kinds of behaviours that will be expected of them. Increasingly, employer brands are highly values-based, though of course the notion of a single employer brand, defining what the organization offers potential employees, is largely obsolete. If anything, multiple brands targeted at different employee segments may need to co-exist and be delivered in reality if they are to maximize the possibility of retaining an engaged and high-performing workforce.

Conveying the right message is therefore vital, as long as it is genuine, of course. The Webrecruit survey found that over 80 per cent of candidates look beyond pay and benefits in their quest to find a great place to work. Instead, they are attracted to other factors such as career prospects, the working environment, what an organization stands for, and how it serves its clients. Generation Y, in particular, looks for opportunities for professional growth and generally prefers to learn in a mobile rather than static environment.

For the following case study I am grateful to Robert Taffinder, Senior Manager Resource Partnering, and Stephanie Tapner, Manager Resourcing and Case Management, at Nationwide Building Society.

CASE STUDY Agile recruitment at Nationwide

Nationwide Building Society is rare among financial services organizations: it has emerged relatively unscathed from the 2008 financial crisis with its reputation intact. As a *mutual*, Nationwide is owned by and run for the benefit of its members (customers) with no shareholders to satisfy (in the way that banks do). However, in the wake of the 2008 financial crisis, in common with all financial service providers, Nationwide is subject to new regulatory requirements from the Financial Conduct Authority and Prudential Regulation Authority in order to avoid such crises being repeated.

In response to the changing context, Nationwide recognized the need to build up its first-, second- and third-line risk roles in order to retain its traditional focus on customer interest and to meet the new regulatory requirements. Similarly, new generations of customers expect to be able to transact 24/7, remotely, securely and conveniently, through tablets and other mobile technology. Nationwide's innovation strategy is simple; they are investing in technology, which makes life better for their members and their people. They are using digital innovations to better connect their people with their members and ensuring that members have access to their experts – anywhere and at any time.

However, Nationwide's recruitment practices were fairly traditional and relied on advertising on its careers site, posting vacancies on job boards or using recruitment agencies. Finding and recruiting such scarce talent would be a major challenge using conventional methods and in the face of the current 'war for talent'.

In response to these challenges the Resourcing Delivery team decided to build upon existing good practice and adopt a new way to attract potential candidates both cost-effectively and innovatively. The new approach began with research, listening closely to a wide range of people with different backgrounds, skills and capabilities, looking at emerging trends with respect to people's behaviour and perspectives on Nationwide's brand. Candidates' expectations were clearly starting to shift; lifestyle and balance appeared more important than salary. Social media was becoming a key means by which potential candidates now interact, so digital tools would be part of the solution. IT support would be needed to support the recruitment team in using the careers site to advantage and getting more candidates through the door.

The challenge was how to make Nationwide stand out as different in the jobs market. Ironically, though Nationwide has a good story to tell, the society's cultural modesty meant that many people did not know about it. So it was important to develop a strong and authentic story about Nationwide, about what being a mutual is all about, demonstrating what it stands for, sharing success stories. The aim was to surprise potential recruits, and one initiative – a video developed for internal recruitment purposes titled 'Haircut' – certainly caught people's imagination and was shortlisted for an external award.

In true agile style, a variety of other initiatives was developed through a three-phased approach that allowed for feedback and further development over a six-month period. Elements were added based on what the business was saying was great. So, for instance, the traditional careers site was made interactive, with an employee blog so that people can add their comments and their feedback can be acted on. A variant on the job website Glassdoor (like TripAdvisor for candidates, so that anyone can see reviews about an organization and what current employees say about it) was developed and allows the team to respond to things that need improving with respect to recruitment processes and to learn from why people leave the organization.

The team itself has become agile and empowered and has come a long way in a short time. There is a great deal of collaborative working with other departmental functions such as Brand, Marketing and IT. Data analytics and reviews from the careers website provide useful intelligence, which resourcing consultants use to select the right kinds of attraction channels to reach specific types of skill set.

For the resourcing team, the challenge of success is that people expect more of you. It is important to manage expectations, look at internal platforms and what they can deliver, use data/evidence and communicate/renegotiate priorities on an ongoing basis, pushing back if necessary. The key to ultimate resourcing success is being clear what you stand for, as Robert Taffinder points out: 'if people are put off by that, it's not a bad thing. I'd rather have fewer candidates of higher calibre than have to deselect more people who would not operate well in our culture.'

Onboarding

Having struggled to attract and recruit the best, many organizations often lose new hires within weeks. Turnover can be as high as 50 per cent in the first 18 months of employment.[21]

Organizations have traditionally offered new recruits induction training to introduce them to company-specific information, compliance require-ments and ways of working. Onboarding, also known as 'organizational socialization', goes further than induction and refers to the whole range of ways in which new employees are welcomed into a firm and acquire the knowledge, skills and behaviours they need to become effective organi-zational members. Many companies begin the onboarding process during recruitment, before the new employee formally joins.

The ways that firms bring new staff in – and the environment they create for them – communicate, model and form the culture. Unless new employ-ees are made to feel valued from the outset their motivation on arrival is likely to drop off dramatically. If new hires feel welcome and prepared for their new positions, they gain the confidence and resources to make an impact within the organization, and ultimately to help the company to con-tinue carrying out its mission. The active involvement of line managers in onboarding is vital. Being introduced to new workmates in person and via social networks helps them to become culturally attuned to the company. 'Buddies' and mentors may be assigned to support the new arrival with relevant information and encouragement. These socialization techniques lead to positive outcomes for new employees such as higher job satisfaction, better job performance, greater organizational commitment, and reduction in occupational stress and intent to quit.[22]

There is also some evidence that employees with certain personality traits and experiences adjust to an organization more quickly.[23] These traits include 'proactive personality' – the tendency to take charge of situations and achieve control over one's environment. I refer elsewhere in this chapter to 'learning agility', a similar concept. Researchers have noted that role clarity,[24] self-efficacy, social acceptance and knowledge of organizational culture are particularly good indicators of well-adjusted new employees who have benefited from an effective onboarding system.

In order to increase the effectiveness of an onboarding programme it is helpful for one person to 'own' the onboarding process, oversee all departmental stakeholders,[25] and to monitor and measure how well new recruits are adjusting to their new roles, responsibilities, peers, supervisors and the organization at large.

Build strategies – growing the talent pool

Tapping into new sources of talent is a key priority as organizations gear up for growth. So it is important to combine internal development and external recruitment in filling talent pools.[26] Instead of hiring new people with a narrow skill set to meet a temporary need, leading companies strengthen existing people with additional skills to build a more agile workforce capable of responding to new competitive threats and capitalizing on new opportunities. This facilitates the management of quantitative risks associated with ensuring there is sufficient talent to meet organizational needs and not an oversupply – which represents a waste in resources. It also ensures that the organization has the requisite skill set required at a point in time.

For such employees a commitment-oriented HR system seems appropriate.[27] The emphasis for HR practices should be on building the motivation, commitment and development of those in the talent pool, shifting from a short-term 'transactional' psychological contract towards a more long-term 'relational' psychological contract.[28]

Identifying high potential

In large talent pools the challenge is to distinguish between those who have the ability to perform at the relevant level now and those who have future potential for more senior roles. Conventionally organizations have used variations on a 'nine box grid' to assess performance and potential and to identify their current and future 'stars'. However, use of in-year appraisal ratings to define performance is risky given the instability of the measure. Moreover, 'potential' is often confused with 'ready for promotion', which begs the question of 'potential for what?' The process often ignores business critical expertise and functional mastery. Increasingly firms are using psychometric tests to determine the nature of potential, rather than relying mainly on current performance assessments. Test provider SHL argue that three components that have proved to be robust in identifying true high-potential employees are: *aspiration* to rise to senior roles; *ability* to be effective in more responsible and senior roles; and *engagement* to commit to the organization and remain in a challenging role.

Learning agility

To perform in this new environment, individuals will need greater resilience and agility than ever before in order to be able to reinvent themselves for future, as yet unknown, challenges. According to Miller, learning agility is gaining favour as a meaningful indicator of potential since it enables leaders to thrive on diverse, intense and varied challenges.[29] While the job and the person should be a good fit for each other, in these more fluid times, experience alone will not accurately predict a perfect match. Diversity of thinking is needed; leaders must be able to develop a corporate culture based on inclusion and a mindset of encouraging diverse viewpoints.

In assessing a person's learning agility HR can work with line managers to find out:

- What characteristics does a promising employee bring to challenges?

- How do they manage an unfamiliar situation? Do they get excited by matching their attributes against the demands of a task?

- What is the individual's likely career path – the type of position and highest level in the organization that they can attain?

Companies such as IBM look for a combination of cognitive, behavioural and attitudinal qualities that they expect to see in their leaders present and future. Leaders should:

- Have depth and breadth in technical and global business knowledge.

- Be known as a true thought leader in their area of expertise.

- Be able to tackle difficult problems head-on and know when to seek input and guidance from others.

- Be a natural visionary who is not intimidated by taking calculated and informed risks.

- Be able to see the bigger picture without losing sight of the small but important things.

- Have multicultural and multilingual aptitude – able to deliver results and value to global clients and stakeholders from different locations.
- Be able to inspire self and others; instil a sense of meaning and purpose in others.

And have:

- generational 'savvy' – able to bring out the best in an age-diverse workforce;
- change management expertise;
- comfort with ambiguity;
- dilemma-flipping ability;
- immersive learning and organizing skills.[30]

Developing people

In the long run, when talent is scarce, developing people will prove much less costly than recruitment. While holders of business-critical roles will still be given extra development support, the shift taking place is towards nurturing a broader spectrum of talent, finding talent in unexpected places, with exclusive and inclusive talent approaches existing side by side. So by offering real-time development for everyone, for instance via peer coaching and team learning, and investing in employees at junior levels, such as via apprenticeships or the chance to study for employer-based qualifications, employers send strong positive signals to employees about the company's priorities and about how it values them.

Providing training and development has been regularly cited as one of the most important factors in creating a positive work environment, which ultimately affects employee performance and retention. Development gives staff a sense of progression within the workplace and is likely to lead to greater commitment and engagement. Training employees and making them more effective and productive helps to build organizational flexibility and resilience, which have a direct impact on the company's success and profitability. This is about taking a long-term view, helping people and organizations to develop the capacity to improve and adapt to the changing needs of the business.

By forging creative collaborations with learning providers or other organizations keen to create shared learning opportunities for their workforce, firms can contain costs and increase the value of learning. Formal courses are increasingly geared towards skills not just knowledge, with participants selected based on their motivation to learn and managers' support in applying the learning. Developing line managers as coaches, providing tools for self-assessment, holistic succession planning and innovative career management are just some of the tools in the new 'war for talent'.

Increasingly, too, training and development aims to increase people's self-awareness and ability to thrive in more fluid work environments. The popular focus in recent years on emotional intelligence is being complemented by insights from mindfulness and neuroscience.

Career resilience

The nature of careers is also changing. In the past people were expected to be loyal to one company; today people are likely to pursue their professional objectives and personal goals through multiple companies. Of course, organizations must accept that many people will move on – but need to mitigate the risk of loss of key talent. Consequently some turnover of staff, including those with business-critical skills, should be expected. While organizations have been advocating career self-management for years, in today's environment many people feel ill-equipped and unsupported and may lack the skills and mindset to become more career resilient.

Typically companies are reluctant to articulate a longer-term view of career, and career support has declined in real terms. While organizations might want employees to be willing to adapt, embrace change and take greater ownership of managing their career, few appear to have recognized the link between equipping people to manage their career and organizational agility. Some organizations at least are starting to feel the need to articulate a clearer 'career deal' and better information about career paths. Equipping employees to manage their career by providing career support should be an explicit part of organizational strategy. Ironically, if you train people and set them up with contracts, making them more employable and giving them the flexibility to move, they tend to stay.

Agile succession planning

For many organizations the biggest risk factor relates to the organization's vulnerability after an unplanned departure of a top manager. Not surprisingly, succession planning for top roles forms part of corporate governance. Despite this, very few organizations are able to mitigate the impact of valued people moving on. The Corporate Executive Board's 2011 survey of 33,000 corporate leaders in 23 countries revealed that almost half – 41 per cent – were struggling to find qualified executive leadership.

Succession planning typically focuses on developing employees for certain types of roles – especially by expanding their career experience and functional skills – thus growing credible candidates for real jobs when they fall vacant. It also involves the longer-term development of talent pipelines to meet future business needs.[31] Akin to workforce planning, part of its developmental purpose is diagnostic – to identify where pipelines are weak and the specific skills, knowledge or experience lacking in the workforce.

However, succession planning is not always fully integrated with other talent management initiatives – plans are often created in a vacuum, which leads to duplication of work. Succession plans should be closely integrated with high-potential talent assessment processes and leadership development to ensure leadership continuity – and make it work successfully.

Succession planning has itself been through something of a metamorphosis in recent years. Traditional succession planning was arguably too focused on the long term – people don't stay in jobs 5–10 years any more. There is growing recognition that some senior professionals and experts are a source of competitive advantage and there are also shortages of individuals in operationally critical but not necessarily 'senior' roles. For all these workforce groups external recruitment is seen as too risky to meet business needs with the speed, quality and increasingly specific skills required. Moreover, as organizations get flatter, with fewer vertical promotion possibilities, succession planning needs to allow for lateral movement and skills development.

Succession planning is adapting to meet these changing needs. Many organizations are moving towards integrating succession planning with broader talent management approaches. And although succession planning remains primarily focused on senior leadership and management roles it is increasingly used for selected 'critical' roles at a range of levels where the organization is vulnerable. Planning for these selected roles should take place at appropriate levels of detail – often for groups of jobs not single posts – and with relevant time frames. There should be a mix-and-match approach to filling vacancies, blending the open job market with managed career moves, identifying and using external as well as internal successors as appropriate. In particular, agile succession planning involves individuals in planning and delivering their own skill and career development.[32]

The corporate centre is usually directly responsible only for small numbers of very senior roles, but also ensures appropriate devolved processes are in place within regions, divisions or functions. Succession or talent reviews, also called forums or succession committees, are becoming more strategic in scope and can enable job filling and development actions for succession candidates to help them gain specific skills or wider career experience – often in a different function, unit or location.

A formal process

In planning for succession a typical approach is as follows:

- First define the scope: what roles are critical to the organization? How far down should succession planning reach?
- Then define what current positions look like and what current competencies exist.
- Next define the future state: what competencies are needed? What gaps exist between the current talent pool and the future needs?

- Identify talent: who are high-potential candidates? What is their level of readiness?

- Develop talent: are development objectives aligned to meet succession requirements? What tools and resources are needed to implement development plans for individuals?

- Track development: how do you monitor and measure the success of an individual's development against their plan? Which external factors serve to impede or enhance individual success?

Succession planning must be integrated with other people management processes, especially assessment and actions for job filling and development.

Towards a more 'agile' succession approach

There are signs that a more 'agile' form of succession planning is emerging from the well-established 'developmental' approach. But what does agile succession planning look like? This approach assumes that change will happen. It draws heavily upon career planning and management to help create an informed, relevant and realistic view of succession. Rather than linking succession plans too strictly to organizational structure or specific roles that are subject to too much change, a person-based, pool-based approach is much more flexible.

At the same time it involves identifying successors for selected roles where the business is vulnerable – not just senior management – and planning for these selected roles at appropriate levels of detail, often for groups of jobs not single posts, and with relevant time frames. So 'emergency' and 'ready now' successors are in primary focus in addition to those with short-term (one to two years) and longer-term (usually three to five years) potential. Every effort must be made to identify those hard-to-replace individuals whose knowledge and skills are vital to the organization and put in place strong engagement and retention plans. External as well as internal successors should be identified where appropriate, recognizing the long-term trend towards involving individuals in planning and delivering their own skills and career development. In an agile succession process, vacancies can be filled by combinations of managed career moves and the open job market.

Evaluating experience through the lens of learning agility adds a 'leading indicator' to the equation and yields better succession planning decisions. Properly applied, learning agility can help companies to develop a deep bench-strength of talent and an understanding of how best to use that talent.

Increasing transparency

Today the very idea that organizations can manage talent may be an outdated conceit.[33] From the employee's point of view, agile succession planning must take account of their goals, aspirations and preferences. So an agile process should be genuinely two-way and involve input from the chosen 'successor' and all relevant parties. It is important to build talent dialogue into how you do business and use continuous feedback instead of intermittent spot checks. So get the facts – use multiple approaches such as surveys, coaching, exit data, focus groups – and analyse them.

Tools such as social media may have an increasingly relevant role to play in helping people to understand 'what's in it for me?' Focused career conversations between individuals and line managers or HR can help people to clarify their motivations and what they want from their work at this point in their lives, and help them to take stock of their personal appetite for learning. Yet in practice many line managers neglect to have regular career conversations with successors or high potentials. Many are reluctant to talk about their talented employees in succession forums for fear they will be poached by other departments or, worse still, from outside the company.[34]

Companies facing this problem need clear, unambiguous senior management endorsement that the talent pool is a company asset, not an individual executive's plaything. To help managers overcome their initial resistance, it is useful to train them to identify and develop talent, evaluate them on how well they do this and reward those who are most successful at developing and exporting talent. It is important to institutionalize these practices through KPIs and reporting, keeping the process 'live' by frequently updating executives on what is happening and communicating successes. People will support a succession plan much more enthusiastically if they can see that it works in reality. It's about building a talent management culture and mindset, developing a clear definition of 'successful leadership' for the future.

Succession planning should expose future leaders to opportunities to acquire a versatile set of skills and experiences; development opportunities should be meaningful and allow individuals scope to demonstrate their performance, potential and motivation. Such development opportunities might include short-term high-risk positions, rotational and global assignments, project roles, lateral moves or 'temporary promotion', from which they can move on quickly, develop their skills further and apply their learning in the next experience. People can also grow in 'real jobs' and learn to handle problems, deliver and prove their worth.

As succession planning becomes more agile, it will become a key mechanism for managing business risk and for speeding up responses to shifting business demands and increasingly diverse employee aspirations.

Conclusion

So the truth implicit in the old cliché 'people are our greatest asset' is becoming evident as companies compete to attract and retain the best people.

Capable and often multiskilled knowledge workers can pick and choose who they work for, so assumptions behind old-style organizational processes such as workforce planning and succession planning, which are designed to protect the organization's longer-term interests, must now flex to accommodate the interests and aspirations of a more mobile and demanding workforce. As we have discussed, in today's workplace:

- *Definitions of 'talent' and 'high potential' are broadening* beyond the select few future leaders.
- People processes should be *owned by the CEO* and managed by HR.
- They must be *developed with people, not done to them.*
- *One size does not fit all.*
- Analytics can help to source people; *relationships retain them.*

A multigenerational workforce will look for new working arrangements, career routes and development opportunities. This will impact on flexible working policies, on styles of management, social media policies and so on. Workforce design should also reflect the changing nature of careers and be geared towards developing change-readiness in the form of employee agility and career resilience. It should inevitably feed into learning, development and career strategies and related career deals. Since it is unrealistic to expect to retain all the 'key talent' an organization requires, talent processes must become more open, transparent and inclusive, with development geared towards creating a wider talent pool. By investing in the workforce, organizations are more likely to reap the benefits of innovation and high performance.

A more sophisticated estimate of the minimum supply of skilled staff required will take into account not just cost but also how future productivity demands can be met without destroying people's work–life balance. Success depends entirely on people's skills, ability and willingness to give of their best. The best calculations come to nothing if key people move on too quickly. So workforce strategy should involve an understanding of how staff will need to be managed in order to retain their motivation and performance.

In the next chapter we consider how employers can create a context conducive to employee engagement, the vital driver of employee commitment and performance. In particular we consider what executives, line managers and HR professionals can do to make their organizations employers of choice.

- Have the competencies that are required for your industry changed – and have the human resource practices of your firm kept pace?

- Is there a good process for developing needed competencies and making sure people can have meaningful and developmental job experiences and career paths?

- How effectively do line managers hold career conversations?

- Who 'owns' talent management in your organization?

- Is your firm developing the needed leadership capability at all levels and the lateral leadership capabilities required for success in a complex world?

- When opportunities are identified how are participants selected?

- In the last year, what feeder groups were available for each identified promotion?

- Of the promotions that occurred in the last year, were the selections reflective of the pool of eligible candidates?

Notes

1 Source: *The Future of Work* (2014): published by the UK Commission for Employment and Skills (UKCES).

2 CIPD (2014): *Managing An Age-Diverse Workforce*, CIPD, London.

3 Howe, N and Strauss, W (2007) The next 20 years: how customer and workforce attitudes will evolve, *Harvard Business Review*, July–August, pp 41–52.

4 Aon Hewitt (2014) 2014 Trends in Global Employee Engagement.

5 Deloitte (2014) [accessed 30 August 2014] The Deloitte Millennial Survey, *Deloitte* [Online] http://www.deloitte.com/assets/Dcom-Italy/Local%20Assets/Documents/Pubblicazioni/gx-dttl-2014-millennial-survey-report.pdf.

6 SHRM [accessed 30 August 2014] Globoforce Employee Recognition Survey (2012), *SHRM* [Online] http://go.globoforce.com/rs/globoforce/images/SHRMFALL2012Survey_web.pdf.

7 [Online] http://businesscasestudies.co.uk/companies/#axzz37MJAn4W9.

8 Couzins, M (2013) [accessed 15 January 2015] CIPD 2013 highlights: Unilever, Facebook and HMRC, *Personnel Today* [Online] http://www.personneltoday.com/hr/cipd-2013-highlights-unilever-facebook-and-hmrc/.

9 Kaplan, RS and Norton, DP (2001) *The Strategy-Focused Organization: How balanced scorecard companies thrive in the new environment*, Harvard Business School Press, Boston.

10 Chambers, EG *et al* (1998) [accessed 30 August 2014] The War for Talent, *The McKinsey Quarterly* [Online] http://www.executivesondemand.net/manage mentsourcing/images/stories/artigos_pdf/gestao/The_war_for_talent.pdf.

11 Arthur, MB and Rousseau, DM (1996) The boundaryless career as a new employment principle, in *The Boundaryless Career*, ed MG Arthur and DM Rousseau, Oxford University Press, New York, p 5.

12 Boatman, J and Wellins, RS (2011) *Global Leadership Forecast*, Development Dimensions International, Inc., Pittsburgh.

13 Bersin & Associates (2011) *Talent Watch Q1: Global growth creates new war for talent*, Bersin & Associates, Oakland, CA.

14 CIPD (2012): Resourcing and Talent Planning: Annual Survey Report 2012, CIPD, London.

15 Tansley, C *et al* (2007) *Talent: Strategy, Management, Measurement*, CIPD, London.

16 Collings, DG and Mellahi, K (2009) Strategic talent management: a review and research agenda, *Human Resource Management Review*, **19** (4), pp 304–13.

17 Cappelli, P (2008) *Talent on Demand*, Harvard Business School Press, Boston.

18 Deloitte [accessed 30 August 2014] The Chemistry of Talent, *Deloitte* [Online] deloitte.com/straighttalk.

19 The Beginner's Guide to Careers Sites [accessed 30 August 2014] *Webrecruit* [Online] https://rapidrequest.emedia.co.uk/4/Success/25192?submissionID=41 70180&instanceID=1364785&package=EmediaSecure.

20 Ambler, T and Barrow, S (2008) *The Chemistry of Talent, Straight Talk Book No.10*, Deloitte.

21 SHRM (2013) [accessed 30 August 2014] SHRM Survey Findings: Social Networking Websites and Recruiting/Selection [Online] http://www.slideshare. net/shrm/social-networkingwebsitesrecruitingselectingjobcandidatesshrm-2013final.

22 Fisher, CD (1985) Social support and adjustment to work: a longitudinal study, *Journal of Management*, **11**, pp 39–53.

23 Saks, AM and Ashforth, BE (1996) Proactive socialization and behavioral self-management, *Journal of Vocational Behavior*, **48**, pp 301–23.

24 Adkins, CL (1995) Previous work experience and organizational socialization: a longitudinal examination, *Academy of Management Journal*, **38**, pp 839–62.

25 PriceWaterhouseCoopers [accessed 30 August 2014] Best Practices For Retaining New Employees: New Approaches to Effective Onboarding, *PriceWaterhouseCoopers and Saratoga Global Best Practices*, http://www.pwc. com/en_us/us/hr-saratoga/assets/retaining_employees_onboarding.pdf.

26 Cappelli, P (2008) *Talent on Demand*, Harvard Business School Press, Boston.

27 Lepak, DP and Snell, SA (2002) Examining the human resource architecture: the relationships among human capital, employment, and human resource configurations, *Journal of Management*, **28** (4), pp 517–43.

28 Boxall P and Purcell J (2008) *Strategy and Human Resource Management*, Palgrave Macmillan, Basingstoke.

29 Miller, M-A (2012) [accessed 30 August 2014] Seeking the Agile Mind: Looking Beyond Experience to Build Succession Plans, *Avnet Insights* [Online] http://www.google.co.uk/url?url=http://news.avnet.com/download/Avnet_ Learning_Agility.pdf&rct=j&frm=1&q=&esrc=s&sa=U&ei=eWPGVKX5Co3 SaPbjgoAD&ved=0CBQQFjAA&usg=AFQjCNELnrTX1OHLMhIeJay44728 p4zxqg.

30 I am grateful to Bob Johansen, Institute for the Future, for the last two bullet points in this list.

31 Hirsh, W (2012) *Planning for Succession in Changing Times*, Corporate Research Centre, London.

32 Ibid.

33 Sparrow P, Otaye, L and Makramet, H (2014) [accessed 30 August 2014] How Should We Value Talent Management? *University of Lancaster* [Online] www. lancaster.ac.uk/.../WP14-01HowShouldWeValueTalentManagement. pdf.

34 Porr, D (2014) [accessed 28 August 2014] Agile Succession: HR's Toughest Challenge, *Human Resource Executive Online*, Oct 7–10 [Online] http://www. hreonline.com/HRE/view/story.jhtml?id=534354896.

Nurturing employee engagement and resilience

In Chapter 8 we looked at some of the challenges of attracting and developing the agile and resilient people organizations need. Today's economic outlook for many industries looks decidedly mixed so the emerging talent agenda needs to have some flexibility built into it. As we have seen, an agile workforce is a broader, more inclusive concept than focusing exclusively on future top talent.

As organizations struggle to sustain competitive edge in this volatile context, many business leaders will need to set new strategies to increase productivity and innovation. But they cannot effectively execute what is required for future growth without the 'right' people focused on the 'right' things, motivated and 'engaged' with their organization; in other words, people who are willingly investing their 'discretionary effort' in the collective effort. How people feel about their work influences whether or not they release their discretionary effort and makes a difference to performance and innovation.

That is why I believe that especially in today's knowledge-intensive and service-intensive industries – where people are the main source of innovation, production and service excellence – employee engagement or '*the intellectual and emotional attachment that an employee has for his or her work*'[1] becomes crucial to business success. Therefore, if leaders want their organizations to survive and thrive in today's challenging times, they must become intensely focused on improving employee engagement.

In this chapter we consider:

- The central link between employee engagement and performance, commitment and retention.
- What is employee engagement?
- Getting to grips with employee engagement.
- The 'engaged' model.
- An emergent psychological contract.
- Team engagement.
- How HR/OD can help to stimulate engagement and wellbeing.

We look at what is involved in creating a work context conducive to employee engagement and consider the roles played by executives, line managers, HR/OD and employees themselves.

Links between employee engagement and performance

High performance theory places employee engagement at the heart of performance and productivity – especially among knowledge workers – since when people are engaged with their work they are more productive, more service-oriented, less wasteful, more inclined to come up with good ideas, to take the initiative and generally do more to help organizations achieve their goals than people who are disengaged.

Research has correlated employee engagement with higher earnings per share, improved sickness absence, higher productivity and innovation – the potential business benefits go on and on. For instance, a Corporate Leadership Council (CLC) study found that companies with highly engaged employees grow twice as fast as peer companies. A three-year study by Towers Watson of 41 multinational organizations found that those with high engagement levels had 2-4 per cent improvement in operating margin and net profit margin, whereas those with low engagement scores showed a decline of about 1.5–2 per cent. Other studies suggest that highly engaged employees tend to support organizational change initiatives and are more resilient in the face of change.

In Britain's National Health Service (NHS), a meta-analysis of research into the links between patient health outcomes and employee engagement found that patient satisfaction was consistently higher in health organizations with better rates of staff health and wellbeing, and that there was a link between higher staff satisfaction and lower rates of mortality and hospital-acquired infection.[2] The study concluded that health-care employers should try to accelerate increases in employee engagement scores as they appear to correlate strongly with patient outcomes.

Yet the UK is generally reported to suffer from a growing 'engagement deficit' relative to many other countries, including the United States.[3] A global engagement study by Aon Hewitt (2014) found that only just over half of UK employees saw a long-term path with their current company and fewer saw a compelling employee value proposition (EVP) to keep their talents with their current company.[4] Recruitment firms are aware of wide-scale pent-up career frustration and high turnover of key talent can be anticipated in the years ahead. And as many organizations continue to downsize or implement other cost-reduction measures, employee engagement and retention are likely to become major casualties of change.

So while attracting the talent needed for business performance can be challenging enough, retaining talent requires an understanding of the specific drivers of engagement for a given workforce and creating a context conducive to employee engagement.

What is employee engagement?

Definitions of employee engagement abound. MacLeod and Clarke, whilst researching for their 2009 report Engaging for Success, found at least 50 different definitions of employee engagement.[5] Many make the association between engagement and high-performance work practices and other forms of human resource management (HRM).[6] Different definitions focus on employee behaviour (eg discretionary effort), on employee attitudes (eg commitment), on employee feelings (eg enthusiasm), on the conditions of work and what the organization does (eg provides support).

Among the earliest definitions was the association of personal engagement with the 'needs-satisfying' approach to motivation by William Kahn in his 1990 article for the *Academy of Management* journal.[7] He defined personal engagement as the harnessing of organization members' selves to their work roles; when engaged, people employ and express themselves physically, cognitively and emotionally during role performances. Personal disengagement, on the other hand, is defined as the uncoupling of selves from work roles; people withdraw and defend themselves physically, cognitively or emotionally during role performances. Kahn and Heaphy later identified the importance of the 'relational context', which affects how people use varying degrees of their selves – physically, cognitively and emotionally – in work roles.[8]

The psychological concept of 'work engagement' developed by Schaufeli and Bakker is defined as 'a positive, fulfilling, work-related state of mind that is characterized by vigour, dedication, and absorption'.[9] Work engagement describes how workers experience their work: as stimulating and energetic, something to which they really want to devote time and effort (the vigour component); as a significant and meaningful pursuit (dedication); and as engrossing and something on which they are fully concentrated (absorption). The fully engaged employee:

- knows how their job contributes to the overall mission and goals of the organization;
- has a job with enough variety to keep them challenged and engaged;
- is able to use their talents and abilities effectively in their current position.

This form of employee engagement is closely associated with psychological 'flow', a sense of oneness with the activity being pursued.[10] In this emotional state employees feel passionate, energetic and committed to their work. This aspect of engagement is very intense and produces a sensation of 'being at one with the world', has the capacity to banish anxieties and concerns and makes one feel completely focused, satisfied and happy. This form of engagement is thought to produce the highest levels of performance in individuals.

According to social engagement theories, engagement does not exist because of the person or their environment – but in the relationship between the two. The key enabler of social engagement is commitment and trust between employers and employees. MacLeod and Clarke's chosen definition was that engagement is: 'a workplace approach designed to ensure that employees are committed to their organization's goals and values, motivated to contribute to organizational success, and are able at the same time to enhance their own sense of well-being'.[11]

Psychological contract

As we discussed in Chapters 1 and 7, with respect to white-collar work in particular, the psychological contract has been changing in nature and growing in complexity in recent years. Psychological contract theory is part of social exchange theory, according to which reciprocation is pivotal to the maintenance of a healthy contract. Since engagement is the point where business and employee interests coincide, employee engagement could be thought of as a barometer of the state of the employment relationship, manifesting the health of the psychological contract between employees and employers.

Since the mid-1990s many employers have moved away from employment relationships based on the old exchange: long-term job security and gradual career progression up a hierarchy for employees in exchange for loyalty and hard work for employers. Instead a 'new deal' is supposed to have taken its place, according to which employers will expect employees to be flexible, high performing and committed while also managing their own careers and making themselves 'employable'.[12] The basis of this exchange is short-term agreements dependent on performance and mutual value exchange.

Psychological contracts can be dynamic, to reflect changing circumstances and needs. For instance, companies aspiring to become agile now also want employees to show resilience, learning, adaptability and speed. However, if one party (the organization) in the exchange relationship fails to deliver, or unilaterally reneges on its part of the bargain without acknowledgement or renegotiation, the other party (employee) is likely to lose trust and respond by withdrawing discretionary effort or leaving the firm.

A one-sided deal

In practice it could be argued that the mutuality implicit in the 'old' psychological contracts has been largely swept to one side and there is increasing polarization of employee treatment. For key talent, the unitarist assumptions behind the 'new deal' – that 'what is good for the business is good for the people' seemingly hold true. For them, what Denise Rousseau calls '*i*-deals' (or specialized idiosyncratic deals) will be struck. Conversely, for employees with less valuable skills the evolving employment relationship may be breaking down. The drive for organizational agility is often synonymous with cost-cutting. Now that 'more for less' has become the nature of business as usual, employees may suffer a reduced psychological contract in the form of work intensification, pressure and loss of job security. These conditions can lead to poor morale, exhaustion and the risk of 'burnout', which Maslach and Jackson consider to be the opposite pole of the engagement spectrum,[13] so employee engagement is likely to become a major casualty of change.

The consequences for organizations could be severe. First there is the medium-term challenge of retaining key people: UK recruitment firms are aware of wide-scale, pent-up career frustration and, as employment opportunities become more abundant, significant employee turnover can be anticipated.[14] The tougher the measures taken to keep organizations viable, the greater the risk of strained employee relations with 'survivor' employees simply 'hunkering down', doing the minimum necessary to get by. So at the very time when organizations most need employees to be engaged with their work and producing their best ideas, employee engagement and talent retention are at significant risk. Indeed, so concerned was the UK government about the 'engagement deficit' that the Department for Business, Innovation and Skills (BIS) backed the Engaging for Success inquiry (or the MacLeod Report[15]) to explore the assumed links between employee engagement, performance and productivity. The report's conclusion – that the business case for employee engagement is overwhelming – has been strongly reinforced since then as more research is published.

It is vital therefore that organizations reframe the 'deal' to maximize the value for both the firm and its employees over the next few years. In any case, demographic shifts and other factors may force a rebalancing. Findings from many consultancy reports and company engagement surveys suggest that what many employees (especially millennials) want from their employers may be different from what is on offer. The Aon Hewitt 2014 global engagement survey suggests that millennials, due to the sheer size and influence of this generational cohort, may be setting the organizational tone for employee engagement and are likely to be influencing the perceptions of generation X and baby boomer employees.[16] Only 12 per cent of employees are reported to be highly engaged.

So should business leaders be worried? Absolutely: arguably it is before talent shortages start to hit that employee engagement should be recognized as a business priority.

Key enablers of engagement

The MacLeod Report summarized four fundamental 'enablers' of any employee engagement strategy:

- Leadership that gives a 'strong strategic narrative about the organization, where it's come from and where it's going'.
- Line managers who motivate, empower and support their employees.
- Employee voice throughout the organization, to challenge or reinforce the status quo and involve employees in decision making.
- 'Organizational integrity': stated values are embedded into organizational culture; what we say is what we do.

The last of these, integrity, is in many ways synonymous with trust – doing what you say, being ethically and morally bound, doing unto others as you would wish done unto yourself. Trust underpins the psychological contract and Kenexa's 2013 Worktrends report points to integrity being the most important lever of trust, above benevolence or competence.[17] Purcell *et al* analysed the factors most strongly associated with organizational commitment, using the national UK Workplace Employment Relations Study (WERS) data.[18] The most important and influential factor, which applied to all types of employees, was trust in management.

The roles of leaders and managers

The MacLeod Report found that 'engaging managers' and 'engaging leadership' are pivotal to creating work contexts conducive to engagement. Top leaders in particular have a multiplier effect on engagement, since their own approach is very visible and they have control over all the top engagement drivers. Yet it seems that, instead of seeking to understand how to maintain or enhance employee engagement, many UK top leaders simply ignore it, possibly because they are unaware of or do not understand its importance. The MacLeod Report puts it less charitably: 'The issue seems to lie in their unwillingness to "talk the talk" and truly relinquish command and control styles of leadership in favour of a relationship based on mutuality.'[19]

Line managers set the tone for employee engagement. Through their interactions with their teams on a day-to-day basis the organization's relationship with employees is made manifest. The defining contribution of great managers is that they boost the engagement levels of the people who work for them.[20] Yet managers are often unclear as to how to create an engaging context; they may lack the relevant skills or interest and there may be few consequences for doing nothing. Indeed many managers consider engagement to be the job of HR.

Getting to grips with engagement issues

So if managers and leaders are so crucial to employee engagement, how do great managers get the best out of their people? This is why Geoffrey Matthews and I wrote our book *Engaged* (2012).[21] We wanted to demystify this contested topic and provide practical guidance for managers and HR professionals who want to create a work context conducive to engagement.

Surveys are a conventional means of exploring what engages and disengages key segments of the workforce. Cattermole argues that surveys are important because they allow you to measure many different aspects of employee engagement, broadly divided into three main areas:[22]

- Blockers: problems facing employees, eg inadequate IT systems or excessive workloads.
- Drivers: motivating factors, eg recognition, good relationships with managers, opportunities to learn career-enhancing skills.
- Outcomes: beneficial attitudes – employees' pride in their work and organization, willingness to recommend and desire to remain with their employer.

The downside of surveys is that they can be expensive, overly cumbersome and may result in 'analysis paralysis'. There can be lack of management sponsorship and subsequent activity is often misaligned or irrelevant, so that energy is spread too thin and efforts 'run out of steam'.

To avoid these risks, periodic pulse surveys can be used. The initial review of results should be checked and calibrated with relevant segments of employees, key lessons drawn, solutions generated with employees and appropriate focused action taken. Keeping everyone involved and informed is vital. Improvements should be measured and initiatives concluded with a review of the additional learning gleaned as a result of the activity.

More generally, though, approaches to employee engagement should move away from being HR-owned, reactive, periodic and survey-focused towards being manager-led and HR supported. Engaging line managers focus on individuals and teams, proactively building a context in which engagement is a daily part of working life.

What do employees want?

From our own research we know that there is no 'one size fits all' when it comes to engaging individuals. Given that engagement is a personal and individual phenomenon, is it then possible to generalize about what employees want from work and about how managers can influence engagement levels? Many consultancy reports highlight the 'top 10 engagement drivers'. For instance, the 2014 Aon Hewitt survey found a number of shifts under way in what appears to connect generation Y in particular to organizations, with the following increasing in importance:

- Changing career expectations – with the end of 'job for life' people do not expect to make their careers in one organization any more.
- Social media and connectivity in general are driving the democratization of work – people expect to be informed and to have a say.
- Desire for collaboration/co-creation/interaction with employer.
- The importance of empowerment/autonomy.
- Work environment.
- Ethos, brand and reputation.
- Quality of relationships, work–life balance.
- Opportunities to grow and develop.
- Management and leadership.
- Self-awareness.

The survey found that the top employee engagement drivers for all generations – and therefore potential elements of the evolving employment contract – centre on career opportunities, managing performance, pay and reputation and communication. Employees want to work for companies with a solid employer reputation, reward for performance, career trajectories and a collaborative culture.

Similarly, Purcell *et al*'s analysis of WERS data produced the following, often considered the classic building blocks of engagement:

- employee trust in management;
- satisfaction with work and the job;
- involvement in decision making at work;

- climate of relationships between management and employees;
- satisfaction with pay;
- job challenge;
- sense of achievement from work.

These insights offer a useful starting point for conversations with employees about how to create a more engaging context.

The 'engaged' model

In analysing many varied sources of employee data for our book *Engaged*, and recognizing the risk of generalization, Geoff Matthews and I categorized the main factors we believe to be present when people are engaged with their organization, not just their job, as set out below.

Connection

Many people want to work for organizations whose purposes and values they can embrace – this sense of higher purpose appears to be closely associated with motivation, commitment and ultimately the energy and effort workers are prepared to put in. They want to feel part of something worthwhile, that their work is meaningful and that the value it adds is clear since it links to important organizational outcomes. They want to feel that they belong (for a time at least), to have a sense of job security, affiliation and strong workplace relationships. Employees want to be valued for their contribution and to be dealt with in a fair and consistent manner.

As we discussed in Chapter 4, for people to engage with the organization, and not just with their own work, they need to connect with other people, including leaders, as well as having a chance to participate in strategizing. Flatter organizational structures don't solve the problem if the hierarchical mindset is still in place.

Support

In engaging work contexts employees receive appropriate support from management and cooperation from others. The amount and nature of support they need may vary according to age, stage or circumstance; managers must be alert to what support individuals actually require. They may need development or exposure to new opportunities or help managing complex workloads. As a result, employees are able to do their best and they give it their all. Above all, being valued as individuals is crucial. While pay remains important, other forms of recognition and reward – such as flexibility – are also important.

Voice

Given that the risk in the employment relationship is largely with employees, people want to know what is happening in their organization and to be able to influence matters that affect their working lives. In an engaging workplace employees are involved, have opportunities to participate in what is happening and have their voice heard. They are also open to new thinking and embrace diversity and teamwork.

Scope

People want work that is interesting, challenging and that offers meaning, stretch, enjoyment and satisfaction. They also want autonomy, control and task discretion, the chance to develop their skills and careers and opportunities for growth.

The blend and intensity of these different desires will differ according to individual preferences and career needs. In particular, what is happening in the broader organizational context can impact how individuals feel and what they need from their organization.

What does this look like in practice?

To respond to the engagement challenge of this new era we looked at examples of management practice in organizations where employee engagement levels remain high despite the challenging context.

Below are some examples of what we found.

Creating connection

Engagement levels are higher when leadership styles have evolved beyond command and control towards more open, collaborative and participative approaches that act as the foundation for mutual trust and respect. Engaging leaders look beyond the current challenges, anticipate the big business issues and plot a way through to growth, taking short-term decisions with the longer-term in mind. They reshape the work environment and culture to enhance performance and match their special basis of competitive advantage. Engaging leaders actively lead culture change, working to create a shared sense of higher purpose and a positive sense of the future; something to aim for that people can connect with and can really believe in. Purpose is a firm's vision for the value it seeks to create and how that value is created; it defines what the corporation is and does, whom it serves and how it contributes to the well-being of society.

Whilst the causal link from shared purpose to sustained high performance has yet to be proven definitively, there are various pieces of evidence that suggest such a connection. Analysis of survey data[23] indicates that a strong sense of shared purpose leads to high levels of employee engagement. Employees who share a sense of higher purpose are most concerned about how they can accomplish a goal that makes a difference to the purpose. It gives them a compelling reason to come to work. In turn high employee engagement drives sustainable high performance.[24] Bevan et al (2005)[25] and Buytendijk (2006)[26] both found that high-performing organizations have a strong sense of purpose internally and with external stakeholders.

Some forms of organizational purpose appear more strongly linked to high performance than others. The shareholder value idea may have worked at one time, but it now appears outdated, does not fit well with the needs of the 21st century and may be harmful in some cases. While superficially clear and simple, the short-term nature of shareholder value purpose discourages executives from making investments that really might be good not only for society in the long run, but even for the shareholders themselves. So shareholder value in general, and a relentless pursuit of that objective, can have negative social consequences.

Increasingly, there is a return to the historical relationship that holds the interests of society as paramount, and that corporations exist primarily to serve social needs, especially those of the customer. In 2002, Richard Ellsworth[27] published data indicating that companies whose corporate purpose focuses on delivering value to customers are significantly more profitable over a 10-year period than companies aiming at maximizing shareholder value or those trying to balance the needs of all their stakeholders. Springett (2004)[28] also found that a customer-focused corporate purpose produces a strong sense of shared purpose among employees – suggesting that this might also be driving high organizational performance. Part of the explanation seems to be that a customer-focused purpose leads to both a strategic focus and creative capability inside organizations.

As we have discussed previously, some leaders are increasingly advocating an employee-driven purpose as a means to both improve employee engagement and customer satisfaction. To be effective in inspiring people, such a purpose must be authentic and consistently applied. It would not work if, in order to keep prices low, employees are paid at, or close to, the minimum wage, receive few if any benefits, have no job security and are given only enough training needed to do basic jobs that have been designed to be simple and easy to learn. When workers at the bottom of these companies have no opportunities to make a good living or to do interesting work – much less to make a career in them – organizations should avoid declaring that people are their greatest asset.

So how do leaders inspire an authentic sense of shared purpose? Engaging leaders set and communicate a clear direction and priorities (developing what MacLeod and Clarke refer to as a 'strategic narrative') so that employees know what is required and feel empowered to deliver the right outputs without the need for micro-management. They develop self-awareness regarding their own core purpose, values and beliefs – the core which shapes their approach and by which they influence and take people with them when everyone is under pressure. They strive to role model the values and use, and act on, 360 degree and other feedback to show commitment. They nurture leadership at every level.

For instance William Rogers became CEO of UKRD in 2002 and has overseen its transformation into the UK's fourth largest commercial radio group. In 2009, UKRD won a hostile takeover bid for the publicly quoted Local Radio Company PLC. Since then, further acquisitions have been made as the group builds its portfolio of local commercial licences. As William Rogers points out:

> We've tried to create a values-based culture and there are six words that set the parameters for the standards of behaviour we encourage: open; honest; fair; fun; professional and unconventional. It is one thing to introduce a values-based culture; the second thing is backing it up with cash and time. At UKRD every single year, everyone has a full day out of the business talking about what these values mean to them in the workplace. It's also important that everybody understands that the values apply to everyone. All of the senior team takes part in workshops; they're not just there to make a speech. We also provide all of our teams with 'courageous conversations' training, which has led to a massive reduction in how much managers need to get involved in disputes between individual members of their teams. Between 90 per cent and 95 per cent of decisions in this company are made on the ground.[29]

Not surprisingly, UKRD came top of the *Sunday Times Top 100 Best Companies to Work For* list for three consecutive years.

Supporting people

Engaging managers get to know people as individuals, care for employees, create an open and positive work environment and build teams. They execute tasks in an enabling way, aiming to keep staff motivated and developing people's performance potential. They are versatile, able to judge when to involve employees and when to direct them. Engaging line managers set clear objectives so that people know what is required but allow staff to work out how to deliver them. They watch for signs of 'burnout' and aid people in managing workloads by being clear about what can be stopped as well as started. They support people best by designing interesting and worthwhile jobs and ensuring employees have the skills, authority and resources they need to deliver results that matter. They 'declutter' jobs of unnecessary bureaucracy so that people have a clear line of sight through their day job to the purpose, mission and goals of the organization.

Engaging managers strive to deliver on the employer brand, promise and ensure employees get a fair deal. In the current context, old-fashioned carrot-and-stick incentives to stimulate and reward performance are unlikely to be effective. While no organization can guarantee job security, engaging managers can help employees to cope with stress and anxiety during change. Providing meaningful support – even simply listening – not only shows employees whose jobs may be at risk that they are valued, it can also help survivor employees (those whose jobs remain after downsizing) to remain productively focused on their work.

Since some of the human reactions to change can be anticipated, HR can help managers to take actions to minimize the negative impact of change on people and build policies and initiatives that support people in managing their own wellbeing. Employee assistance programmes can help. Therefore managers need to develop more of a coaching style and be willing and able to involve staff in implementing change. When making change becomes part of every employee's job, it can become the spur to innovation and improvement.

Voice

Engaging employers encourage and facilitate the kind of connections that employees want to make today. By doing so, they form communities of like-minded people collaborating on purposes that they share. Especially in tough times, frequent and honest communication is vital for (re)building employee trust, resilience and engagement. Engaging leaders and managers are visible, accessible and approachable; they communicate authentically and consistently about the bigger picture, strategy and direction. They are also willing to listen and act on what they hear.

Communication is not just top-down, but also involves genuine dialogue at organization and team level. Whether dealing with business problems or developing new ideas for growth, engaging leaders take a participative approach, building consensus between different groups and individuals within the business. They make sure that people can see clear signs of progress by marking milestones, celebrating successes, stabilizing what works and sharing the benefits of change.

Scope

Engaging employers provide opportunities for employees to develop their skills so that they can work more effectively and have opportunities to achieve more. Engaging managers work at improving the skills and competencies people really need, focusing in particular on people in new roles. They spot opportunities for employee development and actively coach their teams, involving them in working on real business issues, providing job shadowing and mentoring.

In particular, engaging employers work to clarify career tracks to enable internal (and external) mobility and enhanced experience for key groups and individuals. Engaging managers deliberately encourage people to change roles/re-energize themselves by moving between domestic and international divisions or from one country to another. This allows them to gain new experiences and helps develop different parts of the business – and is also a great motivator. After all, when people feel valued and have opportunities to grow, they are likely to perform well.

One international charity recognized that, while staff are responsible for their own career development, some organizational support should be available to help staff understand how to go about planning their career. They developed career planning support tools based on their competency model that individuals can access and discuss with their line manager. Managers were given skills development to help them support staff with career development conversations and a pool of peer mentors was established so that colleagues can help each other learn new skills and access new experiences. HR acts as facilitator of job and experience moves.

An emergent psychological contract

Engagement framework thinking – connection, support, voice, scope – is potentially the basis of an emerging psychological contract that is founded on equity between employers and employees. Elements of this emerging contract might include the following:

- *Connection*:
  - organizational affiliation;
  - quality of relationships.
- *Voice*:
  - co-creation;
  - access to speak truth to power: mentoring by talent psychology-savvy senior colleagues.
- *Support*:
  - peer support;
  - work–life balance;
  - effective management;
  - a positive work climate.
- *Scope*:
  - self-awareness: with talent psychology-savvy coaches;
  - autonomy and influence;
  - real work: action learning, projects;
  - opportunities to grow.

Any organization that wishes to retain talent should be vigilant to how employees' needs are changing. Ultimately, though, employees are responsible for managing their own engagement. Moreover, if staff genuinely do enjoy scope, receive the right level of support, have voice and feel connected with their organization, it is only to be expected that they can be trusted to get on with the job, be accountable for their performance and 'go the extra mile' for the organization.

Team engagement

Beyond individual engagement, the level of team engagement will also affect performance one way or another. Creating an engaging workplace climate is usually a joint effort. The following case study tells how a partnership between a ward sister and an organization development (OD) specialist in a UK hospital helped a demoralized and underperforming ward team became a well-motivated, healthier and high-performing team that genuinely does put patients at the heart of their work. I am grateful to Tracey Gray, formerly Head of Education at Doncaster and Bassetlaw Hospitals, NHS Foundation Trust, who is the OD practitioner in this short case study.

CASE STUDY Changing attitudes – improving outcomes

These days the UK's NHS is subject to considerable media scrutiny and criticism over poor patient care. Naturally this negative press can be demoralizing for staff. At Doncaster and Bassetlaw Hospitals NHS Foundation Trust serious concerns were raised by major stakeholders about the detrimental effect on patient experience due to the demotivation of staff on one of the wards. The regular metrics of patient care posted on the ward notice board (known as the 'wall of shame') showed an ever downward spiral of staff morale, absence and patient care. The ward staff were feeling undervalued and had mostly come to believe that they were seen as 'problem children' and that this was how things would remain. The risk was that, if ignored, the situation could deteriorate and become another scandal of poor patient care.

An internal OD consultant Tracey Gray was commissioned to work with the ward sister to improve the situation. The work involved listening deeply to colleagues, whom it could have been easier to dismiss as part of the problem, and looking unflinchingly at some very challenging aspects of hospital life.

Key elements and purpose of the intervention

Part of the challenge was how to get team members 'on board' with the idea of looking at their own practice and taking responsibility for improving patient care. Tracey had individual conversations with staff, based on which a four-phase behavioural and educational development programme was designed. Its aim was to improve the patient experience in this specific ward by changing the attitudes and behaviour of staff, resulting in measurable change for the better. The training programme focused on both individual and group values and interventions were chosen to emphasize teamworking and included individual coaching, action learning and workshops. Simulations were designed to vividly bring to life typical problem care issues and help staff to understand care needs from the perspective of vulnerable patients.

Everyone in the team received individual coaching from Tracey, who did not shy away from using the ugly data and demonstrated a passionate belief in the possibility that anyone can change. She listened closely to staff, using neurolinguistic programming (NLP) to understand how they perceived their role and to elicit people's values and beliefs, identifying differences in beliefs – which can lead to conflict. This raised staff awareness and helped people to get issues out and deal with them constructively and systemically, for instance in action learning sets, by using shadowing, and by giving team members new process skills to talk to each other. Thus as OD practitioner Tracey planted seeds of self-help within the team to ensure that potential future conflicts could be addressed positively. Throughout the programme, the emphasis was on helping staff to feel empowered to improve patient care.

The effects

Clear markers were established and there were many beneficial outcomes from these interventions, not least improved staff morale and satisfaction, patient safety and wellbeing. Simple and effective symbols were used to reinforce messages, such as reframing the 'Wall of Shame' as the 'Wall of Praise'. These helped to keep people focused and enable the team to measure visually the progress towards better patient care. As the programme progressed, a positive improvement in the ward's climate became evident. There was a significant reduction in staff sickness and absence, improved staff morale and fewer patient complaints. As the ward team grew in confidence, rather than seeing their situation as remedial, staff members started to feel proud of the special help they were receiving to become a high-performing ward team.

Significant changes were noted in the following months, such as the positive atmosphere on the ward, staff's improved awareness of patient needs and recognition of non-verbal signals, resulting in better patient care. The ward staff grew into a strong team, since they had increased understanding of each other and enhanced process skills. Nursing practice improved and all concerned were proud of what had been achieved: all of this within a short space of time and at low cost. Results were disseminated to the chairperson and executive board members and the team who piloted the first event received certificates of completion and were rewarded with a celebratory buffet and presentation. This will no doubt have reminded the team members of how much they have achieved and just how much patient care on their ward has improved.

Spreading the learning

While the programme's interventions were both bespoke to and embedded within the ward in question, they also offer the potential for scaling into the wider organization, since champions are being developed within different areas who are being trained to become NLP master practitioners. Strong clinical leadership was a key element of the success of this initiative. Tracey worked closely with the ward sister, training her to support and embed initiatives in this ward and potentially others. The upskilling of clinical staff to apply such processes in their teams should help to spread and embed effective practice and behaviours across the organization. Thus not only has the programme had a beneficial impact on improving patients' experience but also the approach taken is very congruent with the humanistic principles and values of OD, which is about working *with* not *on* people to achieve renewal and growth.

Maintaining engagement in change

Of course not everyone is going to be 'up for change' and getting others to share the vision of the future workplace can be difficult. As one CEO commented: '20 per cent are always going to be on board with me and 20 per cent are always going to oppose, regardless of what the change is. The trick is getting the 60 per cent in the middle to first engage and then buy into the change.'

In many cases the notion of 'resistance' to change is perfectly rational, especially if people feel they are going to lose something by the change and have had no say in the decision to change. It is therefore important to take account of some typical human responses to change that can be predicted when change is mooted.

Typical human reactions to change

There are many frameworks for understanding some of the psychodynamics of change, not least the five stages of grief framework (also known as the change curve or transition curve) originally developed for use in bereavement counselling by Elisabeth Kübler-Ross.[30] More recently updated in the context of work environments by John Fisher as the process of personal change,[31] it describes the typical emotional roller-coaster people are thought to go through when faced with a change, especially one that they have not initiated themselves. These include 'holding on' responses – shock, denial, anger; followed by 'letting go' responses of bargaining and depression; and finally the 'moving on' responses – of acceptance, experimentation, new learning and experiences.

William Bridges distinguishes between a change (as a new situation) and a personal transition (the psychological process people go through to come to terms with the new situation).[32] He argues that generally speaking it is not change that people resist; it is the feelings of losses and endings that they experience and that may make the transition process difficult for them. For Bridges, the transition journey begins with *endings* – this is where people have to let go of something and experience a loss. They then enter the *'neutral zone'* akin to an emotional wilderness. Here people grieve the loss of the old and/or do not find the new comfortable and/or need to readjust to new circumstances. As people go through adjustment there is likely to be increased conflict, higher incidence of sickness and turnover, dissatisfaction with leadership, poorer work performance and confusion.

Finally come the *beginnings* – this is where people have worked through their loss, recognize they cannot turn back the clock, accept and are able to come to terms with the new reality. Although people positively reorient themselves to the future, old anxieties may easily be reactivated.

Similarly Kurt Lewin's three-stage theory of change addresses the transition journey and identifies what is happening to people at each stage. This is also commonly referred to as the 'unfreeze, change, freeze (or refreeze)' model.

Unfreezing The unfreezing stage is about getting ready to change. This first stage is about preparing ourselves, or others, before the change (and ideally creating a situation in which we want the change). It involves getting to a point of understanding that change is necessary and getting ready to move away from our current comfort zone. The more we feel that change is necessary, the more urgent it is, the more motivated we are to make the change.

To motivate people to want to change it is crucial that people understand why the change is needed and where it fits into the organization's purpose. Three factors tend to generate motivation – when there is:

- enough disconfirming data to cause serious discomfort and disequilibrium;
- connection of disconfirming data to important goals and ideals causing anxiety and/or guilt;
- enough psychological safety: having enough sense of identity and integrity to go ahead with change.

Disconfirming data shows that goals are not being met or some of the processes are not working: for instance, sales are down, complaints are up, there is high turnover of employees. On the other hand, if I don't feel safe and if change threatens my whole self, or I cannot work out what to do, I will deny the need for change, ignore disconfirming data or rationalize it away. However, once the group is in pain they typically listen to disconfirming information.

Moving Kurt Lewin was aware that change is not an event but a process of transition – the inner movement or journey we make in reaction to a change. This second stage occurs as we make the changes that are needed.

Once people are 'unfrozen' they have cognitively restructured what is happening and are moving towards a new way of being. Many different paths can be followed. People can learn by trial and error, imitation of role models – and this new learning will challenge core assumptions that may need to be refocused.

Refreezing While behaviour change can be stimulated for a while, it will not last long once the pressure is off. This stage is about establishing stability once the changes have been made so that the changes are accepted and become the new norm. People form new relationships and become comfortable with their routines. This can take time. So in this final phase, once the new behaviour and core are fixed they will stay like this until disconfirmation starts again. Indeed Hamel and Zanini argue that in a world that is relentlessly evolving, anything that is frozen soon becomes irrelevant, so what is more likely to occur is permanent 'slush'.[33]

Maintaining resilience

Learning from these different theories of personal transition, leaders must anticipate and watch out for any dysfunctional reactions to change that employees may be demonstrating – and provide support as necessary. Line managers, in particular, shoulder the day-to-day challenge of supporting people and maintaining or boosting employee morale, even though they may themselves be under pressure from every angle, juggling both business as usual and managing change. They too need to feel supported by top management and should be developed as leaders, giving them access to new tools, techniques and ideas. Managers and leaders need to be aware of the impact that their own management style may have on the team, especially during challenging times. For instance, managers who respond to pressure by taking more control may end up disempowering their team. Roffey Park proposes that leaders can manage their personal resilience when leading change by maintaining:[34]

- Perspective: being able to take a step back from a challenging situation, and accept rather than deny its negative aspects whilst finding opportunity and meaning in the midst of adversity.

- Emotional intelligence: individuals not being overtaken by their emotions but allowing space and time to process them.
- Purpose: individuals holding a clear sense of their own values and moral compass to keep centred when all around there is change.
- Connections: leaders who are able to stay resilient in challenging times have a wide network of friends and colleagues to draw on, both to get things done and to provide support.
- Physical energy: individuals keeping physically fit, eating well and taking time away from work to engage in activities they enjoy enables them to maintain energy levels.

The challenge for managers is to make sure that a healthy level of pressure and challenge doesn't tip over into unmanageable workloads that make people feel anxious and overwhelmed. It is essential to communicate openly and regularly about what is expected, to provide support where needed – not least making sure people have the resources they need to do the job being asked of them – and to help people prioritize so that they can perform at their best and maintain a healthy work–life balance. If people are to maintain a sense of control over their destiny it is important to involve your team as much as possible in planning, decision making and problem solving and to keep people informed of developments. People are more likely to feel positive about change, and even be energized and excited about it, if they feel they are involved in creating the way forward. We shall return to the question of how change can be 'managed' in the next chapter.

How can HR/OD help to stimulate engagement and wellbeing?

In any organization that faces ongoing change, employee engagement must be a priority. HR can play a key role in helping to improve engagement levels. Here are a few suggestions:

- Work with line managers to identify and actively address the root causes of employee disengagement. The aim should be to make employee engagement a daily focus for managers rather than simply an annual survey process.
- Help line managers to reduce pressure on people and avoid 'burnout' by (re)clarifying priorities, refocusing workloads onto priority areas and coaching their staff.[35]
- Build a robust business case for improving workplace wellness. Effective wellbeing strategies can help people to make the transition to new working conditions and cope with the demands made of them, and will also show staff that they are valued.
- Retain key players during periods when career opportunities may be limited. Risk management and retention plans should be applied to

key people and jobs where knowledge and skills are in short supply. By creating development opportunities HR can help people to make progress – perhaps through cross-training, strategic project work or continuing education – if not through promotion.

- Motivate younger workers by helping them to build their careers in the organization and also reskilling employees more generally for employability. While staff are responsible for their career development, HR can help staff to understand how to go about planning their careers by:
  - building career planning support based on a competency model;
  - mentorship;
  - improving the skills for managers to support staff in career development;
  - making opportunities available.
- Ensure that companies honour their commitments to employees. For instance, in 2012 all staff at the UK firm JCB shared a £2.5 million bonus pot despite economic headwinds predicted in 2013. Chairman Sir Anthony Bamford said he wanted to reward the hard work and commitment of JCB's 5,000 workers.[36] Playing fair by staff and showing them that their efforts are recognized is a great way to build employee engagement and commitment.

The key to success is creating the right climate and conditions where teams can thrive in the first place. As we have discussed, if people work in a constructive environment where they feel they are achieving something challenging and meaningful, they will be much better able to deal with change and the daily pressures of work. For all its challenges, change can also open up possibilities for development, better work–life balance and growth as people gain new skills, new networks and new responsibilities. Even tough challenges can be opportunities for individuals and teams to become more resilient, if people face these together and in a positive spirit. In Chapter 11 we look at a case study of how one organization is using a strengths-based approach, appreciative inquiry (AI), to help build resilience in turbulent times.

Conclusion

Pressure on employers for a more ethical and *win-win approach to the employment relationship* with employees is likely to increase as time goes by. Social connectivity and technological empowerment pose a real threat to old-style corporate models of organization. As employment patterns shift from lifetime employment to lifetime employability, employers must now interface with an emerging generation of younger workers whose attitudes, demands and expectations of employers may be very different from those only a generation ago. Younger generations have seen the free market model fail, and fail young people in particular. Unless something changes, employer and employee interests may be on a collision course.

So, as organizations plot their way to recovery and growth, today's challenges could prove a blessing in disguise since they highlight that employers who focus on engagement can motivate and retain valued employees. However, rather than attempting to force engagement, it is healthier to encourage it by managing change with a human touch. After all, employees will welcome change if, as a result, they work in a positive environment, are part of a winning team, are more capable and empowered, have learned from their experiences and have the tools to be self-managing. Employers who are forward-looking, who *sustain their investment in people* and continue to develop the abilities of their workforce, are likely to maintain their competitiveness and be well-positioned for accelerated growth when the time comes.

This is the time, above all, where the *'values on the wall' need to work in practice*. So even if business leaders cannot provide job security, they can keep people informed and listen to what employees are telling them. While they cannot provide meaning for their employees, as this is individual and subjective, they can offer a clear purpose for their organizations. They can ensure that values-based behaviours are reflected in appraisals and promotion criteria, and that line managers are recognized for their efforts in engaging employees. They can demand that good intent, in the form of work–life balance, wellbeing or diversity policies, is translated into practice, and make every effort to close any 'say-do' gap of their own.

The engagement-performance potential is there – *delivering the results requires a joint effort*. Leaders, managers, HR and employees themselves have key roles to play since employee engagement flows up, down and across the organization. HR needs to focus on building the foundational context elements – building engaging leaders, delivering a compelling employee value proposition or 'deal' and working with line managers to create a culture of engagement. Employees need to step up to the plate, recognizing that in today's market economy they must continue to develop themselves and do a good job for their employers as they do so. Managers and executives need to focus on clarifying expectations, linking the work of their employees to important organizational results, making those linkages clear and providing support. They need to ensure necessary resources are available, and that employees have a say in what they do and how they do it. In short, managers and executives need to focus on helping their employees succeed.

Ensuring mutual benefits (as well as risks) for both organizations and employees is potentially the most sustainable and honest basis for an employment relationship better suited to the demands of today's volatile global economy. Organizations that do this should reap the rewards of a grown-up relationship with their staff, who will want to invest their discretionary effort in helping their organizations succeed.

Checklist

How desirable is your organization as an employer?

- *Connection*:
    - Do employees feel a sense of belonging? Do they connect with the mission, values, and direction of the organization? With others? Their work?
    - Do managers act as credible leaders?
    - Are managers trusted? Do employees believe that the communication from managers is open and honest?
    - Do managers and leaders lead from a values base and create a strong sense of shared purpose?
    - Do employees understand how their work contributes to the organization's performance?
    - Do employees find meaning and purpose in their jobs? Do they have clear line of sight to strategic purpose and the customer?
    - Do people see positive and worthwhile outcomes from their work?
- *Support*:
    - Is there appropriate management support and coaching?
    - Do employees value their relationship with their manager?
    - Can people experience work–life balance? Are there regular workload reviews? Adequate resources and support systems?
    - Are flexible working policies utilized by people at all levels?
    - Is employee development adding to employees' skills?
- *Voice*:
    - Are communications high quality and two-way? Are employees involved and able to participate in decision making?
    - Do employees feel part of the team?
    - Are people fairly treated? Is there a commitment to innovative diversity and work–life balance policies? Appropriate reward?
- *Scope*:
    - How interesting do employees find their work?
    - Do individuals and teams have the power to shape their work and environment to help them to perform at their best?
    - Are employees stretched and challenged in ways that result in personal and professional growth and progress?
    - Are there clear career progression opportunities?

Notes

1 Heger, B (2007) Linking the employment value proposition (EVP) to employee engagement and business outcomes: preliminary findings from a linkage research pilot study, *Organisation Development Journal*, 25 (2) pp 121–33.

2 The Point of Care Foundation Report on NHS Performance (2014) [accessed 30 August 2014] *The Point of Care Foundation* [Online] http://www.engageforsuccess.org/ideas-tools/point-care-foundation-report-nhs-performance/.

3 Murphy, N (2011) Employee engagement survey 2011: increased awareness, but falling levels, *IRS Employment Review*, 28 November.

4 Aon Hewitt [accessed 26 January 2015] 2014 Trends in Global Employee Engagement, *Aon Hewitt* [Online] www.aon.com/.../2014-trends-in-global-employee-engagement-report.pdf.

5 MacLeod, D and Clarke, N (2009), Department for Business, Innovation and Skills (BIS), London.

6 Truss, C *et al* (2013) Employee engagement, organisational performance and individual well-being: exploring the evidence, developing the theory, *The International Journal of Human Resource Management*, 24 (14), Special issue: Employee Engagement.

7 Kahn, WA (1990) Psychological conditions of personal engagement and disengagement at work, *Academy of Management*, 33 (4), December, p 692.

8 Kahn WA and Heaphy ED (2013) Relational contexts of personal engagement at work, in *Employee Engagement in Theory and Practice*, ed C Truss *et al*, Routledge, Abingdon/New York.

9 Schaufeli, WB and Bakker, AB (2004) Job demands, job resources, and their relationship with burnout and engagement: a multi-sample study, *Journal of Organizational Behavior*, 25, pp 293–315.

10 Csikszentmihalyi, M (1990) *Flow: the Psychology of Optimal Experience*, Harper and Row, New York.

11 MacLeod D and Clarke N (2009) Engaging for Success: Enhancing performance through employee engagement, a report to government, Department for Business, Innovation and Skills, London, p 9.

12 Herriot, P and Pemberton, C (1995) *New Deals: The Revolution in Managerial Careers*, Wiley, Chichester.

13 Maslach C and Jackson, SE (1981) The measurement of experienced burnout, *Journal of Occupational Behaviour*, 2, pp 99–113.

14 CIPD and Success Factors (Feb 2013) *Labour Market Outlook*, CIPD, London.

15 MacLeod, D and Clarke, N (2009) [accessed 30 August 2014] Engaging for Success: Enhancing performance through employee engagement, Department for Business, Innovation and Skills, London [Online] http://www.bis.gov.uk/files/file52215.pdf.

16 Aon Hewitt [accessed 26 January 2015] 2014 Trends in Global Employee Engagement, *Aon Hewitt* [Online] www.aon.com/.../2014-trends-in-global-employee-engagement-report.pdf.

17 Kenexa (2012) [accessed 30 August 2014] Perception is Reality: The Importance of Pay Fairness to Employees and Organizations, a 2012/2013 Worktrends (Tm) Report by Kenexa, an IBM Company [Online] http://www.psyccess.com/wp-ontent/uploads/2013/09/Perception-Is-Reality_WorkTrendsReport.pdf.

18 Purcell, J et al (2009) People Management and Performance, Routledge, London.

19 MacLeod, D and Clarke, N (2009) Engaging for Success: Enhancing performance through employee engagement, Department for Business, Innovation and Skills, London.

20 Michelman, P (2004) Methodology: How great managers manage people, Harvard Business School Publishing, Boston.

21 Holbeche, L and Matthews, G (2012) Engaged: Unleashing your organization's potential through employee engagement, Wiley, Chichester; Jossey-Bass, San Francisco.

22 Cattermole, G (2014) The future of employee surveys, in The Future of Engagement, Engage for Success Thought Leadership Series, Institute for Employment Studies and CIPD, London, pp 31–40.

23 Brakely, H (2004) The High-Performance Workforce Study 2004, Research report, Accenture.

24 Beslin, R and Reddin, C (2006) Trust in your organization's future, Communication World, January–February, pp 29–32.

25 Bevan, S et al (2005) Cracking the Performance Code, Research report, The Work Foundation, London.

26 Buytendijk, F (2006) The five keys to building a high-performance organization, Business Performance Management, February, pp 24–30.

27 Ellsworth, RE (2002) Leading with Purpose: The new corporate realities, Stanford University Press, Stanford, CA.

28 Springett, N (2004) The impact of corporate purpose on strategy, organisations and financial performance, Human Resources and Employment Review, 2 (2), pp 117–124.

29 Faragher, J (2013) [accessed 30 August 2014] Employee engagement: the secret of UKRD's success, Personnel Today, 3 May [Online] http://www.personnelto day.com/hr/employee-engagement-the-secret-of-ukrds-success/.

30 Kübler-Ross, E (1969) On Death & Dying, Simon & Schuster/Touchstone, New York.

31 Fisher J (2012) [accessed 30 August 2014] The Process of Transition [Online] http://www.businessballs.com/freepdfmaterials/processoftransitionJF2012.pdf; Fisher's Process of Personal Change [Online] http://www.businessballs.com/personalchangeprocess.htm.

32 Bridges, W (1991) Managing Transitions: Making the most of change, Perseus, Cambridge, MA.

33 Hamel, G and Zanini, M (2014) [accessed 30 November 2014] Build a Change Platform not a Change Program, McKinsey & Company [Online] http://www.mckinsey.com/insights/organization/build_a_change_platform_not_a_change_program.

34 Lucy, D, Poorkavoos, M and Thompson, A (2014) *Building Resilience: Five key capabilities*, Roffey Park, Horsham.

35 The Conference Board [accessed 30 August 2014] [Online] https://www.conference-board.org/webcasts/ondemand/webcastdetail.cfm?webcastid=2845.

36 Business Bites, *London Metro*, 19 December 2012.

Change and transformation

Change is an inevitable and ongoing aspect of the marketplace that organizations have to succeed in. The speed of change is accelerating, global knowledge is growing exponentially, and disruptive megatrends including demographic shifts and digitization are shaping new competitive agendas. In today's dynamic, complex and global environment, the changes many companies are experiencing are outpacing their ability to respond, with new competitors often emerging from different places, and new regulations and demands being put in place. New approaches for capturing value by innovation (for instance by business model innovation) are becoming mainstream. 'Sense and respond' is the new change imperative.

Conventional efficiency-oriented sequential change management tools and processes appear increasingly out of step with the reality of today's world. Nevertheless some change will still be driven 'top-down' in pursuit of new business opportunities or to respond to external demands.

In this chapter we look at how 'planned' approaches to change can be implemented more effectively and learn from the lessons of failed change efforts about how to mobilize people to want to make the changes needed for business success, since willingness to change cannot be mandated from the top. We will focus on the need both to engage stakeholders and also to help people navigate change successfully and so become more resilient. We consider how approaches to change can flex and move from being sequential and slow towards agile and iterative, thus allowing organizations to change better than the competition and sustain performance over time.

In the next chapter we shall consider how to build an agile culture and create a receptive organizational context for innovation, change and high performance. As discussed previously, what is needed is a real-time, socially constructed approach to change to develop a 'change-able' organizational culture where employees are empowered to innovate, initiate and implement needed changes.

In particular we look at:

- types of change;
- stakeholder engagement;
- mobilizing people for change: 'pull' rather than 'push';
- managing the transition.

Types of change

Firms implement various types of change to deliver their strategic ambitions. Along the spectrum from the small-scale transactional change to transformational change, planning is often a feature of organizational change efforts. These different types of change have varying degrees of complexity and potential benefits and risks.

Transactional, incremental

First there are small-scale transactional changes that typically involve making continuous improvements in an area of work. Then there are incremental changes that are aimed at securing more significant business improvements but within the current business model. Such changes are generally within the 'control' of people who work in the areas concerned and are often initiated by employees themselves. While these tend to be less complex types of change to manage, they can still produce emotional and other reactions from staff who may be unwilling to adopt a new piece of technology, or work in an open-plan environment or be required to share data that they previously 'owned'.

Radical, transformational

Transformational change impacts on all, or significant, parts of the business and is often aimed at changing the business model. Typically initiated at the top, since power is concentrated there, change programmes tend to be endorsed and plotted before launch. Large-scale organization redesign efforts are often planned by consultancies on behalf of executive teams. These types of change offer the greatest potential for major gains or losses. For instance, mergers and acquisitions offer potential gains – such as economies of scale and access to new markets – but these must be offset against the potential losses of key talent, 'corporate memory' and valuable intellectual property; or major customers desert brands if customer service levels change; or the legacy of redundancies leaves remaining staff mistrustful of management. So while the potential benefits should be targets for change there should be an equal focus on mitigating the risks of the downsides of change.

Why should 'managed' change be so difficult? As we discussed in Chapter 2, the main reasons for the high change-failure rate relate to

traditional over-mechanistic approaches to change that fail t(
cient account of the human responses to change. The result: v
and under-realization of potential benefits of change. To avoid
ful effects Abrahamson advocates pacing – interspersing rad
with periods of low-level transactional change in order to ensu
between natural industry cycles and investor and customer horiz(_, as well
as employee readiness for change.[1]

Towards more agile approaches to change

While there is still a place for large-scale change, reorganization and transformation focused on specific initiatives can take years. However, today's
marketplace changes so fast that there are likely to be many complex overlapping changes, continual adjustments and redesigns. The challenge for
leaders is to perceive what is changing in the environment; to work out
the capabilities required to compete and what needs to be done to build
these. The agile approaches to the implementation of projects (discussed in
Chapter 5) can inform the development of change projects. These involve
continuous stakeholder engagement, experimenting and piloting, and short
cycles of activity (iterations) incorporating feedback from users that forms
the basis for adapting or refining the finished product.

So the key to successful change lies in the simultaneous activation of
many different aspects of change beyond the change initiative itself so
that adaptation from within becomes part of the culture. One of the key
models used to guide these efforts is Galbraith's Star Model™, which
aligns strategy, work processes, management processes, reward, systems
and structure.[2] This requires building capabilities within the organization – 'bottom-up' and 'top-down' – for self-regulation, innovation,
engagement and high-impact interventions that accelerate change by
stimulating local initiatives and the creation of connected networks for
learning and sharing. An agile organization design flows from strategy and
will encompass work group design, team structure and accountabilities,
management practices, systems support and aligning reward to agile ways
of working and key outcomes. It is about building an agile infrastructure
rather than managing a specific change.

In initiating a major change we need to:

- Identify what needs to change and why, developing a vision (the 'to
be') and a change approach.
- Identify who will be affected and how.
- Be clear about desired deliverables and initial milestones and develop
plans to achieve these.
- Assess change impact and business readiness for the desired change
(the 'as is') and identify actions to address these. So along with
developing a methodology statement, specifying assumptions,

carrying out a change risk assessment, budget and existing governance arrangements, the organization also needs a Plan B or C in order to address the major change impact/business readiness issues identified upfront and to deal with emergent issues that surface as the change effort proceeds.

Once a go/no go decision has been made, agile leaders understand that they must be seen to champion the change effort and provide active change leadership, aligning people around the vision.

Stakeholder engagement

Maintaining the support of stakeholders throughout is key to successful implementation. Especially for a large-scale change effort, an engagement plan will be needed that identifies the key stakeholders, including employees, whose support will be needed for the intended change to succeed and builds their commitment to and sponsorship of the change. This is about building the case and support for change, focusing on the benefits to be realized by change.

Stakeholders are individuals and groups who are impacted by the change and/or who can influence the outcome. These might include specific stakeholder segments, such as decision makers with governance responsibilities and those who support them. They might be influencers who can affect the course and outcome of the work, even stop it. They may be internal or external to the organization. They may be providers – suppliers, partners who may bring resources and skills you need or customers – who will use directly or indirectly what you deliver. Above all they will include the staff whose work may change as a result of the change effort and whose willingness to deliver the desired benefits will impact on the success of the change effort. In some workplaces employees are represented collectively by trade unions or staff councils.

Stereotypically at the outset stakeholders will vary in their attitude towards the proposed change. Some may be supporters, who understand the reason for the change and are on board with what is proposed. Some may be allies who will support if encouraged to do so. Some may be undecided fence-sitters. Others may be unpredictable 'loose cannons', or opponents of your agenda or even adversaries, opposed to both you and your agenda. There may also be groups of latent 'bedfellows' who may support your agenda but do not yet know or trust you. Finally there may be a voiceless majority who are affected but have little influence or power to stop you in your tracks.

Clearly understanding where specific groups of stakeholders or key individuals may be coming from helps you as change leader to identify influencing approaches that may work to more specifically gain their support. For instance, middle managers are often marginalized during the process of change, sandwiched between senior management who generally initiate major change projects and staff who have to make the changes. By involving managers in identifying the benefits of the changes to them and the organization, they will understand what is being gained – what a 'successful' change will look like – and can more genuinely and enthusiastically communicate the changes to staff and engage them in the change process.

So before developing a change plan it is important to win the support of key stakeholders. This is likely to involve many conversations and discussions aimed at getting people thinking about what better could look like, about potential benefits as well as potential risks of 'to be' and 'as is' operational states. Being open about the potential risks and challenges and dealing with concerns, taking baseline measurements of the 'as is' versus the 'to be', all help build the case for change. Beyond the support of a powerful sponsor, successful change efforts typically need a strong alliance of like-minded change champions who help to drive the change effort to fruition.

CASE STUDY   RBS Choice

I am grateful to Tim Yendell, Head of Workplace – RBS Choice, Design and Moves at the Royal Bank of Scotland (RBS) and Andrea Doel, Strategy Manager, Flexible Working at RBS team for this case study.

Historically RBS Choice, which now features both location and working pattern flexibility, could be seen parochially as being primarily concerned with reducing the property portfolio. Indeed, a previous iteration of the initiative (2006–08) was focused only on optimizing the use of office space. Tim Yendell has led RBS Choice from the outset, and although a property specialist, he wanted Choice to be about more than just space. In 2008, during a period of significant upheaval, a change of thinking started to emerge within the bank and, by 2010, questions were being asked about how organizations would come out of the financial crisis and what shape they would need to be in to be successful in the future. There was also a lot of discussion about the people agenda.

Tim recognized that in order to equip the bank for the future, RBS Choice should be designed to achieve flexibility in ways that worked both for its customers and its employees. If RBS Choice was to realize benefits across the bank, the programme would need to be group-wide, lifting it above the siloed divisional level and getting broader support across the whole organization. He therefore set out to build support for the idea that RBS Choice should be labelled not as IT or property-led, but as a collaborative, cross-divisional initiative that blends HR policies, technology and property solutions.

To win the support of the most senior people in the group was crucial, in particular the strong sponsorship of the board chairperson. Tim set out to engage the leadership of the various businesses within RBS so he developed an 'influencing network' of the group's corporate services, HR and property portfolio strategy directors, who had worked hard to gain support for Choice from their own broad networks within the organization, creating a groundswell of support. For Tim, engaging these sponsors and champions was a question of 'doing your homework, tuning in to things people are interested in, recognizing and understanding their business imperatives'. He also saw that engagement needed to be handled by the 'best voice' in the team, for example, having the HR director convey the message to the HR community.

An important early step was to involve these stakeholders in research looking at the bigger picture around the changing global context of work. The primary driver was to understand the shifts taking place in the ways people were working and how technology is transforming working practices and workplaces. As Tim points out:

> It was important to think about these issues at an organizational level, rather than at a divisional or functional level. It was a question of working out what this might mean for the way we ran or changed the bank. Are we sufficiently prepared for the future? What would be the impact if we don't address these issues? Will we still be able to attract the best to our organization?

In addition to conversations within RBS, research took place with other organizations and sectors that had been through similar change journeys. These concluded that successful organizations of the future will be kinetic and highly networked. Technology is a key enabler, with mobile devices and the ability to work remotely supporting flexible ways of working. Looking at the pipeline for emerging technology and thinking about trends, such as people increasingly using their own devices, allowed Tim's team to discuss how Choice could help integrate this in reality – not treating technology in isolation, but in the context of building a new work culture of transparency, openness and trust.

To address the challenge, Tim brought together an integrated team of specialists from HR, IT, Communications and Security and Risk, in addition to property specialists. While all these functions have different characteristics and expertise, what they had in common was a desire to find a way to add value, while the world around them was changing.

Developing a stakeholder engagement plan

Tim Yendell argues that, in order to move the organization forward in both process and behavioural terms, you have to create campaigns that raise people's awareness of the need for change and stimulate action at the behavioural and structural level. This means being creative – and deliberate – to get the message out and make it visible to the whole organization. One of the fundamentals of this communication is how you tell the story. By sharing real-life examples and case studies of people's experiences of working flexibly, and the impacts this has had on both their personal and work lives, you can bring the story alive.

In developing a communication strategy it is important to identify who is losing what, and what is being lost, as well as what will continue. Then it is about working out the messages for specific stakeholder audiences, the media that will be used, the frequency of messaging and how feedback and change can be monitored. In terms of messages, for instance, the questions to ask are:

- Do these messages speak to their issues and concerns?
- Do they engage the heart and the mind?
- Do they create wins/build support?
- Do they support the movement we want to achieve?

With respect to media it is a question of working out:

- What media works best for this stakeholder?
- What media works best for the messages I need to give?
- What do I want to achieve through communication?

With respect to frequency and feedback:

- How often will I need to engage this stakeholder?
- How will I feed back and monitor change?
- How can I create genuine dialogue?

The acid test for effective communication is that it is: 'fast and honest; tell it how it is'.

We shall return to this story later in this chapter.

Mobilizing people for change – 'pull' rather than 'push'

In order to get 'on board' with a change movement, people need to be personally 'moved' or mobilized towards a shared goal; they need to want to join. If the change is large scale and radical this requires lots of people to be mobilized. As we have discussed previously, genuine buy-in is the product of involvement, not thanks to a tell-and-sell by top management.

Some of the key principles include:

- Involve those impacted early.
- Listen to them and understand what they are saying.
- Keep the conversations going... explore together what different could look like.
- Focus relentlessly on values and constantly demonstrate why they matter.
- Expect new things to emerge – insights, data, priorities – that will require you to adjust your plan.

Building resilience through change is less about increasing the pressure on people to comply with the change requirements and more about a 'pull' approach to unfreezing, based as much as possible on dialogue in which people engage with the change, understand why change is needed and start to let go of the past in order to make room for the new. A contemporary model for change management, AITA, works on the assumption that for change to succeed people must be *aware* of the need for change before they are likely to be *interested* enough to *trial* it, after which point they might *accept* it. As Heimer Rathbone points out, AITA plays particularly well into the generation Y mentality that asks, 'What's in it for me?'[3]

Change on a large scale can only be achieved by building a compelling case and working with employees to create a clear path forward (see Figure 10.1) – one that supports the mission of the firm. This involves starting with *why*?

FIGURE 10.1 The eight key activities for successful mobilization

Communication is essential – 'you cannot overcommunicate' is a phrase used by an experienced acquisition manager who learned the hard way the importance of being as open as possible even though there may be real constraints around commercially sensitive information. The information will 'leak' anyway. For instance, one CEO was surprised to hear that a remark he had made at a private dinner the night before had been tweeted and was public knowledge in his own organization the following morning. So it is better to be proactive in communicating what people want to know – when, or just in advance of when, they want to know it.

There is a wide variety of formats available that provide space for communication, participation and learning, such as:

- Town hall meetings where large groups are given the news and invited to ask how the company-wide shift will affect them.
- 'Hackathons' – online shared spaces to discuss and develop thinking and practice around a shared idea.
- Videos, tweets, blogs.
- Function-wide meetings that include senior management.
- Internal large-scale change events in which 80–120 people receive presentations and break into a sequence of parallel team workshops on various issues. They might participate in a 'World Café' to showcase results and continue discussions and conduct a 'poster session marketplace' that summarizes the 'wisdom of the internal crowd'.
- Reflection workshops in which ideas are collected and rapid prototypes of individual elements of change are discussed.
- Virtual 'jam sessions', ie a website set up for a two- to five-day period where anyone can post comments, responses, suggestions and concerns.
- Physical or virtual 'fireside conversations' with senior management on the case for change, the route that is being followed, early successes and learning points.
- Bringing people face-to-face with the customer or the service user – hearing first-hand the impact of what the organization does.

Leaders need to create a strong strategic narrative that creates the context for change by identifying the organization's adaptive challenge – the *why?* – and framing the key questions and issues that the change effort must address. This provides the rationale for the change and gives employees a strong sense about the purpose of the organization, about the history of the organization and what is good about its past, as well as an idea of the market forces at work today that necessitate change and the responsibility people must take in shaping the future. While perceptions of threat can provide a 'burning platform', the main emphasis should be on the opportunities to be gained.

It is important to be clear about the 'non-negotiables' as well as what people will gain by the change. At the same time it is essential to be honest about the negative aspects. Of course what most people want to know when a major change is announced is: 'Will I have a job?' Even if the answer to that question is still unknown, it is important to communicate the time frame within which such questions will be answered. People should be given opportunities to surface and name feelings and concerns. Management's task is to listen. Sometimes there is a tendency for people to assume that an organizational change effort will affect everything with which they are familiar and value. This is not usually the case in practice, so being specific about the scope of the initiative can help people to get the change in perspective. In communicating how endings are a part of life, the past should be respected while reinforcing the reasons for change. It is also important to explain how people can get involved and help them understand the role they can play.

The importance of involving people

Organizations with low receptive context might experience the same challenges and learn about the same innovations, but lack the cognitive, behavioural and emotional resilience required for taking on board new approaches. If participants do not believe a change initiative will benefit them, are opposed to it, are pressured into using it, or do not think it is a good approach, they will modify it gradually, use it ineffectively and the change initiative may ultimately fail. Any attempt by top management to change the culture by diktat is likely to provoke a response within the informal system but perhaps not the response intended by top management.

From a different sector – higher education – the following case study describes the planned introduction of new organizational structures to enable greater flexibility. The main protagonists in implementing this change – Philip Waters, Secretary and Registrar, and Naomi Holloway, HR Director, worked closely with other members of senior management and used a high-involvement change process.

CASE STUDY   Building agile structures at the
University of Hertfordshire[4]

The University of Hertfordshire aims to develop more agile organizational forms to enable it to become more flexible and responsive to the challenges of the current context. Under the previous vice chancellor (VC), the faculties were made up of academic schools, each with a Head of School, which operated as strategic business units (SBUs). Under the new VC, a review revealed that the faculty structure could be acting as a blockage to flexibility. The VC announced the overall change in July 2011 and a project was set up to remove the faculty structure and locate staff either in professional SBUs or academic schools. Importantly at the outset a commitment was given to no redundancies as a result of this change. A project management group, chaired by the secretary and registrar, was set up to oversee the change programme. HR Director Naomi Holloway is a key player in the 'Agile Project' management group. A major change to the six schools within the Faculty of Health and Human Science was amalgamated into the Agile Project.

New working practices

Eight work streams were established, one of which was 'owned' by the VC and was to determine the top management structure. Other work streams focused on academic structures in the schools and centre, faculty administration, governance, technical staff arrangements, procurement, school management structures and the health and human science change.

As well as simplifying structures, the aim was to ensure that academic areas are professionally run and not to lose sight of the fact that these are academic units whose primary purpose is to educate students, as well as coordinate activities with the outside world. All academic staff must be expert practitioners, undertaking teaching and research, even if they are in management roles. Thus an Associate Dean Research must be a proactive researcher in his or her own right, spending for instance 30 per cent of their time on research and 70 per cent on research management. The intention was to enable academic staff to release time, for instance by providing better administrative support and resolving communication issues. Under the new structure, academic schools would be larger as they absorb administrative staff who were at a faculty level. With respect to support structures, each school would have its own administrative and, if needed, technical support unit. HR, Finance, Marketing, Estates and IT would provide a 'hub and spoke' service through a matrix structure.

A high-involvement change process

A common challenge was how to get communication right. From the outset there was a management commitment to working through issues with staff; key to the success of the new structures was adhering to the values of openness and transparency. A staff survey in 2010 had revealed that staff and trades unions wanted earlier involvement in change projects. When announcing the proposed change, the VC invited any staff who wanted to be involved to connect with the change team. HR provided a vital functional service, leading on the consultative approach and working out the 'how' of mobilizing staff involvement, for instance by putting interested staff in touch with the work stream groups to give evidence or to make recommendations. HR completed feedback loops by going back to staff to say: 'You've told us that you wanted more involvement; here's how you can be involved…'

Union representatives, especially from those areas most affected, were involved in the whole change project from the outset and had an active position in each work stream group, including reviewing the overall blueprints for the organization. Union representatives were given the option of not endorsing a recommendation coming out of a work stream group and such areas became a focus for subsequent formal consultation. HR encouraged work stream leaders to hold sessions with affected staff, advising them on various ways (using OD methods) that they could do this. A 170-page consultation document for the trade unions and all staff was produced after the initial work stream phase and the subsequent consultation period showed that many of the potential areas for conflict were resolved early on through trade union and staff involvement in developing the change plans.

The participative nature of the development of this change programme helped to ease the implementation of the redesign, though it was not without its own challenges. On the whole, people came to recognize that, given the university's strong financial position, the project was not about reducing headcount but to better focus the university's efforts on teaching, research and business effectiveness. Indeed, one trade union representative commented that the involvement process was a potential example of best practice.

Evidence of the success of the engagement process is found in the fact that over 200 staff were involved in focus groups or working groups and were therefore directly engaged in determining the recommendations coming out of the work stream groups. Furthermore, during the consultation phase (three weeks), every affected area held face-to-face briefings for affected staff and over 100 staff provided written feedback on the consultation document.

HR played a key role in helping to manage uncertainty, especially for the leaders of the changes being delivered, many of whom were directly affected. In many ways HR's role was to encourage the team to keep going with the participative approach despite setbacks and, after five months, there was a great deal of staff involvement and engagement. The new structure went 'live' from September 2012.

Culture change

The culture change that the new structure represents is important. People have come to appreciate the need for flexibility; there is a focus on matrix working, especially across the pro-vice-chancellor portfolios of research, international, enterprise and student experience; the 'hub and spoke' model (centralized core and decentralized units) is strengthened through academic experts for the key portfolios being centrally located; and heads of schools have become fully autonomous and responsible heads of strategic business units (SBUs). Similarly, equal weight is now being given to the different strategic portfolios. This is shifting what in university circles is traditional practice; for example, academic promotion to date has been more focused on either a management career or a research career. Now, as Naomi Holloway points out: 'We are working hard to ensure that promotion to the highest level can be achieved not only through research but also through a teaching or commercial path as well.'

These changes reflect the recognition that academic staff time is an invaluable resource of the university and that academic staff expertise should be focused on providing an excellent student experience. Similarly, it is about adding value in professional services by reducing the administrative burden. Thus, the aim is to value staff for what they do best, in a way that should help everyone.

HR's contribution

As Naomi Holloway reflects, on the whole the process of involvement has worked well. The major challenge for HR was to think through the likely implications for senior staff such as deans, pro-vice-chancellors (PVCs) and heads of school. They were expected to both lead change, while also being affected by it, and in the new system are held more directly to account. So HR has worked closely with these leaders, helping them to make wise decisions and getting their buy-in to further change. It is about balancing support for individuals with collective programme leadership.

HR's role during the transition was also to keep the VC informed of how the implementation of the changes was going and about how people were feeling so that, thus informed, the VC could play a part in visibly leading the change. It was also about keeping the unions on board, and building on the collaborative best practice that HR and the unions had established. Most of all, HR's role was what Naomi describes as 'almost like a constant translation job', closing the feedback loops with staff so that they knew their voice had been heard: 'Because of what you've told us, we've done things differently.'

As this case illustrates, it is vital to get those people directly involved in the change process who are going to be most affected by it.

Managing the transition

Whatever the change, the transition towards the 'new' involves dealing with endings, addressing the emotional side of change and helping people with beginnings.

Dealing with endings

Letting go of things that employees value can be traumatic and people tend to 'hang on' to the past for as long as possible. Sometimes it may be necessary to dramatize endings, with symbolic acts showing that some aspect of the past is over. For instance, when one high-street bank was taken over by another, on the day the acquired branches were relabelled with the new company logo staff were given a party and allowed to take away memorabilia with the old firm's name on. It was only some time later that staff in the acquiring firm realized how much life had changed for them too. They regretted that this particular ending had not been recognized by management so that the staff had been able to 'mark' the transition.

Addressing the emotional side of change means 'being there' for people, ensuring people have many opportunities to talk, ask questions and discuss their feelings. Middle and front-line managers in particular should be kept in the loop so that they can play their part in keeping people focused and feeling supported. They should also be kept up to date about progress – via visits, weekly meetings, the intranet, website, CEO blogs and town hall meetings. The emphasis should be on providing people with what they need to know rather than masses of additional data.

During the transition

Especially if people's jobs are to go, 'survivor' employees may feel a sense of guilt and resentment towards management. Managers and leaders need to be consistent with employees, communicate concern, acknowledge what people are going through, monitor performance (and stress) levels and ensure that issues are dealt with rapidly and transparently. And, of course, redundancies should be handled through as fair and transparent a process as possible.

Typically people become overwhelmed with work during a transition, especially if they are picking up the workloads of departing colleagues. Managers can make the transition easier for staff by installing temporary systems and helping staff to identify the key priorities that must be addressed and what other work (if any) can be stopped, even providing additional support if necessary. Where technology is involved, help desks and super-user support should be available to staff. Relevant training helps to prepare people for new ways of working. Intragroup connections should be strengthened so that people can share ideas and learning. Customers in particular should experience only benefits and none of the downsides of change, so providing good support to front-line staff is vital to ensure they can maintain business as usual even while things are changing.

Leaders in particular need to show visible leadership during the transition, encouraging people and creating energy around the organization's mission and vision. Bridges talks of the '4Ps' – communicating *purpose*, helping people *picture* what changes will look like and feel like, setting out a *plan* for implementing the outcome and showing people how they can *participate* in shaping the future.[5] Hamel talks about how: 'Managers/leaders must leverage the power of shared values and aspiration while loosening the straightjacket of rules and strictures.'[6] Thus they can help to create a positive climate for change by setting out key principles and parameters and empowering others. People should be actively involved in finding creative solutions to emerging problems.

New symbols may need to be created to reinforce the new beginning and help people make sense of an often disparate set of change initiatives, where it may be hard to see what difference they are making. If a change effort is branded, it needs to reflect the new 'business as becoming' and irrelevant change activity should be suspended. Both Bridges and Kotter talk of the importance of early successes – what Kotter calls 'quick wins' to encourage people and help them feel that change effort is worthwhile.[7] These early successes should be celebrated, the achievements of individuals and teams recognized and success stories circulated. As Kotter suggests, the risk is that people may think of these successes as marking the end of the change effort. Instead Kotter advises that the early successes should deliberately be used as a springboard for some of the tougher change work that still needs to follow.

Towards the new

As people start to emerge from the transition, managers and HR need to watch out for people struggling to get to grips with the new system or ways of working and reverting to the old. In some cases it may be better to 'burn your boats', ie abandon the old system altogether so that people are encouraged to learn the new system rapidly. HR can help to provide training in relevant skills that prepare people for new roles. Managers may need to provide plenty of coaching and mentoring, facilitating conversations and getting people involved. Staff who have adapted well to the new should be encouraged to act as peer coaches to their colleagues until competence is developed all round.

Managers need to emphasize learning through change as a form of continuous improvement. So it is important to help people to reflect back on how far the change effort has come, the desired benefits and what has been achieved so far. People should feel a sense of purpose and progress, but the message should be that the change journey continues, and so does the communication. As people grow in capability and confidence they start to see the personal benefits of the new approach and develop greater resilience.

Measuring success at RBS Choice

Finally we need to review learning and ensure that new positive practices are embedded. RBS Choice is able to satisfy both the company needs (savings) and employee needs and requirements (reconciling work and personal life) through the implementation of agile working policies (or flexible working). Success is being measured in a number of ways:

- Customer satisfaction.
- Employee engagement: the RBS annual employee opinion survey 'Your Feedback' – which shows how people are feeling about the organization – now has additional questions about flexible working.
- Projects: post-implementation reviews are benchmarked against pre-project measurement.
- Cost reduction from property savings or recruitment costs.

Win-win outcomes

As we saw in Chapter 9, the typical human emotional responses to change are not to be underestimated. So if people are to embrace change as the norm, they must have a strong sense of the 'what's in it for me' (WIFM) factor. The changing 'deal' must feel equitable. They must be involved in helping to shape the changes and be equipped with the skills and approaches they need to deal positively with ongoing change. It is about building a social movement for positive change, improvement and innovation.

This win-win approach seems to be key to people's willingness to keep on changing and even initiating change. For instance, RBS Choice, originally initiated in 2006 with the aim of driving efficiencies in real estate, is today a global enabler for culture change, evolving the workplace to make it a more collaborative, exciting space. It is geared to serving customers and developing and supporting new, more flexible ways of working, with the work shaped around customers and individuals. This flexible working culture is enabling the organization to respond to the needs of their customers with agility and, at the same time, provides employees with influence and control over their work–life balance. It is nothing short of a holistic programme to future-proof the bank's ways of working within a changing context.

In summary, as a change leader Tim Yendell of RBS Choice argues that a holistic approach to building a more flexible working culture brings real benefits, and that change agents can make a positive difference when they work together. In his experience it is important to:

- Be absolutely clear why you are doing this and what your key drivers are. For Tim this was about customers and employees.
- Have a compelling story and a range of solutions.

- Surround yourself with a professional and articulate team who are as passionate about your goals as you are.

- Find senior sponsors who feel strongly about your initiative and understand how you can support their business imperatives.

- Create a common sense of purpose – it is about being successful together.

- Trust the people around you.

- Carefully plan and deliver engagement and communications strategies that get the best outcomes.

- Move the campaign on – use social media and networks to grow the community of interest.

- Embed the benefits within the organization so that it outlasts the initiative and becomes 'just what we do'.

And don't expect overnight success. As Tim points out: 'It's been a long journey, but it's great to see that we're really making a difference now.'

Conclusion

Since change is an inherent characteristic of an agile organization, it is in everyone's interest to develop the organizational and personal capacity to change in such a way as to minimize the downsides of change and to maximize the benefits. Change is rarely easy, but a successful change experience can help to build employee resilience and the capability of the organization to embrace change as the norm. Key to leading successful change is to gain and maintain stakeholder support, including staff support, and *build momentum for change*.

Change should be done *with*, not *to* employees if at all possible. So valuing people, giving employees a chance to be involved and have voice, to have the right support, learn new skills and develop greater scope are likely to reinforce employees' connection and engagement with the organization. This means being open, transparent and well-targeted in communications, having an *effective process for change* that everyone understands and *reviewing and learning* at each stage of the change implementation.

Leaders and managers should keep faith with employees and provide the support and resources people need to make the transition. At enterprise level, collaborative management – trades union forums, as well as works councils – can become drivers for improvement and innovation through trust, shared commitment to mutually beneficial outcomes and willingness to address barriers to sustainable change.

Checklist

How well is change 'managed' in your organization?

- How much change is necessary in your organization?
- How much change is imposed top-down? How much are employees encouraged to create 'bottom-up' changes to benefit the customer?
- How much can the pace of change be modulated/controlled?
- What has been the effect of the last major change in your organization? What did you learn from this change?
- How conducive to change is the organizational climate?
- How clear are people about the rationale for change? How much do they 'buy in'?
- What help can be provided to help people to face up to change?
- How effectively is the 'employee voice' heard and responded to? How two-way are communications?
- What training or other development will people need to prepare them for new roles?

Notes

1 Abrahamson, E (2000) Change without pain, *Harvard Business Review*, July/August, pp 75–79.

2 For details of a more agile approach to organization design, see Cheung-Judge, M-Y and Holbeche, LS (2015) *Organization Development: A practitioner's guide for OD and HR*, Kogan Page, London.

3 Heimer Rathbone, CL (2012) *Ready For Change? Transition through turbulence to reformation and transformation*, Palgrave Macmillan, Basingstoke, p 4.

4 This case study first appeared in Holbeche, LS (2012) [accessed 19 January 2015] Changing Times in UK Universities, *Universities Human Resources* [Online] http://www.uhr.ac.uk/uploadedfiles/Documents/Changing%20 times%20in%20UK%20universities%20%28extended%20version%29.pdf.

5 Bridges, W (1991) *Managing Transitions: Making the most of change*, Perseus, Cambridge, MA.

6 Hamel, G (2009) Moonshots for management, *Harvard Business Review*, **91**, February, pp 1–10.

7 Bridges, W (1991) *Managing Transitions: Making the most of change*, Perseus, Cambridge, MA; Kotter, J (1995) Leading change: why transformation efforts fail, *Harvard Business Review*, March–April, pp 59–67.

Building a change-able culture

As we have discussed throughout this book, nothing is more constant or pervasive than change. So these days the leader's job is less about designing a change programme and more about building a change-able culture – one that allows anyone to initiate change, recruit co-workers, suggest solutions and launch experiments. We have considered how company-wide conversations can amplify weak signals and support the complex problem solving required to address core management challenges.

In Chapter 3 we considered some features of a 'change-able' culture. This is akin to the 'learning organization' concept defined by Senge and others, since experimentation, innovation and learning are characteristic of a change-able culture too.[1] We also have previously considered the importance of the 'receptive context' in which a particular group or organization 'naturally' takes on change and new ideas. Organizations with a high receptive context are seen as ready for change; they can quickly adopt innovative concepts in order to meet the challenges they experience. In a dynamically stable, change-able culture, people are ready and willing to embrace change as the norm; to innovate, learn and produce high performance even while things are changing around them. In other words, in a change-able culture change is viewed as dynamic stability.

In this chapter we consider if, and how, a change-able culture can be built. We look at:

- Can culture be 'changed'?
- Taking stock of culture.
- Defining what 'good' looks like.
- Building emotional energy for change.

- Building a social movement.
- Aligning management and leadership.

Can culture be 'changed'?

There is a good deal of debate about whether organizations *have* a culture, or *are* cultures. I would argue that organizations both *have* and *are* cultures, often made up of many subcultures – such as functional, gender- or age-based – that are changing all the time anyway. Viewing organizations through the lens of complexity suggests that organizations as complex adaptive systems are embedded within other systems within the broader external context and co-evolve with them, which requires constant adaptation, experimentation and pruning. These practices are transmitted by people working within the culture to others who become acculturated to see things the same way. Edgar Schein defines culture as:

> A pattern of shared basic assumptions that the group learned as it solved its problems of external adaptation and internal integration, that has worked well enough to be considered valid and, therefore, to be taught to new members as the correct way to perceive, think, and feel in relation to those problems.[2]

There are many debates about whether or not it is possible to deliberately change organizational culture and I have written extensively elsewhere on this subject.[3] When thinking about changing culture it is tempting to think about changing behaviour, yet behaviour is always partly conditioned by the values, processes, structures, systems and routines that surround it. And while there is a fixed and definable set of rules for pattern formulation, any small change in initial conditions can result in huge changes in resulting behaviour. Even tinkering with just one aspect of culture can be enough to send a ripple effect through other parts of the system.

Of course cultural shifts can be prompted by many things – the arrival of a new CEO, external demands and dramatic events such as the failure of a business model. In any case cultural shifts can and do emerge over time as part of the 'natural' process of adaption, especially within subgroups and networks. Writers from the Human Dynamics Group who view change through the lens of complex adaptive systems consider that individuals and organizations identify and shape emerging patterns in their relationships, behaviours and interactions. Some complex systems exhibit features that are referred to as 'self-organization' or 'emergence'.

According to chaos theory, culture is reducible to two simple concepts: patterns and rules. Under certain conditions, ordered, regular patterns of behaviours or events can be seen to arise out of seemingly random, erratic and turbulent processes. Simple rules are spoken or unspoken guides for behaviours across a complex adaptive system. Chaos and complexity theories also suggest that people operating within the system are free agents who influence each other. Power dynamics can change and new villains, heroes and heroines can become the focus of stories around the grapevine teaching people what is new, and what success and failure look like.

I would argue that culture change can be effected deliberately, to some extent at least, but traditional change management is unlikely to be effective in producing the shifts in 'hearts and minds', behaviour, attitude, norms, working practices and other aspects of culture. Any cultural shift, no matter how well intended, will not take root unless it is accepted by the people who operate it. In practice, any change among and between individuals and their patterns of connections and interpretations changes the culture. In that sense culture change cannot be imposed from above.

The most powerful processes of change occur at the individual and group level, an area that traditional bureaucratic structures often struggle with. Quade and Holladay talk of 'dynamical change' that is unpredictable, characterized by 'multiple forces acting in unpredictable ways, generating surprising outcomes'.[4] For this type of change the concern is to engage people in a new way and build adaptive capacity within the system. Dynamical leaders can see and influence patterns in their systems, understand the dynamics at play, utilize differences for maximum capacity building and move towards sustainable outcomes. They actively work with adaptive alignment to give sufficient structure and stability and build generative interconnections throughout the system – what Kelly calls 'swarmware' – so that local leaders can freely exchange knowledge and resources to make things happen.[5]

For instance, one organization uses a 'Wiki' social networking site to encourage people to contribute ideas while others use workshops, focus groups, interviews and large group events aimed at engaging people in strengthening organizational competitiveness. Increasingly, therefore, there are debates about whether the notion of 'managing' culture change should be replaced by providing a 'platform' for change.

The Star Model™

Arguably, too, 'culture' can be shifted to some extent by altering organizational artefacts such as policies, routines and structures, what Kelly calls 'clockware'. The Galbraith Star Model™ suggests some key 'levers' that managers can control that can affect employee behaviour. Indeed, according to the Star Model™ culture and behaviours are the result of 'design policies' in five specific categories.[6] The first is strategy, which determines direction. The second is structure, which determines the location of decision-making power. Thirdly, processes have to do with the flow of information; they are the means of responding to information technologies. Fourthly, rewards provide motivation and incentives for desired behaviour. The fifth category of the model is made up of policies relating to people (human resource policies), which influence employees' mindsets and skills. The selection and development of the 'right' people – in alignment with the other policies – allows the organization to operate at maximum efficiency. The assumption is that by targeting the desired behaviour, managers can influence the organization's performance as well as its culture.

However, efforts to innovate within the formal system (involving hierarchies) can be aided or undermined by interactions within the 'swarmware' – informal or 'shadow system' involving friends and colleagues.[7] The shadow system includes many 'opinion formers' at all levels who are usually well-networked and are often more influential than top management. In the corporate ecosystem, power is typically assumed to reside largely with the board and executive team and cascade down – the converse of what is needed if a highly mobile and distributed work style is required. Moreover, organizations are usually rife with micropolitics and interests vested in maintaining the status quo. Successfully shifting culture is largely a factor of how willing people are to change their own behaviours and how they influence others.

Let's assume that you are seeking to create a culture more conducive to innovation. Any attempt to shift cultural practice and build new, more useful habits and routines needs to take account of, and embrace, the social nature of innovation and change. After all, a brilliant new product is not usually the property of a single individual or 'skunkwork' group who may have generated the original idea; further creative development and enhancement of the idea also occurs during local implementation and as the idea spreads within the organization.[8] As the proliferation of ideas and learning via social media illustrates, this capacity for creative thought via connections is an inherent ability that we all possess.[9] The culture shifts through the conversations people have, the stories they tell and the new routines that emerge. Thus new sources of value are created through generative relations.

Changing culture is likely to require changing the conditions in which people operate. Therefore to create favourable conditions for new behaviour and practices to emerge, it is important to lead from the edge working with 'clockware' and 'swarmware' in tandem. It is about paying attention to, and seeking to influence, both formal and informal systems, going for multiple actions at the fringes and letting direction arise.

Taking stock

Before you embark on any attempt at cultural transformation it is important to understand something of how networks and influence operate in practice and to put as much effort into understanding your employees as you do into understanding your customers. It's about listening to the shadow system, uncovering and working with paradox and tension. Treat interviews, surveys and suggestion boxes as valuable sources of information. Combine the input you receive with customer satisfaction scores, business metrics and employee turnover rates to isolate the issues that matter most to your employees and your business. It can be helpful to use one of the many frameworks for understanding cultural elements to enable conversations and the sharing of perceptions about how things are.

The cultural web

Among the best-known frameworks for taking stock of an organization's culture is the *cultural web* of Johnson and Scholes.[10] This identifies six interrelated elements that make up what Johnson and Scholes call the 'paradigm' – the pattern or model – of the work environment. The six elements are:

- *Stories*: the past events and people talked about inside and outside the company. Who and what the company chooses to immortalize says a great deal about what it values, and perceives as the 'right' behaviour.
- *Rituals and routines*: the daily behaviour and practices of people that signal acceptable behaviour. This determines what is expected to happen in given situations, and what is valued by management.
- *Symbols*: the visual representations of the company including logos, reception areas and the formal or informal dress codes.
- *Organizational structure*: this includes both the structure defined by the organization chart, and the unwritten lines of power and influence that indicate whose contributions are most valued.
- *Control systems*: the ways that the organization is controlled such as via financial systems, quality systems and rewards (including the way they are measured and distributed within the organization).
- *Power structures*: the pockets of real power in the company. The key is that these people have the greatest amount of influence on decisions, operations and strategic direction.

By analysing the factors in each, you can begin to see the bigger picture of your culture: what is working, what isn't working and what needs to be changed.

Indeed from an organization design perspective it can be helpful to map these factors against the Star Model elements – strategy, work processes, management processes, reward, systems and structure – to explore their inter-relationships.

Surveys and focus groups are often used to initiate constructive conversations about the organization's baseline ('as is') culture, its key cultural strengths and weaknesses that may have a high impact on business strategy. Typical questions to explore include:

- What are we doing well and should do more of?
- What do we do poorly and should stop doing?
- What do our customers want?
- What should our employees expect from the organization and vice versa?

Yet in attempting to mobilize people for new ways of working, it is important to recognize that mechanistic approaches to culture change are of limited effectiveness in a complex system. One will not find much energy for change by assuming that 'culture A' (defined by patterns of behaviour, of thinking and deciding) needs to be replaced by 'culture B', or by overlooking the fact that people have strong emotional ties to the existing culture. Deficit or 'push' approaches to shifting culture should be replaced by 'pull' or attractor approaches.

'Pull': defining what 'good' looks like

Throughout this book I have highlighted the importance of shared purpose as the 'glue' that holds the organization together. Helping people to see if and how their own purpose aligns with that of their organization is crucial to gaining engagement. It is about encouraging employees to care intensely about executing strategic objectives because they matter.

Developing shared purpose

Clarifying the organization's purpose involves asking:

- Why does this organization exist?
- In whose name are all our efforts made?
- How do our origins and original purpose impinge on who we are today?
- What is our 'story'? How important is it to us? When do we tell it?
- What elements of our history and our story have the ability to enrich and inspire us today? What gets in the way of what is needed today?
- What core values do we seek to live, work and be known by?
- What is there great passion for in our organization?

Working with purpose should be an inclusive process. Narrative techniques such as storytelling, in which everyone describes their experience of the organization and what it means to them, can be powerful in surfacing the beliefs and values, key players, symbols, rituals and practices that matter most to people. The big strategic stories are made up of these many smaller stories of personal experience of, for instance, helping the customer. It is about introducing vocabularies that help people to say things in new ways and thus be able to talk about this new way of working. The role of the leader is to listen, be open and connect rather than attempt to control the conversation. As a result managers are likely to have a better understanding of staff, while staff are likely to feel heard and understood and be prepared to put in the effort required to make the difference. We shall consider the various effects of different kinds of purpose on business performance in Chapter 12.

A 'critical few' shifts...

Defining a common purpose is one thing; living it, however, is another. Purpose must be made concrete through a set of quality standards: priorities that will guide front-line staff in delivering the desired customer experience.

So it is important to define a critical few patterns of behaviour and thinking that will be essential to the success of the desired change-able/innovation culture (in particular, how this manifests in patterns of behaviour, of thinking and deciding). These are practices that help people to become skilful and effective at, for instance, communication, innovation, adaptive planning and iterative product delivery. Various studies highlight attitudinal and behavioural elements of a receptive context such as openness to change; collaboration and teamwork; good relationships; involvement; learning by experimentation; employees feeling valued and fairly treated.

Success criteria should be defined by the broadest groups possible. Criteria might include visionary elements or tangible behavioural shifts or both, so that people understand what shift is required, and why. For instance, one group seeking to develop a more innovative culture might propose that, 'in five years from now it should be commonplace that':

- Staff at all levels feel encouraged to think creatively.
- We have moved beyond 'change as a project' and have established a pervasive 'habit for change'.
- We can boast of hundreds of locally generated innovations that have led to service and/or product breakthroughs.
- Innovative ideas that delight customers are generated anywhere in the organization; they spread through the entire system at a speed that rivals cannot match.
- Other organizations look at what we do for examples of best practices in the area of innovation and change.[11]

Whichever criteria are selected, it is vital that leaders are 100 per cent on board with leading or supporting the desired direction of travel. Without their commitment, communication and implementation will soon break down.

A receptive context – are you ready for change?

Understanding what needs to change is one thing: mobilizing people to want to make the changes needed for business success is quite another. Any attempt to shift cultural practice and build new, more useful habits and routines needs to take account of, and embrace, the 'swarmware' or social nature of innovation and change.[12] That is because organizations, as complex adaptive systems, are essentially collections of individual free agents who act in ways that are not always totally predictable and whose actions are interconnected such that one agent's actions change the context for other agents. Employees' collective values and opinions guide behaviour and will to a large extent determine how 'change-able' organizations can become.

Viewed this way, change is a group and individual process. Through discourse practices participants construct the happenings of everyday life, along with roles and relationships, norms, expectations and obligations that define membership of the group. Thus change comes about through conversation. Ideas developed within a group context become a cultural resource for the group as well as for individuals.

Building emotional energy for change

Mobilizing people requires more than rational cognition; it also requires significant emotional energy – those strong positive emotions that drive the movement forward.[13] People tend to be highly motivated when they start off from their strengths and not their problems. Organization development interventions using strengths-based approaches such as appreciative inquiry (AI) can be helpful for individual, group and whole-system engagement (see Figure 11.1).

FIGURE 11.1 Appreciative inquiry (AI)

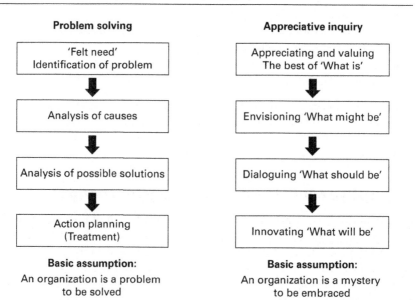

SOURCE © Roffey Park

AI tends to generate many ideas and much enthusiasm for change. The ideas are typically processed and reviewed by an influential project group who can suggest a way ahead to senior management, for instance in the form of a new set of values, plans for operationalizing these or at least a route map of the actions required to bring about the shifts towards the desired culture. The following case study illustrates how the AI approach can be used to good effect as a spur for behaviour change.

CASE STUDY Atkins – building a context where people can flourish

Founded in 1938, Atkins is one of the world's leading design, engineering and project management consultancies; the Burj Al Arab Hotel in Dubai is among its most iconic projects. With a worldwide workforce of 18,000 staff, most of whom are highly educated engineers and scientists, the Atkins culture tends to be technical more than one of openly expressed emotions. Atkins has a nuclear business that supports the entire nuclear power life cycle from fuel enrichment and building new reactors to keeping the existing fleet going and decommissioning. Atkins can anticipate a period of substantial growth as its international nuclear business expands; its nuclear workforce is set to treble by 2017. The rapid growth will mean plenty of change and challenge for employees and more to manage around staff integration and retention.

Previous work on Atkins's identity had crystallized the nuclear business's core values and strengths through a 'bottom-up' engagement process – these were *professional, collaborative* and *motivated*. Caroline Brown, a chartered mechanical engineer by profession and associate director within the nuclear business, was keen to understand how to build upon the strong elements of the Atkins culture during the period of expansion. Caroline made the case to MD Chris Ball to go offline from her existing business-head role to examine how to build on the organization's strengths and create a context in which people can flourish, and so be able to continue to attract, grow and retain the best people. She partnered with Emily Hutchinson, an occupational psychologist with relevant industry experience, and began the work by carrying out research into what other positive work contexts look like. In carrying out research Caroline recognized that key to building a healthy workplace was having connection through a strong purpose – in the case of Atkins's nuclear business the purpose is 'improving lives'. Recruiting the right people and nurturing the skills and talents of staff are other vital elements.

Caroline and Emily worked with each of the business units to introduce and embed some of the relevant practices identified from the research. As Caroline points out: 'Action is not about holding on to a theory but helping it find the right course.'

The practices included:

- *Setting clear direction, share common purpose and values*: although the business strategy was solid, the real purpose (the 'why') needed to be more explicit and shared in a meaningful way. The nuclear board did some superb work to help leaders and everyone in the business to understand how to communicate the why, how and what of the business strategy and this continues to be the platform for various people programmes.

- *Opening lines of communication – 'open minds'*: senior management were concerned that staff were beginning to delegate upwards on business matters. As a business leader herself Caroline was aware that she was privy to financial and business information that other staff had limited access to – a result of recent years' growth. After convincing the board that a real openness was needed again, she helped the operations director to create visual management boards that told the story to staff, putting all of the key business information out there, along with a monthly briefing so that people can 'grab it'. As a result, even quite junior staff are now able to start to ask relevant questions, potentially marking themselves out as possible future leaders.

- *Building on success*: using positive psychology (AI and strengths-based approaches), Caroline and Emily drew on many sources and worked closely with the Atkins Corporate Learning and Development team, who were already starting to pave the way for a strengths-based approach in Atkins. Strengths-profiling instruments are now being used to help staff discover their own and their teams' strengths. Caroline was also able to use her Atkins network to find willing volunteers within the business to trial AI approaches within business-as-usual activities. While there was some initial resistance to the terminology of AI, such as 'discovery', 'dream' (in particular), 'design' and 'destiny', the approaches soon started to be picked up as part of a new way to approach problems and opportunities, which people find engaging and energizing.

- *'Discussing the deal'*: this is about the mutual understanding and implicit agreement of expectations between a staff member and their line manager (the psychological contract). For instance, one high-potential engineer announced that she was going to leave to join another company and one of the reasons that was uncovered was because she wanted more meaningful recognition for her achievements. Of course, recognition is a very individual thing – people have different degrees of hunger for it. However, Caroline firmly believes that it is important that our discussions at work are taken to a level that really matters to staff individually, so that key talent can be retained, but also so that the business can understand what helps their people to work at their best and to have some fun along the way. Accordingly, guidance notes on 'discussing the deal' were developed for all staff with optional tools (prompts) drawing from AI, strengths and engagement questions to help people to articulate what would make a real difference for them at work.

Impact?

Andy Thompson, Director for Nuclear Middle East, piloted a team strengths workshop that included some exercises to visualize a shared purpose as a way of kicking off the expanded team. Following the workshop Andy said: 'It was a fantastic way for us to understand ourselves and each other in a fun and insightful way. We could see straight away how to get the best from each other. All of the team members were very engaged and open, so armed with this insight and our inspiring team purpose we've got the best chance of making our opportunity a huge success.'

While it is early to say, and the general feedback from these initiatives is being evaluated at the time of writing, a positive impact in terms of improved retention is being seen (on top of already very good retention levels to start with). The work is also being shared across Atkins's other businesses and regions, with a steady uptake of the various initiatives.

The next phase of activity will look at intrinsic motivation and growing leaders. Caroline's advice to change agents is: 'Sponsorship and credibility help, but the key thing is to tie everything back to purpose. If you do, brilliant things will emerge.'

So as this case study suggests, people can make surprising shifts willingly if they have been involved, if the process is constructive for all parties and if the outcomes are win-win.

Building a social movement

So real culture change occurs through conversation. Communication is integral to building community and breaking down silos. Essentially, shifting culture is about building a social movement committed to doing something better. Therefore it may sometimes be necessary to go slow in order to go fast. It is usually when people are exposed to new thinking, participate in the conversation and have time to take on board new ideas that they are willing to embrace new ways of working and adopt new behaviours.

Leaders build trust by being transparent in their dealings, asking for help and encouraging involvement. So it is important to widen the circle of involvement, connect people to each other, create communities for action and promote fairness. One of the most important metaphors in culture change is that of a 'learning space', used to convey the notion of a community coming together to concentrate, co-create and learn together. Learning spaces not only provide the opportunity for people – in particular the front-line people – to emotionally engage with the intended change, they can also add value to the thinking and the experiences made along the way.

Learning spaces bring together groups of people whose power may be more informal and is often related to their expertise, to the breadth of their network or their personal qualities. These are the opinion formers within the shadow system who are enthusiastic about the change, who have ideas about how to make it work within some specific organizational segment, and who have the capacity to influence others. Meyerson refers to such people as 'tempered radicals'.[14] The leader's task is to identify and engage these potential catalysts for culture change. Leaders must demonstrate empathy, maintain or enhance the self-esteem of the people they are interacting with. They must listen to employees and ensure there are effective formal mechanisms for employees to express their concerns, either at regular open meetings, through anonymous channels such as internal surveys, or via an ombudsman.

Whatever modes and channels of communication are used, consistency and transparency are key to their effective use. After all, you cannot sit in an ivory tower if you wish to connect. When one CEO first sent out a monthly note to staff asking for their input and then responded to e-mails, staff were shocked that he had actually bothered to read them. As he persevered with this new discipline, staff came to enjoy the regular and personal interaction with the CEO and knew that he had listened to them. Many CEOs now regularly blog and respond to employee commentary and feedback. This opens up a 'skip level' space for dialogue that allows issues to be aired. It also allows provocateurs and mavericks who might otherwise be suppressed to air different perspectives. Old rules and controls can be challenged or relaxed.

Build cohesiveness

Once a community of people who are 'up' for change has come together they can create some new 'traditions' that build cohesiveness. For instance, Covey and Crawley suggest:[15]

- Do some 'city planning': define borders and boundaries. Determine who you are and who you are not. Have welcome signs, reception areas, a distinctive logo, recreation and meeting rooms, and a master plan for five years.
- Focus on what you share in common: share knowledge and information; unite people by focusing them on common causes and concerns.
- Celebrate success: be positive, focus on the strengths of individuals to make their weaknesses irrelevant.

- Take pride in new products and services: build traditions by having ceremonies and annual events.
- Have fun at work: play and socialize together.
- Build meaning into work: be passionate about some shared vision or mission. Tie every new venture to the mission and seek alignment of personal interests behind the vision.
- Take care of your own: when members of the community feel cared for they will be more willing to care for others. Inspire people to give back to the community.

Build in peer support

Of course there is a limit to how many people any single leader can have a one-on-one conversation with, but it is vitally important to keep track of the pulse of the organization to find out if messages are getting through to the front line. One local government body in the north of England has established a change advocates programme. These are volunteers who represent every part of the organization at the front line and at middle manager levels. Following some training their role is to help mediate change, and to work closely with the people affected, encouraging employee engagement. The change advocates meet in monthly network sessions where they can learn more about change processes, share problem areas and exchange ideas. They have also established action learning sets in which trust and other sensitive issues can be safely discussed. As a result there are multiple opportunities for both formal and informal employee voice.

The culture shifts through the conversations people have, the stories they tell and the new routines that emerge. Thus it is about creating new sources of value through generative relations. Once the constructive conversations are concluded, the ideas and insights are documented so that the input can be reviewed, prioritized and acted upon at the functional and leadership levels. But conversation alone will not maintain a social movement for change and innovation for long. People are likely to be motivated to join, take part or stay according to what they perceive as feasible and desirable. This calculation is likely to be based upon what they see as available by way of tangible (money, knowledge, time) and intangible (support, help, endorsement) resources. While the vision is what inspires people for change, it is resources that actually get them moving.

Aligning management and leadership

Strong leadership is a consistent feature of most studies of high-performance working and cultural change. With respect to culture, the leader's role is to facilitate the development of a culture of deeply shared meaning. Edgar Schein considers that leaders are well equipped to transmit and embed culture since they control most of the 'primary' and 'secondary' embedding mechanisms of culture (see Table 11.1).[16]

People are highly influenced by what their leaders say, do, prioritize and reward – so what leaders systematically pay attention to communicates major beliefs. Leaders should recognize their impact as role models, teaching people what behaviour is really acceptable. There cannot be one set of rules for senior management and another set for everyone else. Employees will build up trust in real and sustainable change only when they see it happening at the top of the company. So if leaders want to ensure that their workers are motivated, they must make sure that their own personal values are aligned with those of their employer – and that the organization acts on those values.

There needs to be a collective form of organizational leadership with regard to the development of an innovation culture, with leaders held to account, individually and collectively, for how well and how positively they do this. For example, to encourage innovation 3M Corporation holds senior managers accountable for generating one-third of their division's annual revenues from products that did not exist three years previously; this creates an emphasis on encouraging and nurturing creative ideas from all employees.

TABLE 11.1   Schein's culture-embedding mechanisms

Primary embedding mechanisms	Secondary articulation and reinforcement mechanisms
What leaders pay attention to, measure, and control on a regular basis	Organization design and structure
How leaders react to critical incidents and organizational crises	Organizational systems and procedures
Observed criteria by which leaders allocate scarce resources	Organizational rites and rituals
Deliberate role modelling, teaching, and coaching	Design of physical space, facades and buildings
Observed criteria by which leaders allocate rewards and status	Stories, legends, and myths about people and events
Observed criteria by which leaders recruit, select, promote, retire and excommunicate organizational members	Formal statements of organizational philosophy, values and creed

SOURCE Schein, E (2004) *Organizational Culture and Leadership*, 3rd edn, Jossey-Bass, San Francisco, pp 1–2

Reinforcement

Once the desired cultural shifts have started to happen, they should be reinforced through the formal structures, processes and patterns associated with the creative generation of improvement ideas. It is about changing the context features to change the habits. After aligning on a common purpose, an organization needs to make purpose concrete through a set of quality standards: priorities that guide front-line staff in delivering the desired customer experience.

Then the 'new' practices should be embedded in the organizational system as technology, processes, rewards, structures etc are amended to reinforce the new ways. This is about developing a supportive infrastructure to be consistent with the desired culture change. It is about introducing practices that ease the flow of information, smooth interaction, create transparency and visibility and remove obstacles to these desired behaviours. These include structures to facilitate learning and sharing; availability of key people leading the change; introducing roles that delineate specific skill sets that help to speed up the overall flow; strong administrative support; availability of training and information support systems; clear, simple goals, rewards and performance management systems. For example, Google is renowned for providing employees with a day per week to focus on creative projects of their own choice. Reinforcement occurs through new leadership values to emphasize collaboration and new reward systems that place a higher premium on the behaviour that leads to agility and innovation.

Seeing leaders acting in a new way encourages employees to follow suit and makes common purpose a living reality within the organization. To help the changes stick you need a systematic reinforcement programme combining training, coaching, and 360-degree feedback mechanisms. Develop metrics to track how employees are performing, and intervene when necessary. Training and coaching should evolve over time as the needs of employees and the organization change. And, as we discussed in Chapter 6, performance management and reward can help to shape new group norms and build a receptive context for change and innovation.

Helping people to develop the right skills enables them to do their jobs well; giving them responsibility for managing their own development can lead to greater agility and resilience. Empowerment is a common thread running through a change-able culture. When people are trusted to do their job and are given clear expectations rather than an instruction manual, they feel more valued and empowered – qualities that cannot help but show in the customer experience they provide.

Conclusion

To equip organizations to thrive in an environment of constant change and complexity, their cultures need to be 'change-able', ie ready and able to change deliberately as well as organically as they adjust to changing circumstances.

We have considered the key role of shared purpose and customer empathy in building a change-able culture. Developing a change-able, high performance culture involves 'heart' and 'head', formal and informal approaches to shifting behaviours, for instance by setting new standards, allocating rewards (financial and non-financial), providing follow-up and feedback. It is where Kelly's 'clockware' and 'swarmware' coincide. People need space to make sense of the new and adjust their behaviours. Ongoing dialogue and opportunities for collective reflection provide opportunities for people to take stock and start to co-create the new 'way we do things around here'.

The key to building a change-able culture is *employee empowerment and a fair deal*. If a business wants its staff to participate in the process of change and innovation and also improve productivity, it is unreasonable to expect them to be working 'flat out' all the time. Senior leaders need to develop and communicate clear priorities and accept that it is important to free people up by stopping doing some things – a formal process to review and communicate what will be deprioritized may be needed. HR can help by developing effective work–life balance policies and flexible working opportunities. They can coach managers in how to ensure that workloads are manageable and help managers create time for people to learn.

At the end of the day, if change does not trickle down from the top, it will not last. In the next chapter we look at the significant role of leaders in building this culture and at how 'values-based' leadership can be developed and embedded as a cultural capability.

Checklist

How change-able is your organization?

- How would you describe your culture? What elements of your culture help or hinder you today?

- How well aligned is your culture with achieving your corporate purpose?

- How clear are people about the purpose, strategy and the rationale for change?

- What kinds of communication can help strengthen employee engagement, performance, resilience and agility?

- Do people have the skills, authority, information and resources to be empowered? What needs to happen to increase employee empowerment?

- Do you have well-defined teams that regularly review how they are doing and get to know each other?

- Which communities of practice thrive in your environment?

- Are coherent goals set for quality, innovation, safety etc?

- Are values articulated in a way that shows how they translate into behaviour?

- Are line managers trained in people management skills, including coaching and feedback?

- Are roles designed to provide stretch, be do-able and have line of sight to the customer/purpose?

- Are staff involved in creating new standards and raising the bar?

- Is space created for staff to reflect on customer challenges?

- What do you want your employees' experience of working for you to be in five years' time?

- What do you want your customers', partners' and suppliers' experience of working with you to be in five years' time?

- Do you act on staff feedback – and are staff allowed to make the improvements they identify?

- Do you use hard and soft intelligence about staff experience and morale to seek out problems and target support for solving them?

- Is unnecessary bureaucracy eliminated?

- How clear are staff about what work needs to stop, start, continue?

Notes

1 Senge, PM (1990) *The Fifth Discipline: The art and practice of the learning organization*, Doubleday, New York.

2 Schein, E (2010) *Organizational Culture and Leadership*, 4th edn, John Wiley & Sons, San Francisco.

3 Holbeche, LS (2005) *The High Performance Organization*, Butterworth-Heinemann, Oxford; Holbeche, LS (2005) *Understanding Change*, Butterworth-Heinemann, Oxford.

4 Quade, K and Holladay, R (2010) *Dynamical Leadership: Building adaptive capacity for uncertain times*, CreateSpace Independent Publishing Platform.

5 Kelly, K (1995) *Out of Control: The new biology of machines, social systems, and the economic world*, Basic Books, New York.

6 Galbraith, J (1995) *Designing Organizations*, Jossey-Bass, San Francisco.

7 Stacey, RD (1996) *Complexity and Creativity in Organizations*, Berrett-Koehler, San Francisco.

8 Amabile, TM (1996) *Creativity in Context*, Westview Press, Boulder, Colorado.

9 Weisberg RW(1993) *Creativity: Beyond the myth of genius*, WH Freeman, New York.

10 Johnson, G, Whittington, R and Scholes, K (2012) *Fundamentals of Strategy*, Pearson Education, Harlow.

11 Based on Plsek, PE (1997) *Creativity, Innovations and Quality*, Irwin Professional Publishing, New York.

12 Kelly, K (1995) *Out of Control: The new biology of machines, social systems, and the economic world,* Basic Books, New York.

13 Huy, QN (1999) Emotional capability, emotional intelligence and radical change, *Academy of Management Review*, 24 (2), pp 325–45.

14 Meyerson, DE (2003) *Tempered Radicals: How everyday leaders inspire change at work*, Harvard Business School Press, Boston.

15 Covey, SR and Crawley, JD (2004) Leading corporate communities, *Executive Excellence*, June, p 6.

16 Schein, E (2004) *Organizational Culture and Leadership*, 3rd edn, Jossey-Bass, San Francisco, pp 1–2.

Agile leadership 12

Throughout this book I have emphasized the importance of trust and mutuality as the foundations on which organizational agility and resilience are built. In this chapter I argue that to achieve this we need to think differently about leadership.

In particular I consider two key aspects of leadership theory as key to pulling together a resiliently agile organization. First, values-based leadership stands out since employees need to be led by authentic moral leaders they can trust. After all, as various well-known company disasters teach us, even the most brilliant structures and control mechanisms have proved useless when individual and organizational values have proved to be not aligned. Values-based leaders lead by staying true to their own values, aligning their own and the organization's values, making these pervasive throughout the organization. Shared purpose and values become the 'glue' binding organizations together.

The second key theme is shared or distributed leadership. This type of leadership is frequently referred to as 'horizontal', 'distributed', 'collective' or 'complexity' leadership, and I use several of these terms in this chapter. Given the complexity of the business environment, it is unrealistic to expect that top leaders will have all the answers, especially in knowledge-based organizations, and old-style hierarchical approaches are of limited use. When speed is of the essence, conventional structures that drive decisions towards the centre run the risk of decision making becoming gridlocked. In any case, it is questionable how long organizations can ignore the need for new leadership approaches in the face of rapid technological change, the emergence of Web 2.0 technologies, along with demands for participation from a generation Y who see the world very differently from their forebears.

So in this chapter we look in more detail at the changing demands on individual leaders and how they can help to build a culture of leadership across organizations. In particular we look at:

- Why values-based leadership?
- From 'I' to 'we' – building shared leadership.
- How can agile leadership be developed?

Why values-based leadership?

Management literature is awash with theories about the kinds of leadership required for today's conditions of complexity and ambiguity. Charles Handy writes that a corporation should be thought of as a community of citizens remaining together to pursue a common purpose.[1] In an ever-changing world, agile leaders need to shape organizational communities that employees want to be part of. They have a key role to play in developing the culture consciously since they symbolically represent the collective identity. What they believe and how they act influences the organization around them.

As we have seen throughout this book, 'traditional and hierarchical modes of leadership are yielding to a different way of working – one based on *teamwork* and *community*, one that seeks to involve others in decision-making, one strongly based in ethical and caring behaviour'. This emerging approach to leadership and service began with Robert Greenleaf with his concept of 'servant leadership'.[2]

In leading the changes necessary to implement a strategy, leaders have to bring key stakeholders on board and create alignment. As John Brock, Chairman of Coca-Cola Enterprises notes, leaders today have to work with a wide range of stakeholders, such as shareholders, community representatives, customers and employees:

> I think the role of a business leader today is much more challenging because you've got so many other constituencies out there that you didn't have before. You've got to engage with these multiple constituencies and make decisions in a more consensual way. And that requires a real skill.[3]

It also requires that people trust what leaders say and, as we have discussed in Chapter 2, today there are widespread 'trust deficits' between leaders and 'followers' in many walks of life. To be trustworthy, leaders have to 'walk' the 'talk' on values.

Leaders and values

Discussion about the *values of leaders* goes back to earlier leadership theories. In 1978, for example, when Burns talked of 'moral leadership' he distinguished between two types of leadership – transformational and transactional.[4] Transactional leadership involves developing and maintaining task structures and plans, information management and control systems. It works on a 'give and take' relationship where a leader provides a reward or punishment in return for the work (or its lack) that the subordinate is doing. Transformational leadership is meant to bring about big changes in the lives of followers, thereby making their lives better and more fruitful and improving the society in which the organization operates. In both cases, values-based leaders build a sense of shared purpose and community by never changing their fundamental principles and values, only their approach or strategy in a given situation.

Contemporary theories talk of 'authentic' leadership, 'post-heroic', 'credible' leadership and others. May *et al*, for example, argue that 'authentic leadership' involves: 'the leader knowing him- or herself, and being transparent in linking inner desires, expectations, and values to the way the leader behaves, in each and every interaction'.[5] Knowing oneself and being true to oneself are essential qualities of authentic leadership. Similarly, Goffee and Jones argue that leadership demands the expression of an authentic self.[6] People want to be led by someone real. People associate authenticity with sincerity, honesty and integrity. For Norman, Luthans and Luthans, the authentic leader has confidence, hope, optimism and resilience and also a moral/ethical transparency orientation.[7] Thus values-based management behaviour is consistent with the organization's core values: what leaders say is exactly what they mean.

If leaders and managers want to earn trust and build a more resilient employment relationship with employees, they need to win respect by being open and honest, leading in such a way that the dignity and rights of others are respected. Engagement means far more than having an engagement strategy; mechanistic approaches that lack sincerity will soon be found out. This relationship focus requires social leadership and emotional intelligence, the ability to improve interpersonal dealings within a group, acknowledging and working through historically dysfunctional relationships to create a more collaborative, whole system approach for the future.

In particular there must be a cohesive leadership team at the top since the management team is the most important 'great group' – which now must also be heterogeneous because of multiple stakeholders. Ratan Tata and Mark Wallenberg argue that we should learn from large, enduring firms who have survived many periods of upheaval.[8] Organizations that are in it for the long term choose their leaders according to the challenge at hand; some may have appropriate skills for a restructuring, but different ones will be needed when expansion is called for. As we have considered in this book, leaders must play many roles including master strategist, relationship/network builder, culture developer, change manager and talent developer. While it is unlikely that any individual can play all of these roles, a cohesive management team can.

Of course if top teams are consumed with politics with which their boards may collude, silo-based behaviour is likely lower down the hierarchy. So the top team must model the way forward with respect to values; surface and address political issues that impede collaboration; be open and transparent in sharing relevant information and avoid promoting 'sharks' who achieve business results at the expense of others. As Heifetz and Laurie argue, rather than quelling conflict you need to draw out issues and let people feel the sting of reality.[9] With respect to defining and rewarding success, the *how* should matter as well as the *what*.

Ethics and purpose

Increasingly in public debates the primacy of shareholder value is being challenged and businesses are being prompted to address social issues. Leaders are now expected to be transparent in their dealings, accountable for the ethical practice of their organizations and supply chains. Firms well known for their ethical stance such as Ben and Jerry's, The Body Shop and many others focus on a 'triple bottom line' – ('people, profit, planet') – ie aiming to benefit their communities, the environment, customers and staff as well as investors. The assumption is that companies that do good do well, and vice versa. For instance, in the travel industry, ethical travel matters now. At one time people went on safari without caring much about the welfare of the local people. Now they want to see that their money is funding worthwhile causes: orphanages, schools, research centres. They want to feel they are doing good while having a good – and expensive – time.[10]

Collins and Porras highlight the shareholder value paradox, drawing distinctions between long-lived successful 'visionary' companies who take a longer-term view and take stakeholder perspectives into account, and companies driven purely by short-term shareholder value considerations:

> Paradoxically, the visionary companies make more money than the more purely profit-driven comparison companies.[11]

These shifts are reflected in a Roffey Park study on the differential effects of different kinds of corporate purpose on business performance and on employee motivation.[12] Firms with a customer-focused purpose outperformed those with a shareholder purpose or a mix of purposes. Employees of customer-oriented firms tended to experience:

- their leaders as more trustworthy and able;
- the culture as more creative;
- their contribution as better recognized and rewarded;
- more commitment to and from the organization;
- their work as more meaningful;
- less stress arising from their work;
- a stronger sense of purpose.

It is possible that this paradox occurs because of what John Kay calls the obliquity principle: ie by focusing in a direction that matters to employees (such as delighting the customer), the organization obliquely also makes more money than if the focus was directly on shareholder value, which would drive a different set of values and behaviours: 'Obliquity gives rise to the profit-seeking paradox: the most profitable companies are not the most profit-oriented.'[13]

Putting employees first

Interestingly, while putting customers at the heart of company purpose is a powerful and motivating approach, today there is increasing emphasis on putting employees first since it is only when staff are happy that customers will feel the real benefits of dealing with a firm. For instance the Disney Corporation, renowned for its customer experience, believes that creating great customer experience comes down to having great people and treating them well. Looking after your people makes them feel more engaged with your organization and more committed to your service goals.

Vineet Nayyar, the CEO who led giant IT services company HCL Technologies through a profound reinvention, argues that it is essential to invert the pyramid, distribute the work of leadership, enlist the front line and change the DNA of an entrenched organization.[14]

The role of managers and management should be to enthuse and encourage employees so that they can create a different shared value: enhancing employees first and customers second. Nayyar emphasizes the importance of creating an environment of trust where the employees believe what you are saying and are willing to follow you wherever you are going. So, in HCL, all the enabling functions such as HR, Finance and the office of the CEO are as accountable to the employees as the employees are accountable to them.

This commitment is made real in tangible ways. For instance, HCL created an electronic 'trouble ticketing' system where an employee can open a trouble ticket on any of these functions, who must then resolve these issues within a certain period of time. The ticket is only closed by the employees. Similarly, management and managers are as accountable to the employees as the employees are to them. This accountability is evident since the CEO's 360-degree is done by 80,000 employees across the world and the results are published on the web for all to see. This culture unlocks a huge amount of energy in the corporation.

In summary, in a context where simplistic either/or solutions may not be appropriate, resiliently agile leaders must reconcile the leadership dilemma, being both:

- short-term *and* long-term focused;
- congruent *and* flexible;
- supportive *and* directive;
- task *and* people focused;
- business as usual *and* innovation;
- helicopter-view *and* feet on the ground.

In particular, agile leaders need to build a culture of shared leadership in order to strengthen the potential agility and resilience of organizations.

From 'I' to 'we' – building shared leadership

In fast-changing times it becomes even more critical to distribute the leadership load and a more collaborative approach to leadership is needed, with leaders who can motivate and coordinate a team-based approach. The most crucial test of an agile organization is how well its members make the right decisions at the right time to produce the results needed. So the shift taking place is away from leader–follower relations to a shared leadership model that depends on the collective efficacy of formal and informal networks, where expertise is the driver of change, and leadership is broadly distributed such that people within a team and organization lead each other. Collaborative working is undertaken between individuals who trust and respect each other's contribution and are jointly responsible for leading the organization. *How* leadership is distributed is more important than *whether* leadership is distributed.

Shared leadership is characterized by two main properties – emergence and interdependence – that are constantly being renegotiated according to the changing needs of the organization.

Embracing distributed leadership will require mindset shifts for people at all levels but especially for top teams. Agile leadership is less about directing others what to do and more about creating the conditions to empower and enable others to make the right decisions that generate results. People may also require new skills, or at least a different skills emphasis, if they are required to act in new ways. Communication across the organization – lots of it – and the ability to move quickly to apply solutions are essential.[15] According to research by the Work Foundation, outstanding leaders are self-aware and authentic and put their leadership responsibilities first, their own needs second.[16] They put 'we' before 'me'.

On the journey towards shared leadership

To iniate the move towards shared leadership often a strong senior leader needs to design the distributed model. The task for leaders is communication and sense making, arming decision makers and employees with the tools to find, filter and focus the information they need. After a transition period, this leader – or a top leadership team – still steps in from time to time to make key decisions that keep the firm aligned with external demands. Centralized leadership also weighs in when lots of local decisions are getting in the way of economies of scope and scale, or when time constraints require a short circuiting of more consensus-based decision making. In short, top-level formal leaders still play a key role, but their responsibilities are changing.

Successfully introducing shared leadership in organizations within a traditional command and control structure will depend on the degree to which senior leaders are willing to 'let go' of their overarching control and embark on their own transformation journey (as we shall discuss later in this chapter). Top leadership must actively champion and enable distributed leadership based on a shared vision. This common purpose should be reflected in formal and informal aspects of organization. This involves handling relationships with employees, management, boards, suppliers and partners, building coalitions of support, countering resistance to change and communicating the vision to staff and wider stakeholders. As distributed leadership becomes the norm, people at all levels are likely to engage in collaborative action, accepting leadership in their particular areas of expertise.

For instance at Disney, the purpose of 'We create happiness' is embedded in the first day of training for each new recruit and is brought to life through real-life stories of how staff have put the purpose into practice so helps create an organizational mindset. Purpose is also made concrete through a set of quality standards that guide front-line staff in delivering the desired customer service, striking a good balance between standards and freedom and by the promotion of high-performing individuals. Providing guiding principles ensures that the protective functions of alignment, control and risk mitigation are also distributed. Giving front-line employees responsibility and autonomy creates a sense of ownership that inspires them to do everything they can to improve the customer experience. When they see a problem, they fix it without waiting to be asked. Customer insights from front-line staff are fed up through the hierarchy through robust channels to leaders who can act on it. Bringing in people who are 'up for' distributed leadership helps to mobilize other people, so hiring for attitude as well as aptitude is important.

Shared leadership may also be a more fluid feature of organizations, in which leadership is based on relevant expertise. If it is to emerge 'bottom-up', for instance through networks, an open culture is needed within and across the organization, where groups agree how they will work together and team relationships are built on trust, mutual encouragement, support and protection. In such cases both formal and informal leaders may need to develop clear parameters for the team effort, blurring the distinction between 'leaders' and 'followers'.[17]

Shared leadership is facilitated by collaborative environments and empowerment mechanisms such as participation and delegation, which encourage the sharing of functions and result in the development of leadership capacity to sustain improvements.[18] Shared purpose, common goals, values and beliefs act as parameters for empowerment. When team members have similar understandings of their team's main objectives they are more inclined to both speak up and invest themselves in providing leadership to the team and responding to the leadership of others towards collective goals.

Supporting teams

Shared leadership can also be institutionalized through formal team structures. The use of self-managed teams (SMTs) – for instance quality circles, task forces, communications teams, new venture teams, and business brand teams – appears to be increasing since these are most effective at resolving difficult and complex problems, increasing productivity and heightening creativity in work settings. Widely used in such well-known companies as Google, HP, Wal-Mart and Pepsi-Cola as well as among many smaller firms, they have been credited with achieving conceptual breakthroughs and introducing unparalleled numbers of new products. Shared leadership enables team members to express their different abilities, thus allowing different types of leadership behaviour to be exhibited in a single team.[19]

Teams need *voice* – where team members have input into how the team carries out its purpose.[20] Successful distributed leadership companies work to increase the voice of front-line workers and also to inject more lateral and external voices into the generation, vetting and selection of ideas.[21] Procter & Gamble (P&G), for instance, augments its internal R&D with its 'connect and develop' programme, which invites suggestions from networks outside the company to boost innovation and find new markets. Similarly collaboration is not left to the preferences of individuals, but built into structures, reward systems and HR practices. At Cisco, cross-functional councils and boards were created to quickly make strategic decisions and respond to new opportunities. Senior managers must act as role models – a significant portion of their compensation is based upon peer ratings of how well they collaborate.

Teams need social support – the extent to which team members actively provide emotional and psychological strength to one another. When team members feel recognized and supported within their team they are more willing to share responsibility, cooperate and commit to the team's collective effort. Effective teams also have found effective ways to surface and resolve conflict.

Teams may also need help from senior management. On the journey towards shared leadership, teams will face impediments, not least fear. After all, taking an initiative and learning something new can be scary, triggering the 'fight' or 'flight' instinct. If management leaves teams floundering, teams will be discouraged. Leaders need to provide support without removing responsibility, in order to build ownership; for instance helping people to work through their fears in 'safe' contexts such as focus groups and 'brown bag' lunches; removing practical barriers to shared ownership; building an internal support system; encouraging communities of practice where like-minded people get together and support each other.

External team coaching can help teams to make coordinated and task-appropriate use of their collective resources in accomplishing the team's task. Coaching can foster independence and a sense of self-competence among team members, nurture collective commitment to the team and its objectives, and increase the possibility that team members will demonstrate leadership and personal initiative. Researchers distinguish between two particularly useful types of team coaching; those that reinforce shared leadership (supportive coaching), and those that focus on identifying team problems through task interventions (functional coaching). Functional coaching is needed when teams lack a strong shared purpose. The role of an external team leader is to do whatever is not being adequately managed by the team itself.

Team effectiveness and business performance

Many studies have found a positive relationship between shared leadership and team effectiveness and performance.

One company with a long-standing history of innovative business and a progressive management model is WL Gore, founded by Bill Gore in 1958. Best known for its Gore-Tex range of high-performance fabrics, it makes over 1,000 products and employs 9,000 in 50 locations. When Bill Gore started the company he wanted it to bring innovative products to the market. He sought to understand the human element in innovation and many of the company's current practices derive from his insights. For instance, the company operates as a lattice or a network, not a hierarchy, and associates (staff) can go directly to anyone in the organization to get what they need to be successful. There are no job titles, since this would imply that some people have authority to command others in the organization. Associates are all owners in the company; they are free to decide what they want to work on, since WL Gore works on the principle that this is where they can make the greatest contribution. But once associates have made their commitment they are expected to deliver on their promises.

At WL Gore leaders are appointed to positions of authority because they have followers. The voice of the organization determines who is really qualified to be a leader, based on the willingness of others to follow. They use a peer review process to identify the individuals who are growing into leadership roles. Who are associates listening to? Who do they want on their leadership team? WL Gore adopts a predominantly 'grow your own' talent philosophy in order to create a robust and loyal culture but mix it selectively and judiciously with external hires. At Gore, leaders emerge and once they are in a leadership role they understand that their job is to bring out the strengths of their teams and to make their colleagues successful. Leaders know that their 'followership' comes from their peers, and that they can easily lose this if they don't live up to the company's values.[22]

Go slow to go fast

At WL Gore some of the most impactful decisions are made by small teams. Teams are encouraged to take a lot of time to come together, to build relationships and trust. The firm invests in making sure that teams are effective; as a result, people know they have the authority to make decisions and are responsible for the outcomes.

There are 'rules of engagement' – the norms of behaviour and guidelines everybody must follow. Every associate understands how critical these values are, so when leaders make decisions, they must sell the 'why?' in order to get the organization to move. The company believes it is better to spend more time up front ensuring that associates are fully bought-in and committed to achieving the outcome. So it is less a problem of alignment as one of involvement, since associates are owners and they feel responsible for business outcomes.

A similar philosophy is reflected in 'holacracy', a distributed authority system that has been implemented at Zappos. In contrast to a conventional management model this is a radical 'self-governing' operating system where there are no job titles and no managers. Instead of a top-down hierarchy there is a flatter 'holarchy' that distributes power more evenly across a hierarchy of circles, which are to be run according to detailed democratic procedures. Employees can have any number of roles within those circles. A set of 'rules of the game' provides an infrastructure for building empowerment into the core of the organization so that everyone becomes a leader of their own roles and a follower of others', processing tensions with real authority and real responsibility through dynamic governance and transparent operations.

What happens to top leadership?

So what are the implications of embracing shared leadership for people in formal leadership roles? It is clear that building distributed leadership requires active support from the top leaders – without that, initiatives from the floor tend to be ignored and people may give up trying to make a difference. Gone is the heroic leadership model with a monopoly on the vision; it is replaced by a commitment to building shared visions with a range of stakeholders. This brings many benefits – it exploits the diversity of perspectives and experiences, draws on strengths and builds potential in the organization. This leadership model is about stimulating teamwork, which is far more achievable in complex times whereas being seen as the source of all wisdom will often end in failure.

For many leaders, of course, adopting this approach is challenging because of the skill and risk involved and for the shift in power structures it represents, which some may find uncomfortable. Instead of direct control it is about exercising influence. Rogers and Tierney argue that this is particularly the case with leaders of professional service firms, where many organizations are less orderly than they were, with minimal job descriptions and blurred lines of authority, and leaders face a day-to-day struggle to define and implement strategy.[23] They are held accountable for matters beyond their control.

Employees too may feel uncomfortable with a shift towards shared leadership. Some may continue to expect senior management to 'lead' and be unhappy about taking on more responsibility; others may expect that 'anything goes' and that all their ideas will be acted on even if they are irrelevant to the organization's needs. To avoid chaos, at any point along the journey leaders need to exercise the 'loose-tight' approach – managing both the expansion of thoughts that gives rise to potentially creative alternatives and the honing of a viable option. Looseness usually dominates the early stages of the innovation process; in the later stages, tightening becomes more important in order to scrutinize the concepts and bring the selected ones to the market. A balanced approach and clear signalling about when the balance is shifting – and why – avoids confusion.

To shift to a distributed leadership model requires strong conviction from senior leaders and a willingness to make fundamental changes within their organizations. Long-standing practices may need to be revisited and the current values of leaders and managers put under the spotlight. Other system elements must be reconsidered:

- What is rewarded within the organization?
- How are leaders selected?
- What consequences are there for leaders who don't live up to the desired values?

This journey will not be an easy one, and there will be many forces that will fight the change. And yet the potential benefits of this approach are significant, as the case study below illustrates. It describes how one CEO stimulated the journey towards a positive culture of shared leadership and accountability, and for the study I am indebted to Andrew Lycett, CEO of RCT Homes, and to Sarah-Ellen Stacey, formerly HR and OD Director.

CASE STUDY   RCT Homes

RCT Homes became Wales's largest housing organization when it took over the ownership and management of Rhondda Cynon Taf Council's entire housing stock in December 2007. This followed a successful vote by tenants to transfer their homes to a new independent organization in order to drive investment and service improvement. As well as almost 11,000 homes, RCT Homes also inherited 290 staff from the local authority, with a further 60 new staff recruited.

RCT Homes is a new type of housing organization – a community mutual – whereby tenants can take part in operational decision making, determining how resources are allocated and how services are delivered. From its inception RCT Homes was charged with 'supporting the social and economic regeneration of the communities it serves'. This brought with it a need to transform the culture that most of the workforce had been used to and to create an environment where staff could flourish and be empowered to achieve excellence while, at all times, putting their tenants first.

CEO Andrew Lycett said: 'I recognized from the outset that we needed to think differently if we were to achieve a paradigm shift in the way staff and tenants were to be empowered.'

Signals of change

The approach to bring about these shifts was both planned and emergent. From the outset, for staff who were transferring to the new organization there were clear signals of change. The original aspiration of the tenants was captured in 90 separate 'promises' that had been made in the Transfer Offer document. This was used to set change agendas for every aspect of the business and required everyone to be involved in delivering change. All teams were expected to involve tenants in service reviews and standard setting, and in appointing staff for customer-facing roles. For staff used to dealing with tenants only over transactional issues, such as rent payments and arrears, this was a very different approach.

Plans were put in place for a series of organizational development interventions to give momentum and clear direction to the cultural transformation that would be required within the new organization. Key activities in the first six months built the foundation for conscious change.

The first significant action was to bring together staff, board members and tenants in four half-day workshops to develop RCT Homes's vision and values. The list of promises provided the *why* or the reason that RCT Homes had been established. This process of establishing RCT Homes's vision – 'To provide the best services, designed and delivered with our communities' – defined what it aimed to achieve. Six values – empowering, trustworthy, proud, enjoyable, bold and excellent – outlined *how* the organization would do it. This purpose gave clarity to staff, tenants and other stakeholders about the journey ahead.

Setting the baseline

Having set out its goal and aspirations, RCT Homes wanted to understand its starting position. What was it like to work at RCT Homes in the early days? How far would it need to travel to achieve the vision and values?

The organizational development (OD) team spent the first six months really getting under the skin of the organization in order to understand this, drawing invaluable information from feedback from focus groups, the vision and values workshops, a newly formed staff forum and an inaugural staff survey, conducted in April 2008. The weight of the findings showed that, while staff were proud to work for RCT Homes, a number of sizeable obstacles needed to be overcome. These included:

- managers not listening to their staff;
- lack of fun and recognition for work well done;
- a culture of blame and mistrust;
- 'silo working';
- staff feeling disempowered;
- instability and insecurity;
- poor customer and performance focus.

Many of these themes were also reflected in the results of a comprehensive customer survey that was conducted concurrently, being returned by almost one-quarter of all tenants, enabling a clear causal relationship to be drawn between organizational culture and outcomes for customers. So with this clear 'evidence' everybody understood the need for change. This was the first time that either survey had been conducted within housing services, increasing its power in terms of raising understanding of the starting point for the journey ahead.

Developing the organization

It was clear that OD interventions were needed in order to turn around each of the obstacles listed above. This was not a one-off cultural change programme that had a start and finish date, nor was it about exhorting staff to work harder. Change towards great performance, customer service and empowerment was promoted on multiple levels using a range of initiatives, actions and events. Key organizational messages were layered through everything, providing consistency and reinforcement, incrementally building momentum towards changing the organization.

Employee communications

Employee communications were pivotal in reinforcing the clarity of direction and a sense of progress. RCT Homes worked with an external consultancy that specialized in employer branding, marketing and communication. A new way of communicating was developed under the theme of 'We're better together'. As well as the strapline 'promoting partnership: higher performance and trust', the 'tone of voice' and language used in all communication became more informal and conversational. RCT Homes consciously avoided 'corporate speak' and formal language. For instance, what had formerly been 'the staff handbook', became 'Nuts and Bolts' and an infrequent staff newsletter became 'Update', a regular colour publication with a popular magazine style and contributions directly from staff. Launched in 2008, it includes regular features such as interviews with winners of RCT Homes's 'Esteem' staff recognition scheme, a spotlight on a team or function, celebrations of customer service excellence and a 'You said – We did' section explaining how staff suggestions have been used to implement service improvements.

A bright-yellow plus sign (chosen to depict both positivity and togetherness) is used in office signage and merchandise created to promote the values of the organization. The connections between the different OD activities, initiatives and events were underlined by the use of similar titles such as the 'Leading Better Together' management development programme and the 'Performing Better Together' appraisal system.

Within its first year, RCT Homes launched a number of groups, schemes and initiatives to directly address issues around voice – staff-recognition, empowerment and customer-driven performance. See Table 12.1 for some examples.

Thus a positive common language was forged that helped employees to see how these different processes contributed towards achieving the vision. OD activities continue to reinforce progress towards the vision. RCT Homes's annual conference for all staff continues to act as a tool to transform the organization, share business success and promote continual improvement. This event has team involvement each year; this enables teams to report back on their successes and see their part in the bigger picture. It is proving to be a real touchstone of progress within the organization as a whole.

Developing leadership

Improving management and leadership was key to moving things forward. RCT Homes's executive management team recognized very early on that managers were not aware of what was expected of them. Low confidence was evident in the first staff survey when managers themselves rated the organization's management lower than did any other staff group. The findings indicated that many line managers did not recognize themselves as being managers or leaders – that was widely viewed as someone else's responsibility further up the chain. Some difficult decisions had been made, including making changes to the executive team along the way. The organization needed to invest heavily in equipping line managers with the skills, knowledge and behaviours to enable them to lead their teams effectively. So began the 'Leading Better Together' programme for all leaders and related activities. First, leadership behaviours were aligned with RCT Homes's values and shared with everyone. They were

TABLE 12.1 Voice schemes and initiatives

Scheme/Event/ Group	What is it?	To tackle...
Esteem	Recognition scheme where staff nominate colleagues who have gone the extra mile to exemplify RCT Homes's values.	Appreciation and celebration of great performance. Further embeds the values of the organization.
Staff forum	Group of staff representing different parts of the organization – seeking input to decisions and testing ideas.	Empowerment. Seeks views beyond the line manager/staff relationship.
Voice	Suggestion scheme for staff to put forward their ideas for service and business improvement.	Staff empowerment and enabling managers to listen.
Job well done	A team reward scheme for meeting targets over a quarter. Rewards could include anything from a night of ten-pin bowling to a fish-and-chip supper.	Raising awareness of performance targets, while encouraging fun at work.
Additions	Range of discount benefits, including childcare vouchers and cycle-to-work scheme.	Recognition and reward for staff.

brought to life in 360-degree feedback and in the organization's 'Performing Better Together' appraisal system. Managers began to discuss with their own line managers not just what they had been doing but how they had led their team.

RCT Homes also considered what could be done to sustain and embed learning. Bimonthly 'Leading Better Together' events (which at the time of writing still continue) bring together all managers – from team leaders to the chief executive – for a half-day session. These events enable the executive management team to add the *why* in relation to strategic business direction and decision making. The agenda involves managers in decision making, reinforces key business messages and gets managers working together. The events have proved invaluable in sharing business performance and celebrating success.

Another activity that has helped to sustain and embed improvements in leadership has been the development, in-house, of a 'How to...' toolkit for managers. The range of guides covers communicating effectively, conducting a 'Performing Better Together' review, involving teams in service development plans, managing stress, holding effective meetings and much more. The language is user-friendly and the toolkit offers real case studies from internal teams offering very practical lessons on how to excel.

Customer service

The 'blame culture' identified in RCT Homes's initial staff survey proved a particularly challenging hurdle. RCT Homes wanted to encourage more open and effective conversations and actions in the area of high performance and customer service excellence, but staff were concerned about the consequences both of being honest about their own development needs and of taking different approaches from the norm. When teams saw benchmarking data for the first time, comparing RCT Homes's performance against other similar organizations, conversations began to change.

A great deal of OD activity remains focused on continuous improvement. All staff go through a customer service learning programme 'Being the Best', developed by Mary Gober International Ltd. This tackles service excellence not just in terms of skills, but also in terms of an individual's mindset, language and demeanour. Staff are encouraged to welcome complaints as 'real gold' and emphasis is put on a 'can do' mindset.

Again, mobilizing people for improvement is one thing, embedding new practices is another. RCT Homes made the intangible tangible. The drive for customer service excellence was supported by the modernization and restructuring of RCT Homes's customer services centre, new service level agreements, the introduction of regular customer satisfaction surveys and a range of new performance information that managers are encouraged to share with their teams. Service development plans identify key performance targets and 'Check and Challenge' events bring together staff from different teams to discuss progress against key shared goals. Individuals discuss performance and customer service in their 'Performing Better Together' sessions and in team meetings.

A positive working environment

The personality and working environment of RCT Homes changed considerably over its first five years. The 2008 staff survey revealed that staff were very loyal and had a strong sense of being part of the 'RCT Homes family', but there was little sense of fun or enjoyment in the workplace. Group activities such as local community volunteering, charity fundraising, sport and leisure activities have proved to be key to creating a more relaxed and open working environment. Not only have they brought together individuals from completely different areas of the organization, they have also provided opportunities for staff at different levels to work together and build trust in less pressurized environments. They have also encouraged the establishment of a more empathetic relationship with customers.

Every year RCT Homes supports Business in the Community's 'Give and Gain Day' by offering the whole organization the opportunity to contribute a day's voluntary work to local community projects. The sense of teamwork, pride in the local community and simple fun is evident throughout the day. Team-building and development events often include an element of volunteering on RCT Homes's estates and every year one of the 'Leading Better Together' sessions is a volunteering opportunity. Teams right across RCT Homes have put real energy and effort into myriad charity and fundraising events, including Children in Need, Comic Relief and numerous local events. In total, RCT Homes staff have contributed more than 3,500 hours of voluntary work in the local community and in 2012 their volunteering took them even further afield when a team of tradespeople from RCT Homes's repairs service raised thousands of pounds to fund a trip to Uganda, where they led pupils from Pontypridd High School in the building of a hostel for rural schoolgirls.

The vast majority of voluntary activities come from ideas generated by staff themselves – and the impact on their loyalty and pride in their impact on local communities has been palpable. In 2012, RCT Homes became the first housing organization ever to be named 'Responsible Business of the Year' by Business in the Community in Wales.

Health and wellbeing

An emphasis on health and wellbeing has also been a vehicle of organizational change. RCT Homes has encouraged individuals to start sports or social teams and many of the charitable events have included sporting achievements or endurance events, such as taking part in Wales's Four Peaks Challenge and a 24-hour sponsored cycling event. Healthshield – a health plan providing contributions towards dental, optical or medical treatment – was introduced for all staff during 2010. Staff sickness levels reduced from an average of 14 days per employee per year to less than eight – a saving to the company of more than £150,000 a year. Determined not to rest on its laurels, RCT Homes is working towards the Welsh Government's Corporate Health Standard.

Results and benefits

The benefits are substantial.

RCT Homes's staff surveys have provided evidence of significant change in the workplace. Overall staff satisfaction figures have increased by an average of 25 per cent since RCT Homes began operations. When RCT Homes was awarded Investors in People Bronze status in 2012, the assessors highlighted quotes from staff including:

- 'There is a faster pace to things now. You don't have all the answers yourself so you have to collaborate with others in order to get things done.'

- 'We are encouraged to see ourselves as one team working for our tenants.'

- 'It feels different to what it used to – the attitude is more caring; I feel proud to be part of the organization.'

- 'It's a great place to work.'

RCT Homes's investment in community regeneration and training opportunities has had a major impact on many lives. Jason, a trainee in facilities management, said: 'I wouldn't be where I am now. I would be unemployed without the confidence and qualifications.' Most importantly, the changes have been felt by RCT Homes's tenants and customer satisfaction increased significantly – all this during a period of unprecedented growth when RCT Homes's annual turnover increased from less than £10 million in 2008 to nearly £49 million in 2012 and its breadth of operations has grown to incorporate four subsidiary companies delivering a very diverse range of technical, charitable, development and social enterprise activities.

As this case study suggests, top leadership working from a strong sense of purpose and values, supported by a capable OD specialist, can help to develop a culture of shared leadership focused on doing the right things for the tenant/customer.

How can agile leadership be developed?

Senior managers have usually spent many years developing rules of thumb, instincts, crisis management models and metrics that have made them successful in traditional ways of working. Top teams often prefer to hold on to what they have done in the past even if this means they act as operational managers rather than strategic leaders. As we have discussed, agile leaders must be able to lead in complexity, be a relationship/network builder, culture developer, change manager, talent developer and enabler of shared leadership. Some leaders, therefore, may need to develop new skills, open their minds to new approaches to leadership, learn new techniques, receive 'fresh knowledge' from outside their system and step out of their comfort zone.

As Marcel Proust points out: *'The only real voyage of discovery consists not in seeking new landscapes but in having new eyes.'*[24]

Look outside

Top leaders must develop systemic understanding and gain insights into the 'zeitgeist' and its implications in order to identify what Heifetz and Laurie call the 'adaptive challenge'.[25] Mayo and Nohria argue that the ability to understand the zeitgeist and pursue the unique opportunities it presents for each company is what separates the truly great leaders from the merely competent.[26] These authors found that a lack of sensitivity to contextual factors can trip up even the most brilliant of executives. Without this, a leader's personality and skill are but temporal strengths.

Welbourn and colleagues of the Cass Business School advise leaders hoping to influence systems to:[27]

- have an open, enquiring mind;
- embrace uncertainty and be positive about change;
- draw on as many perspectives as possible;
- ensure leadership and decision making are distributed throughout the system;
- promote the importance of values – invest as much energy in relationships and behaviours as in delivery.

To develop systemic understanding many senior managers go on study trips and do benchmarking visits to companies in other geographies, who may offer fresh insights into key strategic challenges. Some companies send senior and high-potential managers to large business or management conferences, accompanied by a learning facilitator who helps the leadership groups to process their learning at the end of each day.

Organizations are also increasingly running large-scale scenario planning sessions that involve large numbers of staff and managers, opening up minds and garnering collective wisdom on perceived trends and challenges. The creation of an alert, informed and engaged cohort of practitioners is key to the development of a more shared sense of leadership. One medium-sized firm involved its senior managers and high-potential employees below board level in carrying out collaborative inquiry – researching aspects of the business, its environment, opportunities and threats. The firm has since implemented many of the findings to great advantage both in terms of its business results and its reputation as an employer.

Look inside

Whole generations of senior leaders have reached executive roles based on their technical and business prowess. Today's challenges require them to use themselves as instruments to help their organizations to thrive in the new environment. What sets outstanding leaders apart, according to the Work Foundation, is that they think systemically and act long term; bring meaning to life; apply the spirit not the letter of the law; grow people through performance; are self-aware and authentic, putting leadership first, their own needs second; understand that talk is work; give time and space to others and put 'we' before 'me'.

Many of the skills associated with agility have long been identified with psychological and change management studies. Given the importance of relationships, leaders need to be emotionally intelligent and have effective negotiating, influencing and conflict resolution skills. Four key qualities of values-based leaders that emerge from various studies include self-reflection, balance, self-confidence, courage and humility.[28] For instance, Collins highlighted humility as a quality of 'Level 5' leaders of 'great' organizations.[29] Such leaders have learnt to get in touch with what they consider important and have developed their own set of beliefs.

How should such skills and 'awarenesses' be developed? As leaders wrestle with their own development they need to find sources of advice they can trust such as peers, coaches, mentors or colleagues at all levels. For instance, Unilever found that the technical skills of some executives were not keeping pace with the ways in which social and other media can now be used to communicate more widely with employees and other stakeholders; they were therefore unable to plug into new developments and trends. Unilever established 'reverse mentoring' whereby graduate recruits coach and mentor executives in how to use modern media to connect with the workforce.

For Quinn, leaders learn how to handle uncertainty by reflective conversations;[30] Badaracco also argues that change is brought into being through dialogue.[31] Productive deliberation is a chaotic process of zigzagging between feelings, thoughts, facts and analysis, resisting the temptation to grasp hold of a single grand principle or allowing it to tyrannize all other considerations. Action learning sets and peer networks provide spaces for leaders to hone their thinking. Standard Chartered Bank, for example, has experimented with leadership development that provides leaders with space to reflect and engage in dialogue on complex issues that have no easy answers. Similarly, the University of Hertfordshire involves a leading expert on complexity – Professor Ralph Stacey – in leadership development for senior academics and professional services managers based on reflection and dialogue.

In identifying the next generation of leaders it will be important to look beyond the conventional talent pool for leadership, developing a process that scouts internally and externally for people with the potential for leading successfully in conditions of accelerated complexity. This search should be a cross-organizational effort, involving stakeholders in its development. In developing future leaders it will be important to ensure that roles are broad and meaningful 'real jobs' in which people will have a chance to experience and grow through the challenges, develop change management and other key skills and acquire prowess at designing environments conducive to agility, engagement, resilience and great results.

Conclusion

Increasingly, leadership and leadership development are seen as inherently *collaborative, social and relational processes*. Especially in fast-moving times, leadership will be understood as the *collective capacity of all members of an organization* to accomplish such critical tasks as setting direction, creating alignment and gaining commitment. For agile leaders the shift taking place is towards *exercising influence rather than directive control*. Taking this next step will require leaders at the top to gain deeper understanding of the role of organizational systems and culture and how they can be an 'instrument' of change.

In developing communities of leaders the main task for leaders is to *create the conditions* that produce and reinforce collaboration, shared leadership, ownership and accountability at all levels. This will require great communications, strategic conversations and the *creation of cross-organizational networks* united by shared purpose. This is about leading consistently from a basis of shared values, removing obstacles to empowerment, designing structures that facilitate the flow of information, ease interaction and create transparency. It is about upskilling people through new experiences, training and coaching, ensuring that the reward systems recognize team, as well as individual, contributions to overall performance.

The outcome should be a change-able culture in which people can thrive, bring the best of themselves in pursuit of a common purpose and renew themselves and the organization as they do so.

One company I worked with wanted to encourage leadership at the front line but there was concern that there could be too much power distance between those at the top and the front-line workers. The top team had recently clarified the organization's new customer-centric values, but some high-potential managers recognized that if current senior leadership were to remain remote from the daily realities of the organization they were unlikely to be effective or inspirational people managers. Their recommendations to top management as follows make a useful checklist:

- Involve high potentials and senior managers in stepping up to more actively play a role in running and developing the business – usually a role held by top management – so that top management can be more externally focused and strategic.

- If senior managers/leaders become disconnected from customer experience they should go 'back to the floor' – to understand more specifically the customer experience – not only in induction.

- Managers should lead the customer-centric and change agenda and engage with the people who make front-line decisions. Managers should learn how to delegate effectively and develop teams (who can work across boundaries), expose them to new thinking (especially in the light of changing channels), help them become aware of their decision-making bias etc.

- Hold managers accountable for how they are developing people and managing change.

- Don't force technical experts to manage people as the only way to get on – develop other career possibilities.

- Longer term – recruit in or build the management capability we want (people with diverse experience).

- Reinforce customer-centricity through offering a leading people experience to staff.

- Create a life-cycle map about staff in order to assess the quality of people experience at each stage and identify relevant improvement processes.

- Take a fresh look at the competencies required over the next three years: eg change leadership; also taking new values into account.

- Review the whole approach to managing performance to align with new values; focus on behaviours and contribution – including how managers develop people etc – and get people to account for their contribution in customer outcomes.

While top teams may not always like what they hear, they must be open to messages from below and not 'shoot the messenger'. And by institutionalizing new practices, behaviour should start to change at all levels, including at the top.

Notes

1 Handy, C (2002) What's a business for? *Harvard Business Review*, 80 (12), December, pp 49–56.

2 Spears, LC (2004) Practicing servant-leadership, *Leader to Leader*, Fall, pp 7–11.

3 Gitsham, M (2012) [accessed 19 January 2015] The Changing Role of Global Leaders. *Harvard Business Review Blog Network*, 14 February [Online] https://hbr.org/2012/02/what-it-takes-now-to-lead-a-bu.

4 Burns, JM (2012) *Leadership*, Open Road Media.

5 May, DR *et al* (2003) Developing the moral component of authentic leadership, *Organizational Dynamics*, 32 (3), pp 247–60.

6 Goffee, R and Jones, G (2005) Managing authenticity, the paradox of great leadership, *Harvard Business Review*, December.

7 Norman, S, Luthans, B and Luthans, K (2005) The proposed contagion effect of hopeful leaders on the resiliency of employees and organizations, *Journal of Leadership and Organizational Studies*, 12 (2), pp 55–64.

8 Tata, R and Wallenberg, M (2014) The power of enduring companies, *McKinsey Quarterly*, September.

9 Heifetz, R and Laurie, DL (2001) The work of leadership, *Best of HBR*, September.

10 Morris, W (2014) Towards a new luxury, *The Sunday Times*, 21 September.

11 Collins, JC and Porras, JI (2005) *Built to Last: Successful habits of visionary companies*, Random House Business, London.

12 Springett, N (2005) *Shared Purpose,* Roffey Park, Horsham.

13 Kay, J (2004) Forget how the crow flies, *Financial Times*, 17 January, p 21.

14 Nayyar, V (2012) [accessed 19 January 2015] in *Employees First, Customers Second: Why it really works in the market*, ed K Moore, Forbes Leadership 5/14/2012 @ 12:01 pm [Online] http://www.forbes.com/sites/karlmoore/2012/05/14/employees-first-customers-second-why-it-really-works-in-the-market/.

15 Kingsinger, P and Walch, K (2012) [accessed 30 August 2014] Living and leading in a VUCA world, *Thunderbird University* [Online] http://knowledgenetwork.thunderbird.edu/research/2012/07/09/kinsinger-walch-vuca/.

16 Tamkin P *et al* (2010) *Exceeding Expectation: The principles of outstanding leadership*, The Work Foundation.

17 Silva, DY, Gimbert, B and Nolan, J (2000) Sliding the doors: locking and unlocking possibilities for teacher leadership, *Teachers College Record*, **102** (4), pp 779–804.

18 Bowerman KD and Van Wart, M (2011) *The Business of Leadership: An introduction*, Routledge, Abingdon, p 333.

19 Bergman, JZ *et al* (2012) The shared leadership process in decision-making teams, *The Journal of Social Psychology*, **152** (1), pp 17–42.

20 Ancona, D and Backman, E (2010) [accessed 30 August 2015] It's Not All About You, *Harvard Business Review Blog Network*, 26 April 10:55 am [Online] http://blogs.hbr.org/2010/04/its-not-all-about-me-its-all-a/.

21 Carson, JB, Tesluk, PE and Marrone, JA (2007) Shared leadership in teams: an investigation of antecedent conditions and performance, *Academy of Management Journal*, **50** (5), pp 1217–34.

22 Hamel, G (2010) [accessed 30 August 2014] Lessons From a Management Revolutionary, Gary Hamel's Management 2.0, 18 March [Online] http://blogs.wsj.com/management/2010/03/18/wl-gore-lessons-from-a-management-revolutionary/.

23 Rogers, P and Tierney, T (2004) Leadership without control, *European Business Journal*, **16** (2) pp 78–82.

24 Proust, M. *Remembrance of Things Past*, Vol. 5 – The Prisoner (originally published in French in 1923, and first translated into English by CK Moncrief).

25 Heifetz, RA and Laurie, DL (2001) The work of leadership, *Harvard Business Review*, **79** (11), December, pp 131–40.

26 Mayo, AJ and Nohria, AN (2005) *In Their Time: The greatest business leaders of the 20th century*, Harvard Business School Press, Boston.

27 Welbourn, D *et al* (2012) *Leadership of Whole Systems*, The Kings Fund, London.

28 Kramer, HJ Jr (2011) *From Values to Action: The four principles of values-based leadership*, Wiley, San Francisco.

29 Collins, J (2001) *Good to Great*, Random House, London.

30 Anding, JM (2005) An interview with Robert E. Quinn entering the fundamental state of leadership: reflections on the path to transformational teaching, *Academy of Management Learning and Education*, **4** (4), pp 487–95.

31 Badaracco, JL Jr (2006) Leadership in literature, *Harvard Business Review*, March.

Conclusion

As the pace of transformations in the business environment continues to accelerate many organizations will struggle to keep up, become too slow to respond to what the marketplace now demands and may ultimately go under. Symptoms of organizational atrophy – internal focus, rigid thinking, slow decision making, risk aversion, command and control management styles, organizational politics – are everywhere. Organizational agility is in short supply.

In this book we have considered how this gloomy scenario can be avoided and how greater agility and resilience can be built, where there is a will to do so. The 10 key themes we have examined are as follows.

1. Context counts

I have argued that, if organizations are to survive and thrive in this environment, leaders must be committed to building their organization's resilience and ability to adapt. True agility seamlessly intertwines adaptability, speed, innovation, resilience and renewal. While the degree of agility needed by different organizations will vary according to their situation, what is common to all is the need to keep actively focused on external context trends, anticipate how these will affect the business and its customers and to proactively put in place actions to capitalize on opportunities and mitigate threats. This external focus must percolate throughout the organization, and channels for pooling and sifting the collective intelligence must be found.

To survive and thrive in this confusing landscape, and optimize company performance over time, organizations need to be ambidextrous, effective both now and in the future. So the quest for short-term cost savings and efficiencies – which tend to undermine organizational resilience – must be deliberately balanced by the pursuit of longer-term value generation, innovation and multiple transient advantages. This involves building the new capabilities, routines and practices that will make the organization more resilient and equip it for a sustainable future. New definitions of success must be found that weigh quarterly results and investor dividends in the balance with potentially more important outcomes for a wider set of stakeholders.

2. Agility = mindset

By now I hope it is clear that I believe organizational agility to be more than just a set of tools and activities: it is a state of being. As with all living systems, organizations need to be change-able in order to thrive. They need to be aware of the bigger picture, sense the right time to move, find new propitious spaces in which to thrive, be constantly experimenting and learning from what works and what does not. An agile mindset is needed that is open, alert and flexible, that reframes change as the norm, as dynamic stability, as an inevitable part of the organization's life journey. Like living organisms, organizations must find new sources of nourishment and keep fit (literally and metaphorically) in order to gain the suppleness required for responsiveness and free movement. They need to develop and practise new routines that allow the unfamiliar to be 'managed' in such a way that leaves scope for specific innovative responses to exceptional situations.

An agile mindset is needed by managers, and by functions such as HR, IT, Internal Communications, Finance and, of course, the workforce itself so that agility can be embraced as the new norm. Leaders in particular must become agile and embrace new leadership approaches since they have a disproportionate impact on the success or failure of their organizations. This may require leaders to develop new skills – and, since nothing is certain, the ability to live with ambiguity and make good decisions fast. Leaders must be able to bring people with them through change, remain true to values and lead from a basis of shared purpose. I agree with Hamman and Spayd that the task for leaders is: 'Fundamentally... as much about the interior – of individuals, of organizations – as it is about the exterior. It is as much about developing people as it is about building systems. It is as much about creating an agile culture as it is about adapting structures and processes.'[1]

3. Collective awareness and collaboration

In previous chapters we have looked at various aspects of organizational agility and resilience. We have considered agile approaches to developing and implementing sound strategies. This requires a clear and unambiguous focus on customers – existing and potential – and the development of customer relationships that allow for some co-creation. We have seen that these strategic processes – strategizing, scanning and implementing – require collective awareness and informed effort, an ongoing proactive search of the environment for opportunities that can be capitalized on and threats that must be mitigated.

We have looked at Agile principles, methods and working practices with their short iterations and feedback cycles allowing for responsiveness to changing customer needs. We have seen how the principle of simplicity rather than complexity applies, particularly with respect to finding solutions that are fit for purpose rather than oversophisticated, aligning work with appropriate funding. These agile principles and methods should arguably be spread across the organization, including business functions. Even the grand 'set-piece' change programmes must adapt to ensure greater relevance.

We have considered how agile organizations are dynamically connected with partners across this changing business landscape. As people work across increasingly porous organizational boundaries they have to navigate complexity. To work well with partners, and create effective connections that enable organizational flexibility and reach, people need sophisticated relationship and trust-building skills. Company policies too must become culturally sensitive and adapt in order to ensure they are aligned to different geographical, cultural and business contexts.

4. More democratic approaches

Today's global business environments are fast-paced and operate 24/7. The notion of centralized decision making is becoming increasingly anachronistic and impractical. Given the growing demands for employee participation, and the need to gather collective intelligence, more democratic approaches to management and leadership are required. Leadership styles must evolve beyond command and control towards more collaborative, participative approaches based on mutual trust and respect. Employees must be willing to step up and play a proactive role in furthering their organization's goals. However, if the change of leadership approach is not authentic and the hierarchical mindset remains in place, employees will soon learn not to trust management. Shifts in management approach must therefore be authentic and values-based. Developing disciplines around what must remain 'tight' (ie under top-down controls), and what can be 'loose' to allow for employee participation and task discretion, avoids confusion and enables the right blend of innovation and risk management.

5. Culture building

Culture building become central to the agile leader's task. Trust is the constant theme. Without it, people are likely to be cautious, slow to respond, unwilling to share their best ideas and defensive when change is needed. Open, agile and high-performing cultures are underpinned by shared purpose, values and guiding principles. In such a context the organization becomes a change-able community of leadership at all levels involved in a common effort. This is about creating a social movement for change and innovation, where change and innovation can be initiated by anyone, not simply at the top.

Stimulating culture change requires top-level commitment. Leaders must raise awareness of the need for change, promote dialogue, connect people with each other, create communities for action and widen the circle of involvement so that agility and resilience spread throughout the organization. We have looked at how communications and tools such as social media can be used to enable these connections to be made. The leader's task is to listen and provide a sense of coherence. Above all, senior managers must recognize that their attitudes, behaviour and priorities teach people what is really valued. They must recognize that they have a responsibility to reinforce the organizational values and new practices so that rather than 'do as I say' they model 'do as I do'. The aim should be to bring consistency and strengthen what works – while everything around that can change.

6. An enabling context

Leaders must create an enabling context for change and innovation, including resources, structures, systems and processes and especially clarity about goals and roles so that people know what they are doing. Leaders also need to set parameters for experimentation so people know where change is needed and ensure there are effective processes for sharing learning and evaluation. They need to establish system constraints, including shared purpose, so that risk can be managed. They should reinforce the desired direction using communications, recognition and rewards.

HR policies such as performance management and management development should be reviewed from the position of being values-driven, enabling autonomy and responsibility. When new initiatives or policies are introduced the focus should be on measuring outcomes, rather than just a defined output that reduces to a number the value and complexity of the result. Similarly when people are working remotely, it is important to work towards outcomes/products, mapping achievement rather than time worked. With respect to performance management, perhaps the most important part is not only people having the conversation around performance but also a conversation about their careers leading somewhere.

7. Agile people

We have looked at the importance – and challenge – of bringing in, developing and retaining agile (and mobile) 'talent'. We have seen how HR processes relating to talent management are becoming more agile as organizations struggle with talent shortages, varied fields of operation and more diverse workforces. We have seen how important it is to link the personal and professional from the outset of a staff member's journey as they join an organization.

We have discussed the vital importance of employee engagement and considered how being true to one's values is particularly important when leading employees through periods of major change. We have also discussed how employees are often viewed as a cost. Today's working conditions can be highly pressurized for employees who are often beset with demands – for dynamic ideas, customer service, innovation – and required to do 'more for less'. When this happens, people's engagement (and health) may suffer and organizational resilience be undermined. HR, managers and employees themselves all have key roles to play in ensuring that a better balance is struck that enables employee engagement, health and wellbeing. As we have noted, some leaders are increasingly coming to the view that employees should be seen as the primary stakeholder, since when they are engaged in shared purpose they produce better outcomes for customers and their employer. So in order to strengthen resilience, organizations must pay careful attention to employee needs and seek to achieve win-win outcomes for employees and the business.

8. A more mutual employment relationship

The emerging employment relationship must be two-way: what does the organization expect from you, and what do you expect from the organization? Trust is the vital determinant of the employment relationship. When trust exists there is greater accountability and less need for direct control. Work should be designed around engagement principles, geared to improving employee involvement in decision making at work, the climate of relationships between management and employees, employee development, satisfaction with pay, job challenge and a sense of achievement from work.[2]

People may need flexible working arrangements at different ages and stages of their lives. Wherever possible, the organization should seek to accommodate rather than deny employees this flexibility. They may need support with their development needs/career aspirations. So organizations should look creatively at shaping opportunities for people, for instance helping staff to move around the organization by putting a greater emphasis on capability and competency rather than experience in a particular area.

9. Becoming 'organizational citizens'

In recent times the very role, purpose, nature and legitimacy of organizations, professions and institutions are coming into question. Organizations are more obviously than in the past accountable to, and part of, their communities. Today there are rising public expectations that companies – including across their supply chains – should act in more ethical and more financially, socially and environmentally responsible ways. So organizations must become responsive and proactive with respect to their communities, and demonstrate their responsibility towards the environment and to stakeholders such as customers, suppliers, employees and shareholders in all aspects of their operations. As the RCT Homes case illustrates, when organizations voluntarily extend their efforts beyond their statutory obligations and take further steps to improve the quality of life for employees and their families, as well as for the local community and society at large, their corporate social performance and reputation are likely to improve.

10. When all else changes, purpose and values act as glue

As I have said throughout, drawing lessons from long-lived organizations and from many of the case examples featured in this book, shared purpose and values are key to organizational agility and resilience. They not only provide coherence and legitimacy, they act as a mainspring for renewal, improvement, change and learning. They provide people with a real line of sight to the point of it all that is motivating and uplifting. They act as the foundation of trust, the vital enabler, on which agility and resilience can be built. When the purpose is uplifting and provides worthwhile benefits to stakeholders, including the community, it can galvanize employee energy, enthusiasm and high performance. When this happens, resilience and agility – ie change-ability – become part of the DNA, flowing through every aspect of the organization, acting as the mainspring for sustainable performance, innovation, renewal and health. That way, agility and resilience become the 'gift that keeps on giving' – to everyone's benefit!

Notes

1 Hamman, M and Spayd, MK (2014) [accessed 30 August 2014] Being an Agile Leader, a White Paper, *Agile Coaching Institute* [Online] http://www.agilecoachinginstitute.com/wp-content/uploads/2014/05/Being-an-Agile-Leader-ACI-White-Paper-Mar-2014.pdf.

2 Purcell, J (2013) [accessed 30 August 2014] The Future of Engagement: Speaking up for Employee Voice, *IPA*, October [Online] http://www.ipa-involve.com/news/the-future-of-engagement/.

INDEX

CPSIA information can be obtained
at www.ICGtesting.com
Printed in the USA
BVOW06s0950100118
504962BV00001B/37/P